The Poorhouse

The Poorhouse

America's Forgotten Institution

David Wagner

ROWMAN & LITTLEFIELD PUBLISHERS, INC.
Lanham • Boulder • New York • Toronto • Oxford

This book is dedicated to
the memory of
Richard A. Cloward
(1926–2001)

ROWMAN & LITTLEFIELD PUBLISHERS, INC.

Published in the United States of America
by Rowman & Littlefield Publishers, Inc.
A wholly owned subsidiary of The Rowman & Littlefield Publishing Group, Inc.
4501 Forbes Boulevard, Suite 200, Lanham, MD 20706
www.rowmanlittlefield.com

P.O. Box 317, Oxford OX2 9RU, UK

British Library Cataloguing in Publication Information Available

Library of Congress Cataloging-in-Publication Data

Wagner, David.
   The poorhouse: America's forgotten institution / David Wagner.
      p.   cm.
   Includes bibliographical references and index.
   ISBN 0-7425-2944-4 (cloth: alk. paper) — ISBN 0-7425-2945-2 (pbk.: alk. paper)
   1. Almshouses—United States. 2. Poor—United States. 3. Public welfare—
United States. I. Title.
   HV61.W34 2005
   362.5'85—dc22

                                                                    2004015137

Printed in the United States of America

♾™ The paper used in this publication meets the minimum requirements of
American National Standard for Information Sciences—Permanence of Paper
for Printed Library Materials, ANSI/NISO Z39.48-1992.

Contents

Tables and Boxes

TABLES

BOXES

Acknowledgments

In many senses this book represents a continuity for me personally; I was a history major in college, fascinated by the past, and was admitted to a Ph.D. program in history. Life takes us on various turns, and while a masters student in social work at Columbia, I met Richard A. Cloward, whose impact on me, in addition to his and Frances Fox Piven's critically important work, was also personal, in that he always emphasized and counseled a broad social science and historical connection to ground one's work. I later studied labor history and, through a mix of labor studies, a Ph.D. in sociology, and teaching social welfare, came to a fascination with how those excluded from the headlines and textbooks of history lived their lives. For many years now I have taught an "Introduction to Social Welfare" class that begins with the almshouse/poorhouse. My academic work on homelessness and poverty and activism in the community with these groups provided me with some sensitivity as to how those at the bottom of society see those further up the class hierarchy.

My students at the University of Southern Maine have been my teachers, forcing me to make the past relevant to the present and to help them appreciate the continuity of American policy from the Colonial times to contemporary ones. One student in a class on homelessness, Miles Rightmire, who works for the City of Portland, stimulated the immediate impulse to study the poorhouse by alerting me to recently archived material in that city.

Yet each work provides something new, and the kindness of complete strangers and a couple of acquaintances gave me a new appreciation for

New Englanders, sometimes initially quite reticent and shy, and yet very accommodating to others. In several areas I studied, invaluable assistance was provided. In Worcester, Massachusetts, Arthur Tirella, once briefly my opposite as an administrator of the Belmont Home, the City Nursing Home in the late 1970s and 1980s, while I was a union representative in that city, was gracious in his help with the papers the home had inherited from the old "Home Farm" in Worcester. In Haverhill, Massachusetts, Greg Laing, the head of Special Collections at the City of Haverhill Library, proved a valuable guide to a very valuable collection of documents there. In Lewiston, Maine, the Landry sisters, particularly Gertrude Landry Mynahan, were enthusiastic participants in providing memories and papers and suggestions for other leads. In Rockingham County, New Hampshire, the Hilton family shared the papers of their parents and uncle, letting a stranger comb through their lives. Also, Eileen Roblee, the very efficient executive assistant to the County Commissioners' Office patiently allowed me access to records.

Additionally, I would like to thank David Rushford, the City Clerk of Worcester, and the staff of the Worcester Room at the Public Library and the Worcester Historical Society; Bill Barry of the Maine Historical Society, an eager ally and guide into Portland and Maine history; Sandy White of the City of Haverhill Auditor's Office for escorting me through the city vaults there; Sheila Foley, a teacher in Carroll County who was excited about the project and phoned and e-mailed for connections; Kathy Armstrong and Kathy Garry who work for the County Commissioners' Office of Carroll County; Karen Ardagna of the Rockingham County Nursing Home Medical Record Department for her enthusiasm; Marge Webster, County Commissioner, and Forrest Painter, administrator of the Mountain View Nursing Home, both in Carroll County; Barry Rodgrigue of the Lewiston-Auburn College of the University of Southern Maine and Douglas I. Hodgkin, professor emeritus of Bates College, for material on Lewiston; and Gerry Cayer, director of health and human services in Portland, and Doug Gardner, director of the Barron Center in Portland, for their help. The staffs of the Lewiston Public Library, Maine Historical Society, and Portland Room of the Portland Public Library were also invaluable. Marie Roy of Lewiston at no cost translated French documents on the Lewiston Farm into English.

I am indebted to Angela Desrochers for her research assistant work; her assistance was vital particularly for the histories of poorhouses in Lewiston and Portland, Maine. As usual, my wife and colleague Marcia B. Cohen, a professor of social work at the University of New England, played a major role as my first reader and advisor. I am indebted also to those academics and writers who found time in their busy life to read the manuscript in various forms, particularly John Buell of Southwest Harbor,

Maine; Robert Fisher of the University of Connecticut; Frances Fox Piven of the Graduate Center of New York; Ingrid Sahlin of the University of Gothenburg; and Sandra Wachholz of the criminology department at the University of Southern Maine.

Finally, I would like to thank the staff of Rowman & Littlefield Publishing who were a pleasure to work with and did their work efficiently and cheerfully: Alan McClare, my editor; Alex Masulis, assistant editor; and Jenn Nemec the associate editor for production.

1

+

Poorhouse, Almshouse, Poor Farm: Buried American History

Into such a house, none shall enter voluntarily; work, confinement, and discipline, will deter the indolent and vicious; and nothing but extreme necessity will induce any to accept the comfort which must be obtained by the surrender of their free agency, and the sacrifice of their accustomed habits and gratifications.

—English Poor Laws on the workhouse[1]

There was a cheerful feeling of activity, and even an air of comfort, about the Byfleet Poor-house. . . . The inmates were by no means distressed or unhappy; many of them retired to this shelter only for the winter season, and would go out presently, some to begin such work as they could still do, others to live in their own small houses; old age had impoverished most of them by limiting their power of endurance; but far from lamenting the fact that they were town charges, they rather liked the change and excitement of a winter-residence on the poor-farm.

—Sarah Orne Jewett, "The Flight of Betsey Lane"[2]

Major American institutions often fade from memory. Many of us grew up hearing our parents exclaim, "You are driving me to the poorhouse!" Many of us remember the card in the Monopoly game that says, "Go to the Poorhouse! Lose a Turn!" Throughout parts of the country, particularly the Northeast and Midwest, we drive past streets named "Poor Farm Road," "County Farm Road," or "Town Farm Road." Despite these remnants of a not-too-distant past, few Americans know much about what a "poorhouse" or "poor farm" was.

The idea that special institutions existed in America that housed the poor comes as a shocking revelation when I mention it to my students, even those who would be nonchalant about passing a homeless shelter or nursing home. The idea strikes many as a little strange and repugnant, particularly when it is revealed that millions of elderly people, physically and mentally disabled people, single mothers, and children found themselves in these places along with unemployed able-bodied people. And when they learn that such places existed for as long as three hundred years, and for more than a century were a key component in the care for the poor, disabled, elderly, and others in need, they are often further shocked.[3] Although the critical 1960s and 1970s brought out of oblivion the history of many groups previously treated as marginal to the American story—African Americans, American Indians, women, working-class people, and gay and lesbian people, for example—with some exceptions, the treatment of the poor and the disabled and elderly never quite made center stage of either the popular or academic literature.[4]

This book is in part an attempt to remedy this gap. Although it does not seek to be a definitive work on the poorhouse, I hope to open new roads to the old byways and even to old physical structures and spaces that still exist in many communities. Up the street or down the road in many cities and towns still stand hospitals, nursing homes, mental hospitals, and boarding homes that were once poorhouses. In fact, all over the nation old poorhouses are being turned back to one of their original functions: serving as homeless shelters. The famous Bellevue Hospital in New York City started as an almshouse in 1816, and now again houses a men's shelter; in Boston, the harbor islands that housed the poor in almshouses, houses of correction, and reformatories in the nineteenth century now host a large homeless shelter.[5] In other towns and cities, structures that once aroused dread and fear have come and gone. In one New England city I studied, a large lot of land, once the poor farm, is being sold to Wal-Mart, while in another New England county, the poor farm still operates but now with prison labor.[6]

The loss of this history suggests, too, a whole other side of the history of the poorhouse or poor farm. As the quote at the start of the chapter from a story by Sarah Orne Jewett, the noted American nineteenth-century writer, suggests, the poorhouse was a community for many people. Not only was its role important to those who stayed there but in some counties and towns, the poor farm also grew to play a major role as an agricultural center, a producer of revenue for government and of food products for the poor and others. No wonder some communities called their farms "our pride" in the late nineteenth century and well into the twentieth century.[7]

The history of these institutions—sometimes called almshouses, some-times poorhouses, sometimes workhouses, sometimes poor farms, and, later, often city or county homes or infirmaries—is interesting and deeply important. Millions of Americans, perhaps tens of millions of people, spent at least some time as "inmates" in these institutions. Moreover, as impor-tantly, their neighbors talked in hushed tones and in fear of their own fate at the "specter of the poorhouse." Unless they were in the top one or two percent of society in wealth, they knew that the poorhouse could well be their future, and this dread structured their daily lives and actions. There was, after all, no Social Security, unemployment insurance, Medicare, or food stamps. Secondly, the poorhouse is important because many other major institutional settings in America grew out of it: the mental asylum; the prison and penitentiary; the orphanage; the state school for the "feeble minded" (later the retarded); the nursing, old age, and boarding home; homes for unmarried women; and even, in many cases, medical hospitals.[8] Deeply intertwined with the history of the poorhouses, then, is not only the history of poverty but of old age, sickness, physical and psychological disability, alcoholism, child welfare, widowhood, single parenthood, treat-ment of deviance, unemployment, and economic cycles. As noted, poor farms also had an independent history as farming enterprises and were a source of municipal and county income. Finally, this rich story is deeply important to understanding ourselves, and particularly how groups of people, poor as well as middle class, elderly as well as young, are adept at surviving and creating community in all sorts of places, including these stigmatized settings. The story of the poorhouse is not a depressing sob story, though it contains many things we regret; it is just as profoundly, and perhaps more importantly, a story of how poor people and others came to change the nature of an institution until its old form was greatly abandoned. It is a story of hope as well as pain.

WHAT'S IN A NAME? CONFUSING TERMS

This chapter begins with two very different quotes; one, although from England, is a widely cited quote about the horrors of the workhouse made well known at least in academic circles by Frances Fox Piven and Richard Cloward in their book, *Regulating the Poor: The Functions of Public Welfare* (originally published in 1971). The second quote is from a short story ("Betsey's Flight") in the late 1870s of noted writer Sarah Orne Jewett. Al-though the second quote is from fiction, its description is similar to some that I heard while talking with elderly people who had lived in New En-gland poorhouses and poor farms in the twentieth century, and parallels some accounts of life in the New England poorhouses I studied.

Clearly, there were vastly different experiences of the same institution (as there are, of course, with any institution, e.g., a school or place of employment); still, there were two very different concepts reflected in the first quote and the second. Although often used interchangeably even by social scientists and historians, as well as by eighteenth- and nineteenth-century Americans, the words and origins of the "poorhouse" or in older English "almshouse" (these two words are essentially synonymous) must be distinguished from the concept of a "workhouse" or a "house of correction," which is reflected in the reference in the English Poor Law quotation.

It would appear that two totally different ideas—hospitality and punishment—oddly enough became confused, at least when European institutions crossed the Atlantic to America. In medieval Europe, before the poor and other groups such as the "mad" were stigmatized, hospice or a place of hospitality was a central part of European society in which a stranger—often poor, sometimes just a wanderer—was welcomed. While all sectors of society played a role in hospitality, the monasteries came to play a key role in care of the poor. The hospice idea grew into its many offshoots, including not only the word *hospice* (today usually used for programs in aid of the dying and terminally ill) but also *hospital*, which emerged out of the hospitality idea, and *hostel* or (later) *hotel*, again a place for travelers. Alms as charity was similarly a social obligation in feudal Europe. The term *almshouse* in its original usage conjured up a house in which poor people or wanderers or others could be aided. An almshouse or poorhouse can be interpreted as simply a house for those who need aid, and the development of hospitals, asylums, orphanages, and nursing homes from this institution makes clear sense.

But a more punitive tradition arouse in sixteenth-century Europe. By the time of the Reformation, Europe was changing drastically, and initially in the areas where Protestantism first triumphed, such as Holland, Switzerland, Germany, and England, a harsher treatment of the poor and those who were deemed unproductive ("indolent" or "vicious") developed. Medieval society's obsession with alms and a static traditional society that protected the poor grated on the new Europe, soon to include Catholic nations such as France, influenced by both the Catholic Counter-Reformation and the rise of capitalism. Out of a new consensus that suggested "repressing" pauperism and beggary came another institutional invention, the workhouse. The workhouse was meant as a correctional institution in which actual discipline (cells, bread and water, instruments of punishment such as the ball and chain and later the treadmill) was to be imposed on the "unworthy poor," usually men of working age, who were vagrants, beggars, "indolent," petty criminals, or intemperate. They would be housed only on condition of hard work. The presumed lazy or deviant person (although in fact even workhouses came to often include families or individuals just out of work during slack times) was to be put to work, even if it were "make work," to press proper morality on them. The discipline of work along with mandatory bible reading and other character-building activities would supposedly help reform society and produce a compliant workforce.

Where workhouses were built in the United States, mostly in the larger Eastern seaboard cities, there indeed can be little confusion as to their punitive intent. In Portland, Maine, the Maine Historical Society still displays the ball and chain from the old workhouse, and there are drawings of some small barred cells built there in the late 1700s. But generally in America, where social welfare was an intensely local proposition for three hundred years, the confusion between workhouses and poorhouses never left the public imagination or academic writing. Dickensian images of the old institutions for the poor are often based on the workhouse, yet most American communities never had workhouses. The speeches of nineteenth-century reformers promoted poorhouses for the "worthy" or "deserving" poor along with workhouses for the "undeserving." But in an agrarian society with low population density, no massive building of workhouses ever ensued (unlike England). As immigration grew and population increased, the poor, the aged, the widow, children—in short, people of all types—found themselves in poorhouses or receiving other types of relief (described later in this chapter). Many towns and cities gave up their efforts early on to actually punish the poor. Reformers were outraged not necessarily by the harshness of the poorhouse but rather by its indiscriminate "mixing" of the "indolent and vicious" with the widowed, aged, infirm, children, and other "deserving poor" all housed together in one place. They complained too that work was often not enforced, and poor people came and went as they pleased.

Further complicating things are other terms that came to be applied in place of *poorhouse*. Around the middle of the nineteenth century, many poorhouses came to be termed *poor farms*. Poor farms were, in part, simply a name for a rural poorhouse or a city farm basing its economy on farming. But as I shall explore in chapter 3, poor farms may also have had less of a repressive origin than the original poorhouses. In an agricultural society that promoted the ethic of work above all else, farming was one area where men and women, young and old, could share the work. Moreover, for financially vigilant towns and counties, there was another advantage. The superintendent's salary (the superintendent was the man hired to run the poor farm, usually with his wife, entitled "the matron") could hopefully be supported by the successful sale of produce and other farm products. The operation would be self-sustaining, or in the hopes of many nineteenth-century officials, actually make money for the town or county (a few, but only a few, ever did make a profit). Poor farms, like poorhouses, varied tremendously in their nature from region to region, county to county, and town to town. Some poor farms, as Jewett describes, were rather homey places and came to be greatly appreciated by the "inmates," particularly in the cold winters. Poor farms were by no means limited to rural areas, as some urban areas devoted many acres to their poor farms (or city farms), a term they sometimes used along with *almshouse*, the latter to describe the actual structure the poor lived in. This produces considerable terminological confusion; in some areas I studied, I found that the farm (such as the county farm in New Hampshire) even in the twenty-first century was well known, while buildings that once housed the poor (e.g., the almshouse or poorhouse) were not well known.

Late in the nineteenth century, with further population growth and the development of specialization and professionalization, as well as in an effort to reduce the stigma of the poorhouse, many towns and cities renamed their institutions *city home* or in counties, *county home*. Officials found that the change fooled few, and they often complained in their reports that despite improvements people "still talk of it as the poorhouse." By the Great Depression, although there were still some institutions labeled "almshouses" and "poorhouses," as well as many that were "almshouse and city farm" or "city farm and hospital," the majority were either "county or city homes" or were in the process of a medical transition to a "city infirmary" or "city home and hospital." Although some citizens considered these terms euphemisms as well, they did mark an important turn toward the transition of most poorhouses into hospitals and old age, boarding, and nursing homes by the post–World War II period.

Most fascinating in my own research is the how the term *inmate* lingered into the 1960s and 1970s, at least in New England. For example, although New Hampshire poor farms changed their names to county homes, their records speak of "inmates" in 1960s and 1970s (those in the house of correction were "prisoners," not "inmates"). Even more interesting is the public hospital and nursing home, where cities and counties referred to residents as "inmates" until slowly they became "patients." Arthur Tirella, former administrator of the Belmont Home in Worcester, Massachusetts, remembers his amazement when as a young employee there in 1980, an aging physician gave a speech thanking the "inmates" (a.k.a. patients) of the city nursing home, which had inherited the old inmates of the city's poor farm.[9] The institutional stigma that developed in the almshouse may still structure our experience in many unconscious ways when we enter institutions such as nursing homes.

SOCIAL WELFARE (SUCH AS IT WAS) BEFORE 1935

For three hundred years before the passage of the Social Security Act of 1935, which provided not only pensions for the aged but also unemployment insurance and some federal welfare programs, the choices of poor, disabled, elderly, and others in need were fairly bleak. With no modern social welfare, any hope of aid rested on the Elizabethan Poor Laws developed in England and taken lock, stock, and barrel into American law. Despite the myth of American prosperity, periodic depressions and unemployment, disasters such as fires and wars, injury, and ill health produced plenty of adversity in America before the Social Security Act. If Mrs. Jones found herself widowed because her husband was killed in battle with Indians or if Mr. Smith was too old to work his farm and had no children to work it, both would have no choice but to submit themselves to the will of the overseers of the poor.

The term *overseers of the poor* originally came from English churchwardens who were chosen to judge applicants for parish aid. As the Elizabethan system became a public one, overseers became elected officials. In some towns and cities, the councilmen, selectmen, or freeholders served as overseers, whereas other cities and towns had separate elected officials. Overseers, at least until around World War I, tended to be the elites of the towns or cities, rarely having any firsthand experience with poverty. Mrs. Jones and Mr. Smith would hope in knocking on Overseer Brown's door (or, in New England, actually pleading in front of a town meeting for aid) that Brown was sympathetic, a fellow religionist, and had no personal or factional feud with them.

If Mrs. Jones and/or Mr. Smith were accepted as worthy people who had fallen on hard times through no fault of their own, and their infirmities were likely to be temporary, and most importantly, they held legitimate settlement within the boundaries of the town or city in which they were applying for aid, they might be helped through *outdoor relief*.[10] Outdoor relief is any aid that requires no institutionalization or removal from the home. As a few items from late eighteenth-century Worcester, Massachusetts, records indicate, often the aid was payment to suppliers in town or other citizens who provided aid:

[Voted that] Saml. Eaton be allowed 3 sh. 8 pence per week for keeping his mother the current year, if she lives.

Connilius Stowell to supplying Thomas Gleason with milk, 147½ Quarts at 2d.

Simion Duncan for moving a poor woman to Grafton [Mass] and her Effects And Finding them 11 sh.

Joseph Wheeler Esc. Sundries supplied the wife of Nathl. Kimball including a waggon [*sic*] to remove her to, Haverhill 17 sh 1 d.[11]

Two other methods of aiding the poor existed. One was boarding them out and the other was auctioning them off to the lowest bidder. Boarding out occurred in many towns in early America to care for the old and ill, and also with poor youth or disabled people "with strong back and weak mind" who could do farm work. Among the bills found in the Northern Massachusetts town of Haverhill, Massachusetts, in the 1790s were:

> Town of Haverhill for boarding Old Mr. Jeremiah Haseltine, one dollar and thirty-three cents per week. For boarding Old Mr. Lacount, one dollar fifty cents a week.
>
> Received of the Selectmen of the Town of Haverhill their order for twelve dollars in full for bringing up James Malcomb an indentured prentice to me Jonathan Hunkins.[12]

Perhaps the most shocking to us today is the auctioning of the poor to the lowest bidder. The ever-frugal early New England Yankees clearly prized economy above all else, and built in few safeguards against abuse that might occur when a poor person was auctioned off to someone who might use their labor. Historian Douglas Hodgkin cites an auction in the city of Lewiston, Maine, in 1833 where instructions were "to set up the Poor at auction to the lowest bidder, the person bidding them off to be at all the expense [*sic*] of boarding nursing & clothing except Doctors bills & Funaral [*sic*] charges, and return them as well clad as when taken." Hodgkin notes the results of the auctions varied; some people clearly had sponsors, the same family taking the person year after year. But in an extreme case, the widow Sarah Dill was auctioned off for fourteen years and went to fourteen different households![13]

In this context, we can see historically that the potential recipient obviously preferred outdoor relief to being auctioned off, boarded out, or sent to what came to be known as indoor relief (aid in an institution such as the poorhouse or workhouse). No matter how stigmatizing receiving aid was—and it certainly was as much in early America as receiving welfare is today—it was still preferable to have one's residence, freedom of association, and ability to go about one's life while getting on one's feet. Oddly, however, leading reformers saw it differently. Although they criticized the auctions, they saw building more poorhouses as the solution to poverty, and bemoaned outdoor relief as a corrupting and character-weakening process. Later they attacked those city and town officials who would continue to aid paupers with outdoor relief.

John Yates, the author of the influential Yates Report in New York State in the 1820s, which successfully promoted the replacement of outdoor relief with poorhouses, was representative of elite thinking:

The present poor laws, he informed the New York legislature, "tend to encourage the sturdy beggar and profligate vagrant to become pensioners upon the public funds." Their provisions "operate as so many invitations to become beggars.". . . Outdoor relief blunted his proper instincts, or in the words of various overseers of the poor, served to "relax individual exertion by unnerving the arm of industry," and weakened the "desire of honest independence."[14]

The first of many American antiwelfare campaigns was under way, endorsed by political leaders for more than a century (and hardly "conservative" in our modern parlance). Historian Michael Katz notes how such elite consensus, fortunately, never fully persuaded many local politicians who had to run for public office. Elites' pronouncements about cutting outdoor relief never led to its abolition, for at least small sums of cash or in-kind grants continued in most areas.[15] Nevertheless, the formal government policy of numerous counties and localities was that poor people, including the elderly and children, were to be aided only at the poorhouse and not encouraged in "pauperism" by outdoor relief.

Under the constant political pressure of mass universal male suffrage, the growth of the political machine in urban areas among immigrants, the rise of labor unions, and socialist organizing, the consensus against outdoor relief slowly broke down late in the nineteenth century and in the first decades of the twentieth. Veterans of the Civil War were the first to be granted pensions, and by the depression of 1893, many cities and towns provided public works jobs to the unemployed. Another crack in the system occurred when (over the objection of reformers and early social workers) a number of states during the Progressive Era passed "mothers' pensions" so that mothers (of good moral character) would not have to abandon their children and go to the poorhouse, but could stay at home and keep their children. It was not until the Great Depression of the 1930s that "outdoor aid" was accepted by elites and political officials.

PUTTING PEOPLE IN POORHOUSE HISTORY

Box 1.1 provides some of the important milestones in the history of the poorhouse. Although the history noted serves as an important guide for the reader, like most of the history provided to this day in textbooks, it is still a history of elite events and personages: the Yates and (Josiah) Quincey Reports, the actions of Dorothea Dix, the state investigations of almshouses, and so on. As historians and social scientists have argued since the 1960s, it is impossible to know how actual people experienced life by looking only at the official documents or the views of the affluent.

Naturally, this is even more the case with an institution centered on poor people. Even humanitarian reformers such as Dorothea Dix had opinions and agendas that differed greatly from the views of the poor, and they often clashed as well with the local superintendents, political figures, and communities that the reformers criticized.

For the reader familiar with social welfare or American history, several features of this book differ from the existing literature. First, most of the small number of scholarly writers who have treated the poorhouse at all leave the story well in the nineteenth century with the Yates and Quincey Reports, Dorothea Dix, and the effort to remove children from the almshouse.[16] This gives the impression that the poorhouse somehow ends in the late nineteenth century. In fact, much of this book hopes to begin to fill the historical gap from the 1890s into the second half of the twentieth century when most city and county farms continued; others, renamed county and city homes, even city hospitals, still had "inmates." In fact, historians and social scientists have failed to follow the name change from "poorhouse" or "poor farm" to explore exactly what this change actually

---

Box 1.1. Historical Timeline

16th-century Europe: Origin of almshouses, workhouses, and other institutions to confine the poor

1660: First almshouse in New World is Boston's workhouse

1820s: Widespread drive to build almshouses/poorhouses in the East after the Yates (N.Y.) and Quincey (Mass.) Reports

1830s: Dorothea Dix begins her campaign to remove the mentally ill from almshouses

1857: New York State Investigating Committee is the first of many public reports to criticize poorhouses

1871: *Harper's Weekly* magazine publishes its famous "Over the Hill to the Poorhouse" story; title becomes Will Carleton's popular song about the stigma of the poorhouse

1870s–1890s: Campaigns to remove children from almshouses

1910s: Progressive Movement leads to mothers' pensions in many states, helping "morally fit" mothers with children stay out of the poorhouse

1933–1935: Campaign for Social Security Act uses poorhouses and county homes as a major propaganda tool to demonstrate the need for old age pensions

1935: Passage of Social Security Act

1960s/early 1970s: Despite many earlier reports of their demise, the last poor farms and almshouses finally close and/or become nursing homes

entailed. Seemingly, their inquiry ends. Yet in a sense, this would be like giving up studying insane asylums when their names changed to "psychiatric centers." Name changes are not at all unimportant, and certainly the abandonment of the name along with the original aspirations of the poorhouse represented some progress. But in some localities, for decades, there continued to be groups ranging from homeless people, people with disabilities, unmarried mothers with children, people with substance abuse issues, and victims of domestic violence who had nowhere to go. Often they ended up at the public "hospital" or "home." Today those who are not seriously ill no longer end up very often in our medical centers, but in most of the institutions I followed, the renaming of the institution to a city or county home or hospital still allowed non-elderly or ill inmates to coexist with traditional "patients." In one city hospital, in fact, inmates continued to do much of the work at mid-twentieth century.[17]

Secondly, because of an emphasis on reformers such as Yates, Quincey, and Dix, the story of the almshouse/poorhouse/poor farm as presented by most historians and social scientists is an incomplete account. I explore how a great deal of the change in poorhouses can be attributed to how the poor themselves used the system, as well as how local officials and employees of the poorhouses undermined the original goals of the poorhouse. Further, the view of progress, sometimes known as the "Whig" version of history, no longer seems very compelling—if it ever did.[18] Since the late 1970s, conditions for the poor have deteriorated so much that jail, prison, and homeless shelters have become our new poorhouses. Today it can be argued that it was only a brief moment historically when it seemed as if a true deinstitutionalization or the move to "outdoor relief" was the dominant trend. Thirdly, because historians and social scientists have emphasized the repressive origins of the poorhouses, the other major roles they played in their three-hundred-year history have been minimized: they were hospitals, nursing homes, old age homes, maternity and lying-in hospitals, homeless shelters, respite facilities, and domestic violence shelters in modern terms. It is, of course, complex to treat such a multifaceted institution; making simple generalizations about them is inadequate.[19]

The history of the groups of people who were the dramatis personae of the poorhouse—the inmates, superintendents, matrons, and later large numbers of staff—is much more difficult to locate than the history of elites. The poor, in particular, tended to leave few records or diaries, to author no news articles, and to write no reports. Perhaps surprisingly, the feelings of superintendents and staff are not much easier to document. Most cities and towns had annual reports, and in some years in some jurisdictions, the reports are quite revealing of policies, opinions, and goings-on in the year. Often, however, they are strictly official in language, with statistics predominating—a list of crops produced each year at the poor farm, for example, was a staple of these reports. Since super-intendents and matrons were combination farmers and low-level politi-cal appointees, they were rarely writers, and some were even illiterate. Employees on the poor farm were low-paid workers, often working in exchange for board. Some would come from the ranks of the inmates, el-evated to worker.

This book uses a variety of strategies to attempt to capture the history of the poorhouse in six areas. I use official reports, since they provide clues to the doings of these institutions and the changes they underwent over the years. I use newspaper accounts that in some cases provide a very good feel for how the public, superintendents, and sometimes even how the inmates felt; other news articles, of course, focus on elites or the news commentators' own views. By using an intensive approach focusing on a number of poorhouses, I was able in each area to secure at least some personal memories or documentary history. In three localities, I was able to interview (now) elderly children of past superintendents of the poor farm and in one case several former staff members. In one county, I inter-viewed a woman born in the poor farm as an "inmate." In all six places, I discovered primary historical documents in the vaults of city halls, in his-torical societies, or in the attics of people who had worked at the poor-houses or were relatives of those who did. In one county, I found a large stack of letters from the 1930s between county commissioners (the over-seers of the poor there) and families of paupers or paupers themselves. Fi-nally, where "ledgers" or records of the names of inmates are available (usually with age, sex, nationality, sometimes with occupation, sometimes even with notes such as "intemperate" or "idiotic"), it is possible to cross-reference inmates with city and town directories and vital statistics to find out more about the lives of the paupers.

A number of caveats are in order. Without decades of work (if then), it is not possible to construct the actual range of experiences the inmates and others had of even one poorhouse. Rather, I rely on fragments to sug-gest to us what it might have been like for some inmates at a particular place and year. Caution must be used about generalizations. Where rich material was located, in a least some ways, the range of experience with poorhouses broadens and becomes more complex rather than narrow.

Second, an intensive historical study cannot, like a survey, cover the range of American history or geography. I chose to study New England. Although New England's six states and population of fourteen million seems a small part of our nation today, in 1850 or 1900, it was by far more central to the nation politically and, of course, a far greater percentage of the U.S. population as well. Moreover, with the Middle Atlantic states, New England constituted the nation's financial and communication cen-ter. The poorhouse, as with our other institutions such as the asylum and orphanage, originated in New England or in the nearby Middle Atlantic states. For better or worse, the moralism of New England—its puritan history, its role in the American Revolution, and its abolitionist and temperance movements, for example—structures its history or at least its conception of itself. New England's image of itself is certainly a serious one. It took its treatment of the poor seriously, whether repressive, compassionate, or both simultaneously. When the poorhouse was pronounced preferable to outdoor relief, New England built more and more poorhouses. And later, when scandal or investigations became the norm, New England responded quickly, perhaps more rapidly than elsewhere, at least on the brick-and-mortar front of physical infrastructure repair and reform of the poorhouse. Poorhouses were, at least if one believes the highly imperfect censuses on paupers, far more numerous in New England than in other regions, although, of course, the numbers of almshouses reflect to some extent the town and city system used in much of New England as opposed to the county system which prevailed in many other regions.[20]

Yet as with any region, New England is tremendously diverse. Boston, Massachusetts, and Providence, Rhode Island, have little in common with the vast rural stretches of northern Maine, New Hampshire, or even western Massachusetts. Even in the late nineteenth century, industrial cities such as Lynn, Lowell, Worcester, and Fall River, Massachusetts; Woonsocket and Pawtucket, Rhode Island; Manchester, New Hampshire; and Lewiston and Biddeford, Maine, were stigmatized. Primarily composed of French Canadians, Irish, and other European-born immigrants, the more ethnic industrial cities were avoided by Yankees. New England can be divided up north to south, with the southern states (Massachusetts, Connecticut, and Rhode Island) being more or less accurately pictured as more industrial and cosmopolitan than northern New England (Maine, Vermont, and New Hampshire). But New England can be just as arguably divided east to west with its coastal cities from Bangor and Portland, Maine, and Portsmouth, New Hampshire, through Boston, Providence, New Haven, and the part of the New York City metropolitan area that extends into Connecticut on one side, and its more rural or industrial European immigrant cities on the western side of the divide.

Since there are several good sources of material on the origin of the poorhouse and similar institutions,[21] I decided to particularly focus this book on the period from the 1890s until the demise of the poor farms, which in some areas meant the 1960s and 1970s. I found, at least in New England, the 1890s were a turning point both in terms of numbers of inmates (the poorhouses were often quite a bit smaller before this) and in terms of reform of the physical structures and organizational forms of the poorhouse, in that charges of squalor and disrepair of many of the homes were no longer generally characteristic. State laws, moreover, in New

England had begun to expedite the removal of the children and the mentally ill, although, as elsewhere, such removal was never fully accomplished. Since, however, any time period break is arbitrary, chapters 2 through 4 refer back to origins and older history of the poorhouse as well.

SIX NEW ENGLAND POORHOUSES

This book is not intended to represent all such institutions, as indeed any six almshouses out of at least 2,300 almshouses in the nation could not do. Living in Portland, Maine, I was originally attracted to recently archived data at the Maine Historical Society of the Portland almshouse, one of the oldest in the nation. Years before, I had met a student whose mother grew up in the poorhouse in Lewiston, the second-largest city in the state. I was fascinated that the Lewiston City Farm had lasted until 1967, particularly since most textbooks rarely discuss poorhouses at all after the nineteenth century!

Having started my reading and exploration with these two very different Maine cities—the generally Yankee (though increasingly by the late nineteenth century Irish, Italian, Canadian, Jewish, and other immigrant) coastal port of Portland, and the inland Franco-American mill city of Lewiston, I attempted to develop some variety for a book. New Hampshire introduces the county system, different from the rest of New England but similar to many states in the union (where paupers were moved from their towns or cities of origin into a county facility). The two county poorhouses/farms studied also introduce the rural poor. Carroll County, New Hampshire, is still a rather sparsely populated county, just below the White Mountains, centered on Ossipee. It is primarily Yankee and a region of woodworking, lumbering, and farming. Rockingham County is a very varied area on New Hampshire's coast. It includes Portsmouth, one the oldest New England port cities, which was extremely affluent and was central to the first several centuries of American history. The county as a whole was greatly rural in the nineteenth century. Like the southern Maine area, it is a Yankee and Irish area with some additional European and Canadian immigration.

I chose two Massachusetts poor farms to introduce the experience of poorhouses in larger mill cities. Worcester, located in central Massachusetts—today only an hour from Boston, but a world away sociologically—is still the second-largest city in New England. In the nineteenth and early twentieth centuries, it was among the larger American cities and a major manufacturing center of steel wire, tools, and grinding equipment. It was heavily non-Yankee: Irish, Italian, French, Eastern European, Jewish, and Armenian. Finally, Haverhill, located about thirty miles north of Boston, is also among the older cities of the area. In the nineteenth and early twentieth centuries, Haverhill was one of the shoe manufacturing capitals of the world. While less well known, it bears similarities with its neighboring manufacturing centers, Lowell and Lawrence. Haverhill is a medium-sized New England city, similar to Portland, but more ethnically non-Yankee, and had a strong union and socialist tradition, unlike the other cities or counties.

The six poorhouses/poor farms also reflect the diversity of size of poorhouses. The "Paupers in Almshouses" U.S. census editions divided almshouses by size (this count is a one-time count rather than a count of all people throughout the year, which is a much larger multiple). Carroll County reflects the relatively small-sized almshouse (twenty-six to fifty inmates), although as with the others, during depressions, it vastly exceeded this number. Haverhill's and Lewiston's city farms both would be generally placed in the moderate size (fifty-one to one hundred inmates), though again in depression times they held far more inmates. The remaining three (although they varied greatly over the years) would all be considered large by the census; Rockingham County Almshouse often held 200 inmates as did Worcester's "Home Farm" (350 inmates by the 1930s), and Portland's Almshouse ranged from over 200 to well into the 300s. Interestingly, while much of the social welfare literature generally uses Boston, New York, Philadelphia, and other large cities to generalize from, the very large almshouses (those over one thousand) were few.[22]

Some basic facts about the six poorhouses studied are reproduced in tables 1.1 and 1.2. Table 1.1 provides the name of the city or county almshouse, a brief description of the area, the date it originated, and the date(s) the poorhouse either closed or changed into other institutions. The last column is the most complex. With so many name changes, it is hard to know when to declare the "end" except in the case of Lewiston, where the city farm lasted consecutively with the same name until it formally closed in 1967. With the other five, despite name changes, as long as the institution served only the poor, used the term "inmates," and often used at least some inmate labor, I have considered them to be a continuation of the poor farm.

Table 1.2 provides information on the size of the poorhouse/poor farm in terms of the number of inmates they held, and notes whether it included a workhouse or house of correction or was voluntary in nature. I use the term *voluntary* here advisedly, since going to the poorhouse was arguably not ever totally voluntary. Being sentenced to the workhouse or a house of correction, however, usually took a judge's order.[23] As a consequence, the prisoner had a fixed term in the workhouse or poorhouse, while the "inmate" was normally free to come and go.

Table 1.1. The Six Poorhouses Studied

Location	Description	Origin	Ending
Carroll County, New Hampshire	Rural county central NH (Ossipee)	County poorhouse 1870 (towns started their own poorhouses early 19th century)	Still has county farm with work done by inmates from House of Correction; almshouse building 125 years old; County Home changed in 1973 to Mountain View Nursing Home
Haverhill, Mass.	Mid-sized northern Mass. city, once center of shoe industry	1820	Changed in 1937 to "Infirmary" although continued to have "inmates" and poor farm through the late 1940s; became Glynn Nursing Home
Lewiston, Maine	Mid-sized Maine city, Franco-American industrial textile center	1839	Lasted as working city poor farm until 1967
Portland, Maine	Seacoast Maine city, largest in state	Workhouse reputed to be from 1763; almshouse verified from 1803	Changed name to "Home and Hospital" in 1930s though continued also to have inmates, poor farm until 1950s
Rockingham County, New Hampshire	Seacoast NH, mixed rural and more dense; located in Brentwood	County poor farm from 1868; towns and cities had poorhouses from late 18th century	Gradually in 1960s moved toward a medical model, with "inmate" term fading; poor farm until late 1970s; now Rockingham County Nursing Home and Rockingham County Jail
Worcester, Mass.	Second-largest New England city; large manufacturing city in nineteenth and first half of twentieth century	Workhouse attributed to 1772; consecutively run almshouse from 1818	Poor farm greatly damaged by a tornado in 1953, but inmates moved in 1955 to Belmont Home, which also continued a hybrid medical/poor farm with inmates through 1960s

Table 1.2. Six Poorhouses by Size and Voluntary Nature

Location	Number of Inmates 1890–	Voluntary/Correctional
Carroll County, New Hampshire	Average of about 50; as high as 90 in Great Depression	Initially the numbers of those sentenced so few they were integrated with poorhouse residents; later a separate floor for house of corrections; finally becomes Carroll County Jail
Haverhill, Massachusetts	Prior to new building in 1894 in the 40s; averaged 85–115 afterwards, with high of 250 inmates in 1930s	Poorhouse only except for a brief (1891–1898) stint as a workhouse as well
Lewiston, Maine	Range 65–90 most of time, high 115 in depressions, declined to dozens only in last decades	No house of correction or workhouse
Portland, Maine	Usually in the 200 area with high of 300 in Great Depression	Workhouse and later house of correction existed until 1929; few sentenced there after World War I
Rockingham County, New Hampshire	Low of 90–100, usually 150–200 with high of 379 in Great Depression (1935)	Had poorhouse and house of corrections, always separate; today Rockingham County Jail in same complex as Rockingham County Nursing Home
Worcester, Massachusetts	Small until 1890s when averages in 150 range, grows consistently with average of 300–350 in Great Depression and afterwards	No workhouse or house of correction, although there is one reference to a small number sentenced in very early days

ORGANIZATION OF THE BOOK

Chapter 2 describes a number of incidents in the history of the poorhouse in several locales that span from the 1820s to the 1970s. I start in a nonchronological manner for two reasons. One is to highlight the ambiguity and complexity of history as illustrated by the contrast between the repressive story of the early poorhouse and workhouse in the early nineteenth century with the memories of community in some twentieth-century city farms and homes. Secondly, since historians and some social welfare experts have left the history of the almshouse/poorhouse in the nineteenth century, I want to stress the poor farm/poorhouse as an important part of the more recent American history as well.

Chapters 3 through 7 return to a somewhat more chronological treatment of the New England poorhouses. In chapter 3, I explore the idealistic, if often repressive, motives that led to the development of poorhouses, and analyze how the objectives of the poorhouse contained the contradictions that led to its disrepute not long after some of them were built. In chapter 4, I use historical evidence to examine how inmates themselves subverted the purposes of the poorhouse by examining how both long-term and short-term inmates undermined the ideals of the poorhouse founders. Chapter 5 continues the focus on the turn-of-the-century period (1890–1910) and the undermining of the legitimacy of the poorhouse system. Here we see how inmates had the power to force an investigation and widespread news coverage of one city farm, while in another city, inmates threw the overseers of the poor and other politicians into constant conflict with each other. In chapter 6, using particularly rich documentary sources about three poorhouses in the twentieth century, I attempt to identify (directly and indirectly) how inmates continued to use these institutions, sometimes to their own advantage. In chapter 7, I focus on the other group often left out of this history, the officials and employees of the poorhouses and poor farms. From what can be told from the history, generally these were dedicated people who attempted to humanize the institution, and in many cases provided resistance to frugal budgets and harsh proposed policies, sharing some common interest with the inmates.

Finally, in the concluding chapter, I reflect on how the poorhouse was a stigmatized institution that naturally drew few mourners at its end. Yet only a few decades after social welfare historians and social scientists spoke confidently of progress, conditions for those at the bottom of society have arguably worsened to levels worse than in most of the twentieth century. The massive growth in homelessness in the last two decades has led to a new institution, the homeless shelter. These shelters have in many cases produced worse conditions than were the case in the poorhouses, poor farms, and city and county homes discussed in this book. Yet, interestingly, just as the reforms of the early nineteenth century that led to a mass growth in poorhouses, the development of the homeless shelter was in many ways a liberal reform. The growth in homelessness on top of the massive imprisonment of the poor in the last two decades (with over 2.2 million people in jail or prison each night) should at least make us wonder about the claim that history brings progress.

2

Scenes from the Poorhouse

The indigent has no claim to be supported in idleness . . . their poverty generally grows out of an unwillingness to labor, or is occasioned by reckless and improvident habits.

—Maine Supreme Court, April 1834
Upholding Adeline Nott's commitment to the Portland workhouse[1]

Every night there was a card game . . . and then they [inmates] would play the harmonica and tap their shoes and sing.

—Interview with daughters of Antoine and Adrienne Landry, superintendent and matron of Lewiston (Maine) City Farm in 1920s and 1930s[2]

The quotes above indicate some of the changes in institutions for the poor over a century's time, transforming at least some of the old poorhouses. Of course, any institution that spans hundreds of years creates a wide variety of experiences, memories, and historical evidence. In the case of the poorhouse, both misunderstanding and conflict about whether the house was to be an institution of discipline and moral correction or simply a place for the poor to gain comfort and a place to stay (an almshouse in the truer meaning of the word) endured for many years. Meanwhile, major historical changes were occurring in the nineteenth century that affected the relations between poor and working-class citizens of towns and cities and the overseers of the poor and other officials who dominated them. By the late nineteenth century, many poorhouses came to accept as inevitable that most of their inmates would come and go as they pleased.

The following extremely diverse fragments of history show how widely different the experiences of the poorhouses in New England were. The first part of the chapter discusses two incidents in the early years of the nineteenth century. One is the presentation of two petitions from citizens in Haverhill, Massachusetts, asking that certain fellow citizens be placed in "the House that is Located by this Town for persons of this description." The second incident is the harsh removal of one Adeline Nott, a Portland pauper, from the streets to a workhouse in 1834, illustrating the repressive role of the institution. However, years later, changes in society had affected how the poor were treated. As exemplified in the third example, Worcester's overseers were so exasperated by the conduct of many inmates they called "rounders" at the turn of the twentieth century, they not only complained bitterly in their reports but were totally unable to prevent them from occupying city jobs in the warm season and almshouse beds in the cold season.

Later in the twentieth century, examples of poor people finding community and camaraderie among themselves (and sometimes with superintendents, matrons, and other employees of poorhouses, which were by then often known as city or county farms or county or city homes) are more evident than repression. The remainder of this chapter focuses discussion on three moments of time from the twentieth century: the memories of the daughters of a superintendent and matron of the Lewiston (Maine) City Farm from the 1920s and 1930s; a film, letter, story, and memories of the Rockingham County (New Hampshire) Home in the late 1930s through 1940s; and the reports of some former inmates resisting the end of the almshouse in Carroll County (New Hampshire) in the 1970s.

Although I focus on the transformation of the poorhouse, institutional complexity and multiple roles always characterized the poorhouse, as they do nearly every other social institution. Too often, historians and experts speak as if one function, such as social control, on the one hand, or altruism, on the other hand, dominates the history of social life.[3] In fact, in complex fashion, the old poor relief system contained both these functions as well as others.

NOT IN MY BACKYARD: NEIGHBORS' PETITIONS IN HAVERHILL, MASSACHUSETTS, 1820–1821

While the larger cities of early America—Boston, New York, Philadelphia— were among the first to develop workhouses and poorhouses, and were likely to be motivated by a kind of idealism and repression in expanding their "houses of industry" in the Jacksonian period (the 1820s and 1830s), no such idealistic clarity existed in the smaller cities and towns.[4] Haverhill, Massachusetts, then a small village thirty miles north of Boston, specifically rejected a workhouse at a town meeting in 1790.[5] Its decision in 1820 to employ "a practical farmer and his wife to take immediate charge of the [town] farm" seemed motivated mostly by economy and the difficulty of securing enough citizens to board the poor.[6] No great expectations existed in the early documents, and it is not at all clear if citizens understood what the new structure was for.

Whatever the town officials' motivations in starting a poor farm, some citizens of Haverhill seem to have believed that morals and poverty were intertwined, and that certain people were not appropriate residents of their area. In one petition from late in 1820, the citizens did not even know how to refer to the house, but apparently knowing that nearby Rowley had a poorhouse, they thought that two partners in immorality would be appropriate candidates for the new town institution.

> To Capt[ai]n Parker Greenough and Overseers of the Poor of the Town of Haverhill—Gentlemen:
> This is to certify that Whereas a certain woman known by the name of Duchy Tyler wife of Dudley Tyler belonging to the Poorhouse in Rowley from which place she has recently absconded and renewed a former connection with Enoch Eaton of this Town And in consequence have of the peace of the Neighborhood is greatly disturbed and their property rendered Insecure
> We the Undersigned do therefore pray that you would Exercise the Power with which you are Visited and remove the said Enoch Eaton and the said Duchy Tyler to the House that is Located by this Town for persons of this description.
>
> Haverhill December 2nd 1820
>
> Signed in behalf of the Community,
> Samuel Hale
> Ezekiel Hale
> Robert Sargent
> Richard Kimball
> W. Kimball[7]

Given the historical fragment, we do not know the history of Tyler and Eaton, though engaging in adultery certainly would have gotten any Massachusetts couple into trouble in those days. Whether the overseers of the poor of Haverhill decided to place Eaton and Tyler in the poorhouse to "warn them" out of town (which was a common practice toward the poor and also toward those of different religions or unacceptable morals), to send them into a gaol (jail), or to perhaps give them a chance to repent in front of the community is unknown.

Another petition notes poverty and failure to support was itself grounds of complaint:

> To the Overseers of the Poor of the Town of Haverhill,
> The Undersigned citizens of the town of Haverhill represent that [unreadable] Kelly resident in Haverhill, a poor man with a large family from bad habits and incapacity does not, and can not make proper provision for his family who are in consequence in a very destitute and miserable condition, and the said Kelly from his idle habits and his family are a very great incumbrance to the neighborhood in which they live, they therefore pray that you would cause said Kelly to be removed to the place of his lawful settlement or otherwise dealt with as you may see fit or put in the farm for the poor.
> December 11, 1821
> [ten signatures affixed][8]

Interestingly, the literature does not speak of citizens issuing complaints about poor people or suggesting candidates for the poorhouse. While we still do not know how common it was for citizens to issue petitions about the poor and their bad morals, the fragments from Haverhill's history remind us of the early American consensus about poverty, at least among upstanding citizens. With the exception of some cases seen as "deserving" or "worthy" of aid—usually widows and their children, the "lame," "crippled," and "infirm"—poverty was deemed a moral failing, and when it was combined with other transgressions, as in sex and intemperance, moral deviants were not with dealt with very charitably. Poverty and moral deviancy were integrally combined in citizens' minds.

ADELINE NOTT GOES TO THE WORKHOUSE, PORTLAND, MAINE, 1834

While Haverhill in the 1820s was still grappling with the purpose of its poorhouse, Portland, a much larger city eighty miles up the coast, had already had a workhouse for some time (some records indicate since 1763)[9] and those poor who were not deserving were confined there, along with others judged more deserving, including debtors, within the larger poorhouse. In 1834, one Adeline Nott had apparently been scraping together an existence in what was then downtown, begging and scrounging food and other necessities. As we know from our own times, periodically police go on roundups of street people, and constables had evidently begun a crackdown at the urging of local shopkeepers. Two of Portland's overseers of the poor drew up a habeas corpus ordering that she be placed in the workhouse. The warrant read in part:

Adeline G. Nott, now resident in said Portland, is a person able of body to work, has not estate or means otherwise to maintain Herself, and neglects and refuses to do so, lives a desolate, vagrant life and exercises no ordinary calling or lawful business sufficient to an honest livelihood, and in our opinion is liable to become chargeable to the City.[10]

With the city offering a twenty-five-cent reward for Nott's apprehension, finding her was easy. Portland's street urchins went on a hunt and a constable found her cowering behind a warehouse "surrounded by a pack of jeering children." She was taken to the workhouse and placed in charge of one Curtis Meserve, the master. She was cleaned up, given new clothes, and placed in a bed in the attic dormitory room for women. She was set to work washing clothes at the laundry.[11] Much of this scene should be quite familiar to contemporary Americans. Indeed, many homeless people have been forced from the streets, particularly at times of civic events or police crackdowns or during cold weather alerts. Today, the shadow of the workhouse is almost completely paralleled by "workfare" requirements in which a recipient of shelter or federal or city welfare is made to work off his or her benefits at places like the laundries of public institutions! Such work requirements are mandated both by federal welfare laws and by state and local laws in those states that still provide general assistance welfare.

What is most surprising to us now is the legal basis for Nott's incarceration. Absent a finding of illegal activity or grounds for mental commitment, generally homeless people cannot be held against their will for more than a brief period in our contemporary times. What is interesting about the Nott case was that she obtained an attorney, one R. A. Codman. Codman argued that Nott's confinement was unconstitutional, and that no citizen could be committed to a "dungeon or work-house . . . without trial or hearing . . . by persons with no judicial power." Codman also challenged the arrest on the right of the accused to be heard, to confront witnesses against her, and to generally have due process rights. While probably to most of us this seems like an important argument, Justice Nathan Weston, hearing the case in the Maine Supreme Judicial Court, dismissed all the arguments, summarizing that:

1. The Portland's Overseers of the Poor had no criminal jurisdiction [Is dismissed] . . . [her] case is not criminal in nature . . .
2. . . . the indigent have no claim to be supported in their idleness . . . their poverty generally grows out of an unwillingness to labor, or is occasioned by reckless and improvident habits
3. . . . that [she] is likely to claim support as a pauper
4. . . . that if she did not change her habits, [she] would soon be unable to support herself. . . . Overseers had acted within their authority . . . for

her benefit to remove her from the temptation to commit a crime and to teach her industrious habits so she could be restored as a useful member of society as soon as possible.[12]

No doubt the belief system enunciated by Judge Weston in 1834 is still present among some Americans today, and certainly served as a major part of the justification of American social policy for at least a century onward. Rather than America being adequately described as having a laissez-faire government in the nineteenth century, government intervened, often intrusively, into people's lives, particularly the poor. At the behest of reformers from Jacksonian to Progressive times, the state in fact intervened with the poor and a host of other populations "for their own good" to keep them from becoming "criminals" and enmeshed in a life of "dissipation." The workhouse project was very much a moral and rehabilitative one.

Yet the early construction of the workhouse/poorhouse as a quasi-criminal, quasi-rehabilitative institution did not have much historical staying power. Few cities or other jurisdictions were able to maintain a workhouse, and separate facilities for the "deserving" and "undeserving" poor became rare. More importantly, even if the law would uphold such actions against the poor (and certainly laws against vagrancy, tramping, begging, and other status offenses stayed on the books for nearly a century and a half in most American cities and towns), the growth of voting by the poor and immigrants and the development of political machines by the late nineteenth century made the type of harsh action taken against Nott increasingly rare. Some types of behavior such as public drunkenness did seem to continue to be punished by a stint at the workhouse or house of correction, yet the public reward and show of force against Nott did not continue. Politicians were well aware of opposition to the workhouse. Most importantly, the poor found ways to navigate the poorhouse and poor relief system, and employers in an increasingly industrial society came to rely on public institutions for support of the poor in slack times when their workforce was cut, but could still be needed for recall at any time.

UNCONTROLLABLE PAUPERS: THE "ROUNDERS" IN WORCESTER, 1901

While court action sent an inmate to a workhouse, poorhouses, like modern homeless shelters, gained clientele as refugees from the harshness of cold, hunger, and extreme poverty. Yet overseers and other officials, as well as reformers, resented this freedom since the ideology of the poor-house was still centered on the idea of rehabilitation and on transforming the characters of the poor into more perfect moral specimens. In fact, it is fair to say that few issues agitated officials and reformers for much of the history of the almshouse as did the intermittent users of the poorhouse. Writing in 1922, Robert Kelso quoted a nineteenth-century critique of poor men using the almshouses of Massachusetts:

> In winter, they [the poor] seek the towns in which they hope for the best ac-commodations, and the best living; and where the smallest returns will be re-quired for what they receive. . . . Nearly all of them are able, and if kept from ardent spirits, and compelled to work, would show themselves to be able to earn their own subsistence.[13]

Although not a new revelation then that many presumably able-bodied men used the poorhouses seasonally, the charge seemed to gain new hos-tility in the late nineteenth century, perhaps as a result of the depression of 1893 and the increasing number of foreign-born paupers in New En-gland. In the example of Worcester, men labeled "rounders" aroused a long attack from the overseers of the poor. "What [to] do with and how to treat the rounders who make the Home Farm [Worcester's almshouse] their headquarters in the winter each year is a problem that greatly tests the patience and good nature of the overseers," they complained. But the interesting twist was, in Worcester, these so-called rounders had found not just work but city jobs in the warmer season:

> The rounders are able-bodied men, who support themselves from May until the cool nights in the fall of the year force them to seek shelter in a public in-stitution. Some of them are employed in the city departments, where they re-ceive $1.75 per day for eight hours time. Others work on farms in adjoining towns, receiving their board and $20 per month wages. They spend their earnings for liquor, and when their services are no longer in demand they in-dulge in a protracted spree, and wind up by applying to be sent to the "poor-house." Their relatives will not shelter them, and they have their choice of ei-ther the Home Farm or jail. Of course they prefer the almshouse.[14]

The objections of the overseers of the poor in Worcester were not only moralistic—the inmates' seasonal use of the almshouse and alcohol use—but their disruptive effect on the almshouse:

> As a rule, the rounders are a disturbing element in the institution. They live on the principle of rule or ruin; they defy all discipline; the old and feeble inmate who happens to possess a few pennies given by some friend, or who has a small piece of tobacco or pocket-knife, is at the mercy of these

sharks, who watch the opportunity to appropriate for themselves the pocket property of their neighbors. With the return of warm weather, the rounder proclaims his contempt for the "poor-house" and for the Overseers of the Poor, and advises everybody on the premises to follow him, and then, without notifying superintendent or matron of his intention, sneaks off to the city, and in a few hours his name is on the pay-roll of a city department. Civil service is no barrier to him. He always has two reputable citizens who are willing to swear that they know him to be all right; that he resides at a stated number on a stated street, and he passes on and is at once placed on the eligible list.[15]

The dominance of some men within the almshouse over others (if true) would certainly parallel some patterns found in large homeless shelters of today, sometimes even in gang form such as at the Fort Washington Armory Shelter in New York City.[16] It is perhaps more interesting that inmates were able to secure from other departments of the same city seasonal jobs that the Poor Department in Worcester complained about but evidently was not able to halt. From a modern perspective, isn't some work better than idleness? It is well known that in the economy of the time many men could not find employment in the winter, so their effort to be employed as laborers in the warmer seasons might be applauded. But middle-class and upper-class Yankee society saw work and other moral norms in a very different way than working-class or poor people. Moral character stemmed from the willingness to work at all times and all places and at regular times. Nor could the dilemmas of immigrant workers be well understood by the overseers who lived well away from the Irish, Italian, Greek, and other immigrant districts of Worcester. Further, the fact that these men so flouted the authority of the superintendent, matron, and overseers clearly rankled with the authorities since this stance "disturbed" the almshouse, certainly when they also "advised everyone to follow them" out of the poorhouse in warmer weather.

Despite significant barriers to finding out further details about the Worcester "rounders"—the lack of payroll records available in that city and the lack of inmates listed by name after 1899—I return in chapter 4 to some discussion on the winter use of the Worcester almshouse as well as short-term use of other almshouses that so irritated the officials.

Although, of course, not coordinated or organized, the transformation of the institutions for the poor from being quasi prisons, so evident in the case of Adeline Nott, to ones in which poor people at times gained the upper hand was evident by the late nineteenth century. The following three scenes from a city farm and two county homes show how the twentieth-century institution became a community for many "inmates" (since they continued to be called such).

GROWING UP ON THE CITY FARM:
LEWISTON, MAINE, IN THE 1920s AND 1930s

Our natural tendency to divide people into categories can sometimes miss some commonalities. The daughters of Antoine and Adrienne Landry, the superintendent and matron of Lewiston City Farm from 1926 to 1938, grew up at the city farm and shared a certain degree of experience with the inmates of the farm. Merita Fournier, the eldest daughter (she was six to eighteen while her parents ran the farm), remembers sharing some of the stigma of the poor farm as she was made fun of in school by other children, including living with all the pigs. The daughters also shared a common confidential knowledge of who was at the farm, which was not something people broadcast. For example, in this heavily Catholic community, young pregnant single mothers were taken in to the third floor of the brick house on the city farm. Martha Friedman, somewhat younger than Merita, remembers as a young child being told by her mother that the girls "had broken legs and that is why they could not come down." Over the years, the confidentiality kept by Mrs. Landry stuck, and the daughters themselves passed women on the streets whom they recognized, but made no eye contact, much less discussion. In the 1960s, the youngest daughter, Gertrude Mynahan, remembers how the need for a baptism certificate sent a young woman into exploring her past and finding out she was born at the city farm. "You weren't the only one born on the farm," the woman joked with Ms. Mynahan.[17]

The four surviving daughters, all energetic and sharp in their seventies and eighties, speak almost at once about the city farm (their father and mother *never* called it the poor farm, they sternly note), which they praise in the words of Ms. Landry as being "like a commune." It is a description I had not expected to receive of a poorhouse, and some would perhaps wonder if the four were glorifying the past. While no doubt the nearly seventy years that have passed and the experience of childhood may color their comments, it was clear from other accounts that many New England homes did not fit the repressive stereotype.[18]

It is important to remember the families of the superintendent/matron, as well as most employees, lived at the homes, often fairly isolated from the center of cities. Most citizens, unless there was a public investigation going on, did not know much about the city farm and were unlikely to venture to the very edge of the city. Although today one can get quickly by highway to the area where the city farm in Lewiston was, seventy years ago it was tucked away at the edge of town, with little else nearby. The family and employees of poor farms shared in almost all aspects of daily life, and often had no separate building of their own.

Many of the memories of the Landry children are of working along with inmates; the young girls were not at all sheltered from them. They sat in a circle at harvest time and shucked corn with inmates and employees; when they picked wild raspberries, the inmates made them containers out of birch bark to hold the berries; the children joined the female inmates in the sewing room where one year forty quilts were made, and where "no one went around with tears or missing buttons" because Mrs. Landry would insist that even the most battered clothes be repaired. Many of the memories are humorous and evoked shared laughter among the sisters. Inmates and employees were known to frequent the silo and hold a cup to secure the grain alcohol that came out, and it was not unusual to see certain people "plastered" on the ground near the silo. The sisters tell with enjoyment about the farm cook who was an excellent cook but had a drinking problem. She was loved for "how good [she was] to those people. She would have little pies that she would make at lunch." But eventually the Landrys had to warn her as "she would go on a binge and then [our] mom would take over [the cooking]." But one day the cook decided to make soap from leftover food. Merita Fournier laughingly exclaimed, "She was using the same spoon for the soap and the food! And they had to let her go and my mom took over. She had to let her go because they could not take another chance like that. No, no, as much as we liked her, it is a good thing someone saw her!"

As in other farms/homes, long-term inmates are the best remembered and also evoke a fond humor. "Beaucatcher" was a middle-aged woman inmate who always said, "I am going to find myself a beau" (most inmates in the Lewiston City Farm spoke French). One day, Beaucatcher apparently brought some food upstairs, which was prohibited, and threw it out the window. It landed on their father's head. But when Mr. Landry told Beaucatcher that she was not supposed to bring food up there, she denied ever doing so. Their father laughed and protested that, "Well, it fell on my head, so I ought to know." The sisters think Beaucatcher would be diagnosed today as mildly retarded. She loved dolls and stuffed animals, and Mrs. Landry always made sure she had plenty of both. Another inmate who made an impression on the sisters was a teacher who was a double amputee, evidently from being hit by a train. Although some of women remember being scared at first of him, this inmate ended up helping some of the sisters with their homework and reading to other inmates.

Another memory that sticks with Mrs. Friedman is of an Italian inmate whose job was taking care of the chicken coop. The man was getting angrier and angrier as a result of chickens being killed and threatened to murder whoever was doing this. One night the emergency bell rang at the farm. Fearing the worst, their father ran to the coop, which was near the male dormitory, but he inexplicably found that all the male inmates (including the Italian man) had fled. There was a skunk in the coop that gave off an awful smell and it fell to the superintendent to deal with the animal, which the inmates clearly saw as not their task!

Along with humor, of course, there is sorrow regarding the tragedy of the widespread poverty of the Great Depression. The sisters remember many families coming to leave family members, usually elderly people, at the farm. Merita remembers one older man who had a son in Massachusetts and when he found out that his father was at what "he thought was the poor farm," he came to Lewiston with his wife.[19] But the man's father would not go with him. He said, "No, I am happy here." The son cried and cried, and said, "You are at the poor farm!" And the father said, "I do not look at it like that. I am happy, we are well fed. You have children, take care of your children. I am being well taken care of." The father would absolutely not go with his family.

On the other hand, Lorraine Comeau, another Landry daughter, remembers a time when a man drove up to the city farm in a new car and wanted to look around. "He was feeling the bread because he wanted to bring his parents there" and he was testing things. My mother said, "You are welcome to [leave your father here], but let me tell you something, if they die here, it is going to be in the [news]paper that he died at the City Farm and [that] you could have very well afforded to take care of him." The man's guilt was evidently aroused, as he did not leave his father there.

The Lewiston City Farm was located right near the railroad tracks, and many men got off the rails to stay, if only overnight, at the farm. During the Depression, the numbers of men "riding the rails" and "tramping" grew into the millions. It is not surprising that the city farm population rose to twice its former occupancy as the Depression wore on, and Mrs. Landry had to have dinner on the table for as many as 120 guests plus family and employees. Still other poor people were turned away for lack of room. Evidently, the settlement laws broke down some, as the sisters remember many people from Massachusetts and farther away coming off the trains and even by car. It is likely city officials never had an accurate count. The Depression also destigmatized poverty to some degree. Gertrude Mynahan says of her father, "When the numbers were so high the way dad used to talk about it is, look, they [inmates] were looking for work and this is where they would stay until they could get on their feet." Of course, consistent with the tradition of the poor farm, those who stayed more than overnight had to work on the farm, which some willingly did, while others moved on. The sisters noted the inmate community supported the work ethic. Martha Friedman noted, "The others used to squeal on [the lazy ones]." Gert Mynahan added, "'Yes, that guy can work,' they'd say. 'What's the matter with him?'"[20]

Some of the sadder memories for the sisters were when inmates took sick and died at the farm, which, given the age and disability of some inmates, was not unusual. Mrs. Landry always attempted to contact families, but often they were not around or interested. When inmates were ill, the daughters were obligated to go to the room and read to the ill. Particularly if there was no family, the Landry family stayed with the dying, attending prayers, last rites, and funerals. The loss of pride that accompanied "going to the poor farm" also affected the girls emotionally. Martha Friedman "remembers the old folks coming to the farm, and crying, you know. To them it was such a dishonor to be at the farm. They lost everything and the children couldn't manage."[21] One of the sadder stories was Gert Mynahan's memory of a man named Red, who worked on a garbage truck at the farm. In the 1950s, when Mynahan went to visit the farm, he was still there, and when their eyes met "he just started to cry."

Beyond the basic humanity of the home, with its humor and sadness, is the feeling of community that characterized the city farm, at least in the memories of the sisters (and reflected in an earlier paper on the Lewiston City Farm).[22] I was struck at the account of how the daily card game in the men's smoking room awaited the arrival of Antoine (commonly known as Tony) Landry. "Oh yeah," the sisters insisted, "even if he had a meeting, they'd wait. 'When's Tony coming back?' There was a social circle going on." Consistent with French Canadian culture, the sound of harmonicas and foot tapping, and on some occasions, accordions, was a staple of evening entertainment. No doubt the common culture of most of the inmates and employees as Franco-Americans who shared the experience of severe discrimination in Maine explains some of the feeling of the home. And, indeed, when the city farm was criticized, it received support from the French language paper *Le Messager*, one of whose editors accused a politician of attacking the farm on ethnic grounds.[23]

The Landry daughters are extremely intelligent and are aware of most people's ideas of poor farms. Gert Mynahan noted at one point, "Maybe some county farms were mismanaged, but I think the Lewiston Farm was a good place. The food was fine and people were always well-treated and happy there." Drawing on her later experience as a city worker and community volunteer, Mynahan makes an important point: "What I used to see in the boarding homes [in her work as an inspector for the City] is that people were so lonely. There is nothing for them. At least there [the Lewiston City Farm] they had others, they had a smoking room, they had a place to play cards. There was interaction. Another human being [was] there. At the boarding house they would die alone in their room, with no one."

I was fascinated that Ms. Mynahan had made a point very similar to one I had made elsewhere about isolation of formerly homeless people who were placed in housing.[24] I raised the paradox of professional intervention into homeless people's lives, when in some cases it results in placing people into single sterile rooms far from their friends or from areas of the city where they had gone about their daily routines of interaction. For some formerly homeless people, the streets and the community they found there, along with soup kitchens and day centers, provided a close-knit set of friendships and social supports that was more important than just having a room. Given my own set of experiences and conversations with poor people, I was not surprised that for many inmates of the city farm, particularly its long-term inmates, the city farm was a community that they clung to.

THE "HOTEL HILTON": ROCKINGHAM COUNTY HOME

Several things strike me about the Rockingham County home, whose successor institutions still sprawl impressively over hundreds of acres of farmland and a mix of quaint (along with institutional) buildings in rural Brentwood, New Hampshire. One was the focus of the home on reading. The annual reports of the Rockingham County Almshouse and Farm indicate donations were arranged in the late nineteenth century for a library, and in 1908 that "almost everything is read and re-read until it literally falls apart."[25] I discovered a catalogue at the New Hampshire State Library; this little booklet with sixteen pages was undated, but its list of four hundred volumes corresponds with a county report in 1896. The catalogue reflects a fairly well-rounded collection of books from the classics of Cervantes, Defoe, Dickens, Hawthorne, Longfellow, and Thackeray, children's books, travel books, reference books, Bible and temperance tales, and even an antislavery pamphlet. As the quote about the books being read and reread indicates, the inmates did read the books, and increasingly the local communities of Exeter and Epping also provided magazines and newspapers as well as more books to the growing library.[26]

Another thing I noticed was the early appearance of the term *boarder*. By the 1880s, Rockingham County's list of inmates became "inmates and boarders." The term *boarder* would also appear in Carroll County's, Portland's, and Lewiston's poorhouses. Boarders were self-paying clients who sought out the refuge of the institution. By far the largest numbers of boarders seem to be at Rockingham. Most were elderly people and quite a few were couples. The rural nature of much of the county combined with what appears to have been early attention to good medical care may have combined to specifically attract people to Rockingham's county home, and clearly we can see the growth of boarders as a transition to the modern nursing home. As with the growing library, the presence of more boarders certainly gives a different impression from the traditional view of poor farms and county homes.[27]

My first impression of Rockingham's farm was seeing a film, something of a rarity I imagine in the histories of county farms. I viewed the film at the house of Frank Northrup, the nephew of former Superintendent George Hilton and son of Sydney Northrup, the "boss farmer" at Rockingham County in the late 1930s and part of the 1940s. The film, spliced together from footage shot in the 1940s, is about twenty minutes long and is mostly focused on the prodigious farm produce and business capacity of the Rockingham farm, including a large ice-cutting operation and a logging and chipping operation that made the home self-sufficient in fuel and freezing food year-round. What most struck me, as someone interested in the human dimension, was a short scene of a middle-aged inmate named Charlie, who was shown carrying swill over to the pigs. In one scene, Charlie, to the delight of other inmates and workers, chased a pig around the yard. I asked Frank about Charlie and he went into some length about him. Charlie started out as a prisoner at the house of correction.[28] He had only a short sentence and then had nowhere to go. The superintendent agreed to let him stay on, and Charlie even slept with the prisoners, as "he liked the accommodations there." As a child, Frank remembers seeing Charlie smoking his pipe all the time. "Charlie would rarely ever talk, except when he was out on the road. There he would talk with you."

What struck me about the film and conversation was how Charlie would not today be allowed to stay in any facility without payment or state or federal reimbursement. It is unimaginable that Charlie, not a convict, would be allowed in a jail, but neither would he be allowed in the nursing home or psychiatric facility without a medical diagnosis and a form of payment. His only option would perhaps be a homeless shelter, but that would not be an option for the amount of years he spent at Rockingham (which from inmate records was for many years), as almost all homeless shelters are short-term facilities that pressure clients to secure longer-term arrangements. Some shelters now outright prohibit stays over a certain period, such as thirty or sixty days.

Charlie represents a different time when the county home served as a type of "catchall" in which those who wished to stay and work on the farm could. Charlie appeared to me as possibly mentally retarded, but Frank's description of him as "a person with nowhere to go" seems apt. After all, assuming he was mentally retarded, would he have been better off at a facility for the "feeble minded," as they were called then? Most certainly not, not only given the usual reports of these institutions but also today's beliefs that people with disabilities should have a normalized life with all their rights intact. The images of the film show quite a bit not only about Charlie and his fellow inmates hamming it up for the camera but also about how a sense of community tied together the men in the film. It was indeed hard to pick out without Frank Northrup's help who were the inmates, the prisoners, and the regular employees of the county home and farm in the film.

George Hilton was superintendent and his wife, Dorothy, matron, for thirty-five years at the time the Rockingham County institutions were gradually becoming separate and specialized (the jail, nursing home, hospital, farm). Hilton's name, combined with his philosophy of allowing prisoners as well as inmates free rein over the hundreds of acres, garnered the home the nickname of "Hotel Hilton."[29] The Hiltons indeed took pride in treating the groups equally; inmates, boarders, prisoners, and employees all ate the same food. The vast grounds were not terribly difficult for anyone to leave, and prisoners were part of a work crew. Win Hilton, the son of the late George Hilton, laughs about a time when he was working at the farm over the summer and was told to keep his eyes on some prisoners while they cut wheat. "Well, they just escaped under my eyes . . . first one was gone, then another." Still, says Win, "they nearly always found them. It's a small county and not much place to hide." He remembers as a child one day driving with his father in an old Ford and suddenly his father saying, "Hey, there's so-and-so" right in the middle of Brentwood. His father simply ordered him to open the car door and Mr. Hilton grabbed the man and put him in the car.[30]

The laissez-faire nature of security at the almshouse/farm/house of correction/hospital is evident from a letter found in the files of the Rockingham County complex. In a May 14, 1941, letter, County Commissioner Alvin Foss wrote a lengthy apology to Alfred Gosselin, the deputy sheriff of the small town of Raymond, New Hampshire, who evidently passed through the complex and could find no one in charge, after failing to get a telephone response from the hospital.[31] Foss explained the telephone service had been "out of order for a day and a half or so" and that Gosselin's visit to the jail must have coincided with "the turn-key being away from his station for one half hour . . . [so that he could] make rounds as night watchman." More amusing still was Foss's apology for what was evidently a noisy party across from the hospital and almshouse at the nurses' home:

> We cannot, in any degree, permit any boisterousness to be in being there [*sic*], and of course it is our hope that there will be reasonable decorum exhibited there at all times but we also feel that we want the nurses to be as content as possible and we do not want to restrict them any more than the welfare of the whole family at our Institution requires. We cannot have them

be an inconvenience to those sleeping patients and sleeping inmates who are so close to them in the other building, and a word such as you have given me concerning the matter is of great value . . . because it causes us to give this matter immediate attention.

Clearly this was quite a balancing act, running a modern hospital with educated nurses while having an almshouse and a house of correction!

The copious scrapbooks kept by Dorothy Hilton contained many interesting items. One of the most interesting was a story called "County Farm," written for publication by a Dale Scott.[32] Scott (it is not clear if this is a real name or pseudonym) was arrested and sentenced to six months for vagrancy to Rockingham County Farm. He describes his being brought in a police car with a man named Spike. Spike asked the sheriff to stop so he could get a pack of cigarettes. With no handcuffs on, Spike got out. "I thought he was the smart one, that we wouldn't be seeing him again," Scott said. Yet Spike returned and the chief told the author, "You're lucky, Scottie. Brentwood isn't a bad place." After an hour-and-a-quarter drive, the car slowed down "before a large farm of the sort you'd expect a millionaire to run as a hobby. Wide fields, several big red brick buildings, a couple of small white frame cottages. The usual sort of barns. No fences or walls." When they arrived, Scott found out Spike was a carpenter:

> [Lloyd, the turnkey]: "Well, Spike," he said with a grin. "So it is really you. . . . Matter of fact the boys decided that if you didn't show up soon we ought to go out and round you up."
>
> Deadpan, Spike looked at him. "What do you have in mind, Lloyd?"
>
> "An extension on the barn," said Lloyd. "We can't trust the work to anyone but you."
>
> I later learned that Spike was the carpenter, the best they had, and that most of the remodeling around the Farm had been done by him on his various "visits" to Brentwood. Spike hadn't always been what he was but had once been a prosperous contractor. His downfall had been caused by a woman, I believe, but that's Spike's story.

I realized this particular story was based in fact because Frank Northrup had told me about the carpenter who, when needed, was often "picked up" for minor offenses so that work could be completed at the county home.

Scott's story confirms the low security of Brentwood. "Odd as it may sound, we actually had less security than on a regular farm. Russ, the farm boss, would tell us what [was] to be done and how to do it" and left them alone. Despite the growing specialization of the postwar period, Scott suggests there was considerable contact between the county home population and the prisoners at the house of correction. "The old men had the job of setting our tables. They ate at one and we were always kidding back and forth. In the evenings some of the old codgers were likely to slip down to our recreation room for a game of cribbage or so. We got along fine." In fact, Win Hilton notes that despite his mother's dismay ("she did not want me mingling with prisoners"), he always played football and other sports with the prisoners. "It was great, there never was any trouble."

In admitting he "really enjoyed these months" at the farm, Scott recognizes that tough-on-criminal members of the public would object. "Was I treated too well?" he asks. Scott's reply to his rhetorical question is interesting:

> One thing for sure, I hadn't come out hard and bitter. . . . On the contrary I felt sincerely grateful for the chances given to me to prove I was worthy of confidence. . . . Some of the men were repeaters and the majority were there for incidents connected with drunkenness. . . . I will say that after a couple of weeks none of them seemed to miss liquor—and this without the pills and diets of the sanitoriums [sic] where more prosperous inebriates are sent for "cures." Our men certainly didn't become worse for having been at the Farm and moreover as long as they were there the State could have comfort that they weren't costing the tax-payers any money but were making a genuine contribution with their labor. On the other hand, there were quite a lot of us for whom this was a first offense and pretty sure to be the last.

I have quoted from Scott's story at some length because, as with Charlie, the story offers some perspective on the changes in the last fifty or sixty years. While, on a positive note, laws now regulate convict labor and ensure some minimal pay, it is also true that as houses of correction become history, they are usually replaced by high-security prisons even in the low-crime states such as New Hampshire. The process was going on in front of my eyes in Carroll County's jail in Ossipee, New Hampshire. There I stumbled by chance into the house of correction on my first visit, and met an amiable crop of young prisoners who lived in the old almshouse building. There was almost no security. Coming up over the horizon, though, was a massive new jail, scheduled for completion soon, which will have modern amenities such as the already completed electrified barbed-wire fence. Certainly some may claim higher crime rates and different types of crime necessitate the massive increase in number and size of prisons, but the prisoners at Rockingham and Carroll were arrested for vagrancy, drinking, and other misdemeanors, and the majority of arrests today are still for nonviolent offenses.

Lest one imagine the Rockingham home and house of correction as some sort of correctional "nirvana," there were certainly prisoners who felt differently than Dale Scott. To Mrs. Hilton's credit, her scrapbooks include an article on a 1948 prison strike, a large number of escapes, and a

1962 petition and protest by prisoners. All could be read as being critical of Hilton's leadership. In response to the article on the strike and the prisoner grievances, even Win Hilton stressed his father's strictness and his "old school" roots. Both the written record and the family recollections suggest that, if a prisoner did cross Hilton, he faced a tough adversary. Prisoners were given a chance, but if they failed, their terms were extended, they could get confinement or bread and water as meals, and escapees were marked with special uniforms. Win Hilton believed his father would not respond well to prison protests. "These were different times. I don't think he would think well of [this]. We did not have, you know, a notion of due process."

Unlike the Landry family, Win Hilton and Frank Northrup grew up playing with prisoners and inmates but feeling little stigma about it. Both responded that it was only when they grew older that they came to learn the "poor farm" had such a negative connotation. Perhaps it was the success of the farm as an agricultural producer, according to Win Hilton, that gave it a very different image. He remarked, "It was the food on their table!" suggesting many county denizens thought of the Rockingham complex first as a large farm and only second as an institution.

HANGING ON TO THE ALMSHOUSE: CARROLL COUNTY, NEW HAMPSHIRE, 1979

Specialists (as well as the public) have buried the words "almshouse," "poorhouse," and "poor farm" in obscurity. Even social welfare textbooks mention them almost exclusively in reference to the nineteenth century.[33] So I was surprised enough when I visited the Carroll County buildings in Ossipee, New Hampshire, to find an existing almshouse building and a working poor farm (though now worked by prison labor). Still, even though locals laughed and joked that the small county south of the White Mountains was "pretty behind the times," it was not until I went through some newspaper clippings that I saw how recently the non-elderly residents held on to to their home.

Carroll County Home, like most evolving poorhouses, transformed over the course of the twentieth century into a more specialized and professionalized system of care. Admissions, as reflected in the ledger, became more, though never exclusively, elderly people, and the home formally became a nursing home, changing its name in 1973 to the Mountain View Nursing Home. The house of correction was renamed the county jail. But interestingly, as is true elsewhere, several population groups were left out of this transition. Two groups that appear on the ledger a long time (into the 1960s) were children and mothers (presumably single) who gave birth. Children, presumably orphans, stayed only a short time and were placed in foster and adoptive homes. Another group that also appears in several other homes were women and children with the notation in the ledger "for protection." These were domestic violence cases. We have little data on this rather hidden role of the poorhouse, yet most of the ledgers I examined had at least a few entries marked "for protection."

Other groups that often found nowhere to go in either rural areas or even urban areas were those inmates who used the poor farms seasonally, those who were disabled and old but did not want to live in a nursing home, and other adults such as ex-convicts or homeless people who had nowhere else to go. While all almshouses had seasonal dwellers, according to an interview with former Carroll County farm employees who had worked at the home in the 1940s and 1950s, there was a sizable number of folks who lived seasonally in the Carroll County Home.[34] Many people had old drafty homes they could not afford to heat in the winter, lived in homes that were abandoned by absentee owners in the winter, or had families who had trouble caring for them. They lived in the Carroll County Home in winter, but returned to their own homes in warmer weather. One man who lived in Madison, nineteen miles away, came every year in a wooden wheelchair that he pushed himself until he got to the home. It is not surprising that people who chose to come to this institution felt a strong bond of community and some would not give it up when the home evolved into a jail and nursing home.

On May 31, 1979, the *Granite State News* reported that a dozen people were living in the almshouse, an old wooden structure attached to the jail called the "ell." The article at first implies the people are poachers, quoting Russ Whiting, superintendent of the jail, as saying he had had to "arrest several persons living in the annex for being disorderly and created [*sic*] a high risk of fires." Social worker Forest Painter also stated he did not know how the people came to live there and noted that, "Many return to their hometown for the warm months and live in the annex in the winter." Yet the article goes on to indicate they did have county permission as "each resident was paying the county $150 a month for room and board." Though they slept in the almshouse, they ate with the nursing home residents.[35]

A much more descriptive article appeared in June 1979 when a reporter toured the building. There she met Mildred Bisbee, who had lived in the original almshouse for a dozen years. She is described as the housekeeper, yet it is not clear if this was a former paid role or an adopted role. Mildred "in her seventies, will probably go to live with her daughter, but she is sad to see the ell abandoned." Mildred provided a tour:

Escorting us through, she pointed out the former administrator's quarters
. . . showing us each room brought back memories. Some former tenants have

died, some went on to more independent ways of life. In recent years, not all the memories were happy ones. "Loose" or "bad" women who would let men into their rooms have lived for short periods under this ancient roof. Mildred feels sorry for some of the men and women who are unhappy at having to give up their "home."[36]

When she was complimented on the condition of some of the rooms, Mildred replied, "We had a fellow who was one of the House of Correction boys. Then when he'd served his time he stayed on and worked. He liked to paint and fix up and it was a help."

Earlier, the reporter had found "two elderly men rattled around from the recreation room, containing an unused-looking pool table, an ancient refrigerator and antique photographs." The article, while sympathetic to an extent with the hangers-on, noted the dangers of the building, the lack of supervision, and the possibility that "some of the residents . . . being treated for mental conditions and/or alcoholism . . . might be endangering not only themselves but the rest of the complex."[37]

I would not venture an opinion on whether the twelve (or likely more) individuals would be "better off" elsewhere, as reporters, administrators, and social workers clearly agreed, but rather only comment on the ultimate irony of an institution that was developed to "repress pauperism" and punish the poor becoming a somewhat illicit home for the poor in the late twentieth century. The incident suggests the amazing human adaption to institutions; no matter that the intent of counties and cities was to "put the poor to work" or to "classify" them and "place them." Real people find community and find spaces to live, have relationships, and pass the time. The fact that the 1979 incident corresponds to the period when the United States entered a new crisis of homelessness with a new institution—the homeless shelter—may be coincidental, but is also fitting. As the problem of poverty worsened, the institutional choices again worsened, and some have called the shelter America's new almshouses.[38]

3

What the Forefathers Had in Mind: The Purpose and Contradictions of the Poorhouse

Our mission is to furnish everything comfortable for the inmates, kindly caring for the sick and performing all the duties which the unfortunate poor are entitled, but in no way to encourage indolence and pauperism and fill the institution with people too lazy to care for themselves.

—Superintendent Trottier, Rockingham County Farm, 1910[1]

The worthy poor have no just cause to complain; the "deadbeat" element cannot [with]stand personal investigation.

—Worcester, Mass., Overseers Report, 1901[2]

The public usually conjures up a Dickensian vision of institutions for the poor, yet I have presented some scenes from the later poor farms and county homes that are certainly more benign. No doubt, tremendous changes occurred between the early nineteenth century and the late twentieth century in America. What did the inventors of the poorhouse intend? This is a complex question for several reasons. First, somewhat different traditions intersected: one of the European workhouse, modeled straightforwardly as a correctional facility, if certainly more short term than the prison, and two, a vaguer notion of a poorhouse or poor farm divorced from specific correctional intent, but focused on a combination of farm work and shelter. Second, each institution blended a variety of motives—repression, compassion, rehabilitation, and maintenance of a low-wage labor force—with local traditions and economies. I have suggested the term "repressive benevolence" in another work to describe centuries of American social welfare and charitable efforts.[3] Although the development of the poorhouse as well as other efforts at social welfare were self-consciously altruistic, with the "giver" truly believing in his or her own compassion, at the same time, such charity was predicated on the submission, deference, and subservience by the "inferior" party. The poor would receive care if they agreed to reform their characters. Euro-American benevolence aimed to socialize the "deviant" (which in the minds of dominant political and religious leaders included not only the poor but also the morally inferior, such as the intemperate, the sexual woman or girl, or disobedient child) as part of a moral obligation of "doing good." Like the mental asylum, penitentiary, and home for unwed mothers that paralleled or followed the origin of the almshouse, the poorhouses' intent was to reform the deviant and turn him or her into a productive citizen.[4] Finally, we must place the almshouse in the context of history: the almshouse originated in a preindustrial period, yet came to play an important role in the American industrial period between the Civil War and World War II. The contradictions that were present to a great degree when the Poor Laws began were heightened by the contrast of the old system with new conditions of industrial America.

This chapter traces the workhouse/poorhouse tradition as it evolved in the nineteenth century, the mission its sponsors hoped it would serve, and the contradictions that were confronted by the overseers of the poor and other officials during the process of American industrialization. Despite what David Rothman has called the idealistic utopianism of the Jacksonian period, many towns did not embrace the almshouse as anything more than an expedient. But even where high expectations of reform were present, the realities that the poor could be forced neither to enter an almshouse nor to comply with rules once there complicated and changed the poorhouse. At least by the late nineteenth century, shelter came to replace moral reform.

THE WORKHOUSE/POORHOUSE TRADITION

In early America, the workhouse followed the English example and was clearly a correctional institution, as the following duties of John Sebring, the first superintendent of New York City's workhouse in 1736, spell out:

> [To] sett on Work all such poor as shall be sent or committed thither and able to labour; and also disorderly persons, parents of Bastard Children, Beggars, Servants running away or otherwise misbehaving themselves, Trespassers, Rogues, Vagabonds, poor persons refusing to work, and on their refusal to work and labor correct them by moderate Whipping, and to yield a true Account to Every General Quarter Sessions of the peace to be held for this City

and County of all persons committed to his custody, and of the offences for which they are committed.[5]

This complete mixing of the status of poverty with criminality (bastardy, trespassing, runaway servants, vagabondage, etc.), while persisting to a great degree throughout American history, could not completely continue as the young nation grew, and the status of "poor" impacted many people. There were, after all, the old and infirm, lame and crippled, widows and orphans, war veterans, and, as became obvious even to the most conservative observer, people unemployed due to economic depressions. Moreover, while the English workhouse was aimed at enforcing work on a peasantry moving out of a feudal, fixed society, it is hard to argue that American settlers had to be jolted off the land or out of their villages. Even where a workhouse continued operation—and many communities rejected the idea—it was gradually modified from the harshness of 1736.

In the first stage of development of institutions for the poor, between the eighteenth century and the period of large-scale construction of almshouses, it appears that some of the harshest treatments of the workhouse—for example, whipping—were abandoned for punishment by isolation and some emphasis on positive reward. Second, provision was made for the ill and elderly, and even for teaching pauper schoolchildren. By reviewing the rules of two almshouses, we can see how the workhouse idea was gradually altered to serve as a place of both charity (to the "deserving") and punishment (to the recalcitrant poor).

At roughly the time Adeline Nott went into the Portland Almshouse, she would have faced an amazingly detailed set of rules and regulations (see box 3.1).[6] Dated 1839, the rules and regulations show the similarities of the early almshouse to the other "total institutions" (the asylum, prison and penitentiary, orphanage) being invented simultaneously. For example, the accent on the ringing of the bells and time precision, as David Rothman in *The Discovery of the Asylum*, among others, has noted, mirrors the development of the factory and public school at the time, as well as the asylum, prison, orphanage, and hospital.[7]

The detailed rules, regulating almost every action from rising in the morning to eating meals, combined with the restriction on any visiting except on Wednesdays (with permission!) and on any "intercourse between the sexes" would strike us deeply repressive today, even without the constant reiteration in the rules that the "severest" punishment will be meted out. As one reads the rules, one does need to remind oneself that the almshouse was technically not a prison! Still, while Portland's house was a workhouse *and* poorhouse, we see some beginning differentiation and specialization of the institution. First, we note the presence of a "hospital," albeit a primitive one with inmates serving as nurses, an arrangement that

Box 3.1 RULES AND REGULATIONS
for the Government of the PORTLAND ALMS-HOUSE

Admission

Art. I: All persons admitted into the Alms-House, shall be examined, as to cleanliness from Vermin, or any infectious disorder, and kept as separate as possible, until the difficulty is removed. Their clothes and furniture shall go with them unless ordered otherwise.

Rising and the Sabbath

Art. II: At the ringing of the morning Bell, every person, the sick and infirm excepted, shall rise, dress and wash themselves clean, after which if Sunday, put on their best apparel, and attend religious service, at the second ringing of the bell, if performed at the House. The day shall be set apart from all unnecessary labor or recreation. If no minister or other suitable person shall attend to preaching or reading; the day shall be kept by reading the bible or other good books; as a day of rest, without noise or disturbance—all violations punished severely.

Meals

Art. III: The Bell will be rung 10 minutes before each Meal, when every person shall cease from any occupation they may be engaged in, and be ready with clean hands and faces for the ringing of the second Bell, when they will repair to the Dining-Room, and take such seats as shall be assigned them by the keeper, where they must strictly observe decency and good order. Half an hour each will be allowed for Breakfast and Supper, and one hour for Dinner, at the expiration of which times the Bell will be again rung, when every person shall immediately repair to the work assigned them by the keeper. They shall not take any bread or other food with them; they shall not loiter on the way, but shall proceed with alacrity, and at once commence labor. No cooking whatever will be permitted in any room except the kitchen, nor shall any provision be carried into any rooms, those occupied by the sick and infirm excepted.

Cooking

Art. IV: The master or mistress shall weigh and deliver daily the provisions to the cooks, and allow none but assistants duly appointed, to be in the cook-rooms. The cook appointed by the master, shall keep his department and utensils perfectly clean; be punctual in preparing meals, setting the tables, prudent of provisions and wood, preserving fragments for the Pigs. Assistants for the cook, shall obey the head cook, and allow no provisions to be used except at meal times, unless ordered by the master.

Cleanliness

Art. V: Every tenanted room in the house, together with the entries and stairways, cells and cellars, must be swept clean every morning, and scoured once a week, or oftener if necessary, by such persons as the keeper shall appoint. No filth or dirt shall be thrown out the windows, and no person shall in any way dirty the yards or out-houses, and the sweepings of the house shall be deposited by the sweepers in a place or places directed by the keeper. The whole inside of the house to be white-washed spring and fall.

Wash-Day

Art. VI: Washers appointed by the master, on wash days, shall receive, and carefully wash and dry the Clothes, and put them in order and give them to the owners. No washing allowed on other days without permission.

Rising in the Morning, and Retirement for the Night

Art. VII: At the first ringing of the bell in the morning, all the tenants of the house (the sick and infirm excepted) must immediately rise, dress, wash, and repair to their several employments. At 9 o'clock P.M. in summer, and 8 o'clock P.M. in winter, on ringing the bell, every person in the house must repair to their apartments, extinguish the lights, secure the fires, and retire to bed. No person at any time allowed to stroll into any room or entry, not leading directly to his Room unless by permission of the master.

Visitors

Art. VIII: No visitors allowed but by a written order from the overseers, and then only on Wednesdays, except friends of the sick, who may be admitted at any time by written permission. Visitors caught introducing spirits or any other improper articles, shall never be admitted again. No money to be received, or begging allowed in or out of the house by paupers.

Labour

Art. IX: Tasks shall be assigned by the keeper to all who are capable of labour, and those who perform them faithfully and cheerfully, shall be rewarded according to their merits by such indulgences as the Overseers may direct. No work whatever shall be performed by the inhabitants of the house, out of the same, for any citizen of the city except by permission.

Spiritous Liquors, Disorderly Conduct and Profane Language

Art. X: The severest punishment will be inflicted on all those who are guilty of drunkenness, disorderly conduct, profane or obscene language, theft, embezzlement, waste of food or manufacturing stock, or defacing these articles or any waste whatever; and no rum or other ardent spirits, on any occasion or under any pretence, whatever, will be permitted to be brought into the house, unless by a written order of the physician, and then to be dealt out by the master. For bringing or assisting to bring into the house any spirituous liquors, for being intoxicated, or any other breach of these articles, the offender shall be punished with solitary confinement, and fed on bread and water, not exceeding two weeks, nor less than one day, and increased for the second offense.

Solitary Confinement

Art. XI: In all cases of solitary confinement for highly criminal conduct, the prisoner shall be debarred from seeing or conversing with any person, except by permission, and they shall in all these respects, be subject to the severest privations, fed on bread and water, and any tenant of the house, who shall without leave, have any communication with a person so counted, or who shall refuse to assist the master when required to carry these rules into effect, shall suffer the same punishment. All persons confined to the cells shall be previously searched and every instrument taken from them.

(continued)

Intercourse of the Sexes

Art. XII: No communication whatever, except in cases specially authorized by the keeper, shall be allowed between unmarried males and females belonging to the house; and all unlawful connexion between the sexes is strictly prohibited—any violation of this rule shall be subject to the severest punishment by solitary confinement and fed on bread and water not exceeding 20 days nor less than one day.

Hospital

Art. XIII: The nurses who take charge of the Hospital and while actually employed, are exempted from all other duty. They shall keep the apartments, beds and bedding in perfect cleanliness, and shall at all times, by night and by day, pay every care and attention to the sick. No person to be considered as sick or infirm, unless pronounced so by the Physician.

Burials

Art. XIV: Whenever a person dies in the house, the relatives or friends may remove the body and inter it at their own expense, otherwise it will be buried in the ground which now is or may hereafter be laid out for that purpose; the relations and friends of the deceased will be allowed, and all paupers who are able, must attend the funeral at the discretion of the keeper—and any unbecoming conduct will be punished.

School

Art. XV: School hours shall be from 9 to 12 o'clock, A.M. and 2 to 4 P.M. in winter, and from 8 to 11 o'clock A.M. in summer, (Sundays and the afternoons of Wednesday and Saturdays excepted). The most suitable person in the house shall be selected to keep the school; to see that the scholars are kept clean, and behave decently. He shall instill into their minds the principles of morality and importance of the Bible. Rewards will be given occasionally for improvements and good conduct. The children shall be taught reading, writing and arithmetic; and a punctual attendance of the scholars will be required

Dismission and Leave of Absence

Art. XVI: Dismissions shall be made only by the Board, except when committed for short terms, the committee who committed, may discharge them. No inhabitant of the house will be permitted to go out on any pretence whatever, unless by permission of the keeper in writing, not more than once a month (extraordinary cases excepted) and every person so permitted, must return at or before sunset. For leaving without permission shall be punished by solitary confinement. For exceeding the granted permission, not to be allowed to go out again for three months.

Punishment

Art XVII: The keeper will be vigilant in detecting every negligence of wilful violation of these Rules, and will promptly inflict the most exemplary punishment—at the same time, those who conduct well, will receive the kindest treatment, and every reasonable indulgence. All persons confined for aggravated intemperance, or abandoned and vicious conduct, shall be separated from the other paupers, and have such fare as the monthly committee who confined them shall order.

Art XVIII: The master shall appoint suitable persons to take care of the cattle, barns, pigs, &c. and shall regularly look after and inspect their doings, and have a constant and careful eye to the economy of the house, and the discharge of every duty in all departments of the premises, and shall punish delinquents with humanity, but firmness. He shall read these Rules once a month to the tenants, and have them posted up in different parts of the house.

Christopher Wright
Rufus Emerson
Israel Waterhouse
Nahum Libby
Phinehas Varnum
Ezra F. Beal
James Huse
Elisha Trowbridge
Thomas Warren, Overseers of the Poor
April 1839

would have a long history.[8] Second, a school is present with a "suitable person" in charge. The "sick and infirm" are excluded from most rules. Those who obey the rules and labor "will be rewarded according to their merits." While the ordinary poor are to be in one place in the house, "all persons confined for aggravated intemperance, or abandoned and vicious conduct, shall be separated from other paupers." Here, one hundred years after Sebring was hired in New York City to set the poor and others to work with a whip, a slightly more complex system has developed. This system would carry forward the Anglo-American notion of differentiation between a "deserving" class of poor people—at a minimum, including widows, children, the elderly, the infirm, and the crippled—and an "undeserving" class of poor—at a minimum, including those with no settlement (foreigners and transients), apparently able-bodied adults who were not working, and those judged morally deviant.

Box 3.2 shows the rules and regulations in the Worcester, Massachusetts, almshouse twenty-eight years (1867) after the Portland rules.[9] There are some considerable differences. While the focus on labor remains, as well as the power of the superintendent to punish and reward, the constant references to punishment in Portland (including solitary confinement) are gone. The rigid organization by ringing of the bells has gone, and visiting is considerably different, with Sabbath being the only day now restricted. Regulations against "ardent spirits" are still very much present, but those against profane language, disorderly conduct, waste of food, and intermingling of the sexes are no longer specified. The sharpest difference may be that the rules are far shorter, with greater discretion given over to the management (a trend that occurred everywhere, leading to the wide local variation in almshouses), and the distinction is clearly made between "prisoner" or "those sentenced by the court" and the other, ordinary paupers. While the Worcester 1867 rules would hardly attract someone to be a resident of the house, the presentation of the rules seems more rational, with an emphasis arguably more on order than repression.

WAS THE POOR FARM A DIFFERENT TRADITION?

Before expanding our inquiry about all poorhouses, I should raise the possibility that the poor farm had an origin somewhat different from the workhouse tradition of Portland and Worcester (and New York City) noted above. In contrast to the emphasis of scholars such as Rothman, the origins of some poor farms seem not to have reflected the hope for a glorious utopian order that can be found in the orchestrated ringing of the bells in the Portland almshouse. Rothman has suggested that the poorhouse, as with the penitentiary, factory, schoolhouse, and asylum, were all efforts by early Americans to rationalize life along productive lines with hopes of character improvement. But in some of the towns studied, decisions describe pragmatic votes to "get a farm" to "house the poor," citing lower costs than boarding out and, in some cases, a shortage of families willing to board. Haverhill initially rejected a workhouse but the town meeting passed a warrant to buy a farm thirty years later. The following report suggests a modesty of goals:

> A house was furnished by the town in April last, with forty five acres of [land] attached to it, for the accommodation of the poor, and a practical farmer and his wife employed to take the immediate charge of the farm and the poor and with the assistance of such of them as are able to labor to cultivate the farm. It will be perceived that this town has not had sufficient experience to be able to determine what the comparative benefits of supporting them in the poor house or at large, will be; but we believe the inhabitants of this town are generally satisfied that the farm will be, by far, the best method for supporting their poor. We have found far less difficulty in procuring suitable persons to take the immediate charge of the farm and the poor than has been found, years past, in procuring a plan for them in any family that was in any respects qualified to take charge of them.[10]

Like Haverhill, Lewiston kept rejecting warrants at their town meetings to build a poorhouse. At an 1839 town meeting, for some reason, "a suitable farm" was reported found and proponents succeeded in winning a vote to purchase it. After reading the account, it is still not clear whether

Box 3.2 RULES AND REGULATIONS
To be Observed at the CITY ALMSHOUSE
and Farm (Worcester, Massachusetts)

1st. The whole establishment shall be under the general supervision of the Board of Overseers of the Poor.

2d. The immediate direction of the Institution shall be under the supervision of a Superintendent and Matron.

3d. It shall be the duty of the Superintendent and Matron to see that the inmates labor in such a way, and at such times, as they may direct, and that no one shall be permitted to lead an idle life.

4th. The Superintendent shall see that the industrious and deserving are rewarded and the idle and dissolute are punished.

5th. It shall be the duty of the Superintendent to make a monthly report to the Board of Overseers at their monthly meetings, of any information he may be possessed of relating to the interest of the Institution.

6th. No person shall be allowed to visit the Institution on the Sabbath without a permit from some member of the Board of Overseers or the Superintendent.

7th. No person shall be allowed to converse or have intercourse with any prisoner sent to the Institution by the Police or any other Court, without permission of the Superintendent, or some member of the Board of Overseers.

8th. It shall be the duty of the Superintendent to see that all sentences imposed upon persons sent by any Court are strictly enforced.

9th. The Superintendent and Matron shall in no instance whatever, leave the Institution at the same time, without permission from some member of the Committee on the Farm, and not until some suitable person shall be obtained by them to take charge of the Institution during their absence.

10th. The Superintendent is expressly directed to prohibit all persons from bringing or drinking ARDENT SPIRITS upon the premises, without direction of the attending Physician.

11th. It shall be the duty of the Superintendent and Matron to see that all the inmates of the Institution bathe as often as once a week, unless otherwise directed by the attending Physician.

12th. No pauper shall leave the Almshouse without permission from the Superintendent.

13th. The Superintendent is hereby directed to report to the Board of Overseers, any inmate who shall refuse to comply with the foregoing Regulations relating to their discipline and governance.

WORCESTER, February 8, 1867
Adopted by unanimous vote of the Board
George W. Gale, Clerk.

we are talking of the same institutional entity as the New York workhouse or the Portland and Worcester poorhouses. When William Garcelon was appointed to run the farm, J. Holland and his family simply refused to go there. Garcelon took no action, and the Hollands were supported in their home by the town. Moreover, Garcelon himself was woefully unprepared and complained that he could not stay at the farm "until 10 P.M. fixing the beds of the poor."[11] In neither town was there much of a plan, purpose, or ambition displayed by supporters of the poor farm. Although opposition to developing a poor farm may have reflected what some citizens were hearing about almshouses elsewhere, it also may have reflected the self-interest of those who were receiving money to board the poor.

In many New England towns and villages, traditions of a "common" had traveled across the ocean, along with provision by the town and its respectable citizens of wood during the winter to the poor. Some towns and their citizens may also have shared gardens and small pastures with poorer citizens. A suggestion of this communal concept is made in Ethel McClure's history of the Minnesota almshouses, *More Than a Roof*. She cites the Minnesota legislature as associating the poor farm with a community woodpile where a shared store could be worked by any resident. She suggests the idea of people "working off their board and keep" was behind the frequent references to work and manual labor.[12] In other words, a tradition that was not punitive but a kind of shared collectivity may have been at work. Interestingly, during depressions, some communities I studied revived their woodlots, so anyone could come and cut wood.[13] There is no conclusive evidence to prove the point one way or the other; possibly the poor farm was simply a rural or agricultural version of the workhouse, or it may be the poor farm resembled more of a public works program than a workhouse. Perhaps, most likely, is that in the transition of the ambitious motives of the workhouse/poorhouse to the hinterlands, the form was adapted and changed, leaving out some of the mission (both repressive and idealistic) that prevailed in the larger urban areas. In any event, since the poor farm, in fact, came to be the more dominant name and form of the poorhouse by the late nineteenth century, with the requisite inmates, superintendent, and matron, and most importantly, conformed to the four principal functions below, the institutional entities will be treated as one, as least pending new research on the subject.

THE FUNCTIONS AND CONTRADICTIONS
OF THE POORHOUSE

The basic functions of the almshouse, poorhouse, and poor farm can be distilled to four purposes, which may seem simple enough (and very consistent with our current social welfare system), but which on historical examination turned out to be terribly difficult and contradictory to implement. The poorhouses were meant to:

1. Provide a bare minimum existence to the poor in their local area such that they would not starve, but the subsistence was to be minimal and harsh enough to deter the "indolent and vicious," "lazy," and "intemperate";
2. Serve as a sorter of the poor between "deserving" or "worthy" candidates of assistance, those who presumably were poor through no fault of their own, as opposed to those whose habits, morals, or norms and culture placed them in a category of "unworthy";
3. Enforce the work ethic by providing the tools of labor, whether farming or other, so that the poor could be put to "useful work," while in the house; and
4. Enforce the dominant morality of the times with particular attention to preventing intemperance and sexual immorality.

Each of these goals, however, was fraught with contradictions, many of which the overseers of the poor themselves came to recognize (as is clear from their reports). The inmates themselves further subverted many goals, while some goals were less acceptable to superintendents, matrons, and staff than to the town fathers.

HOW BARE AN EXISTENCE? ATTRACTING INMATES WHILE DETERRING OTHERS

There is little question but that the forefathers meant the almshouse to be a last resort against hunger and homelessness, but not at all a comfortable one. Recall one of the initial purposes of "indoor relief" was to reduce the danger of paupers staying on "outdoor relief" (e.g., the dole) and presumably becoming lazy, shiftless, and failing to work. As the quotes opening the chapter suggest, overseers of the poor and other public officials took the contradictory mission seriously, pledging to make the poor comfortable, but not so comfortable that the indulgent and vicious would live there. As early as 1835, a committee of Portland officials appointed to study the almshouse noted that the poor could be well be "us"—yet they took this thought to emphasize how the "virtuous" must be protected from mingling with the "abandoned characters of the race."

A general solicitude should be felt upon this subject; for we all may have a personal interest, directly or indirectly, and although we may now be basking in the sun beams of prosperity, the cloud of adversity may come over us, and find us shelterless, without a home, cast upon the cold charities of the world; and how revolting would it be to a virtuous mind to be under the painful necessity of constantly mingling with many of the most abandoned characters of our race! Let us foresee the evil, and provide for the future. It is very desirable that such arrangements be made for the unfortunate, but virtuous and industrious poor, that they may be rendered comfortable . . . while at the same time we should be cautious not to make the place so inviting as to induce the idle and vicious to desire it as a home, instead of providing for themselves by their own exertions.[14]

How to make the "arrangements" nice enough for the "virtuous" yet not so inviting for the "vicious," providing "a place of labor and strict discipline" with just the bare minimum of food and shelter, produced a number of contradictions for an institution that was not legally a prison or jail. Either an entirely different regimen needed to be carried out with those judged unworthy from those judged worthy, or one group or the other would be confused and treated too harshly or too well.

As the poorhouse separated out in most locales from the institutions of workhouse or house of correction, no legal compulsion governed the potential recipients of the "hospitality" of the house. Certainly, the hard edge of poverty and starvation led many of the poor to use the poorhouse, but *they did not have to stay* long (average stays usually appeared to be in days or weeks). Overseers of the poor, superintendents, matrons, and also a fair number of people in the community who serviced the poorhouse (merchants, local stores and suppliers, other farmers, etc.) had a self-interest in people coming and remaining in these institutions. Moreover, those who continued to believe outdoor relief was character weakening sought to improve the poorhouse.

By the 1870s and 1880s, some of the almshouses studied were beginning to be avoided. The conditions of the house, though supposedly a deterrent to the poor applying for relief, came to be a subject of great upset when overseers felt insufficient numbers of inmates used the house. For example, in 1888, the overseers in Lewiston, Maine, pleaded with citizens to help the poor understand how *nice* conditions at the almshouse were: "If this large class of the poor of our city would be willing to accept the offer, so frequently made to them, of a home in the almshouse, their personal comforts would be very much in excess of what they are now, for in the places which many of them call home it is quite impossible for them or any one to be comfortable."[15]

In New Hampshire, the county commissioners alternated between scolding local officials and enticing them, since it appears that local town politicians favored keeping the poor in their own towns. In Carroll County in 1879, the county commissioners seemed to feel they had room for nearly three times the number of inmates they had on hand:

> With a few exceptions the paupers should be treated at farm, and that while the farm has 52 persons there are ample accommodations for 150 persons. . . . We suggest a visiting committee to be appointed by the convention without compensation to visit the institution at least twice a year, to advise with the commissioners . . . and report to the county press. If this were done we believe that much of the unkindly feeling existing against the institution would give place to real interest.[16]

In Rockingham County, commissioners made an annual appeal to all citizens of the county to come and visit the institution at any time. They felt if this would happen and people would "witness themselves the manner in which the poorhouse was conducted, there would be less prejudice against the institution and less suffering among the poor."[17]

The irony of selling life in the almshouse to citizens and inmates was probably influenced by several factors that separate the latter nineteenth century from the earlier vision of the poorhouse. First, the development of a mobile capitalism in which local areas were competing with each other suggests the argument of Frances Fox Piven and Richard Cloward that the relief system serves the function of "regulating the poor" in relation to the labor market.[18] While the focus of the labor regulation theory has been on the negative deterrence that relief can have, towns, cities, and counties also had the problem of making life *attractive enough* to a mobile labor force in times of economic downturn when many citizens would leave the area for work, but employers still needed workers on hand when production resumed. Simultaneously, of course, relief cannot be made so desirable that it interfered with low-wage work at even the poorest of working conditions. This labor market function led to the contrast between the almshouse's beginnings in often harsh rhetoric and rigorous rules, while by the late nineteenth century, each poorhouse studied was claimed by its city or county to be a "model" and to provide excellent care.

Secondly, reform movements begun in the post–Civil War period in New England led to the inspection of almshouses and placed local officials whose stewardship led to faulty conditions in a bad light. This effort, led by the state boards of charities and corrections, was also affected by other events, such as the increased labor militancy of the 1870s and, as we will discuss, the "tramp" crisis. All had the effect of political officials going before town councils and voters for more money to improve their almshouses. How embarrassing if, in fact, the poor were so alienated that they would not enter! Nor is there evidence that officials were cold-hearted. No one approved of people dying on the streets of their villages or cities. And, in all likelihood, the overseers quoted who believed the slums of the cities or the village shacks of the rural poor were far worse than conditions in the almshouses were sincere.

Finally, the delicate balance between what was believed sufficiently adequate conditions to attract inmates, yet not induce them to "indolence and pauperism," was always upset by the ways inmates subverted the purpose of the house. Seasonal or periodic use of the house, while serving labor market needs, tended to anger superintendents and overseers, but occurred at all homes. Since little work could be done in the winter in New England, there was no time to make the "undeserving" work, for the able-bodied men (and others) often left the home at the advent of nice weather. Other inmates used the house itself as an underground economy, selling wares, or using city or county materials to make money while not at formal employment. These actions drove many an overseer and superintendent to distraction. Clearly pulled in different directions by Protestant moralism and by local labor force needs, officials still disliked the poor's tendency to "get by" through all sorts of improvisation.

THE CONTRADICTIONS OF SORTING THE POOR

No issue would so dominate the history of the poorhouse as the argument about "classification," as it was called, the sorting of "deserving" and "undeserving." This is not to say that the poorhouse invented this distinction present in the English Poor Laws since the early seventeenth century. The poorhouse itself went through three stages in its relation to the deserving–undeserving divide. In its early history, prior to growth in the number of almshouses, the poorhouse was frequently equated with "unworthiness" while the "deserving" poor usually received outdoor relief. This was followed by the period of mass building of almshouses from approximately the third decade of the nineteenth century to the last decade, during which, willy-nilly, many poor people found themselves in almshouses at times, and, depending on the community, on outdoor relief at other times. Finally, during the last chapter of the poorhouse's history, many homes sought to divest themselves of the "undeserving poor" to provide a place for the respectable. If these twists and turns are confusing, they were equally or more so to citizens of the times, including overseers of the poor and other officials who argued vehemently among themselves about the zigzag direction of the poorhouse.

Whether it was in 1835 when the Portland committee found that "the virtuous and the vicious are constantly mingling together, and soon become mutual associates,"[19] in 1870 in North Carolina where a visiting reverend found "the respectable, aged and infirm pauper is shut up with the worn-out strumpet, whose very presence is pollution, and no care is had, in many cases, for the innocence of childhood,"[20] or in Harry Evans's 1926 indictment that poor farms had "living in this mass of insanity and depravity, this prison place for criminals and the insane . . . children and respectable old folk, whose only offense is that they are poor,"[21] "improper classification" was the major indictment against the poorhouse, with the ultimate fear that children would lose their innocence and take on the habits of laziness and intemperance imputed to the broad mass of adult paupers.

But beyond the important fact that one cannot always tell the "intemperate" from "temperate," that seemingly "virtuous" men and women sometimes turned out not to be so, and even the elderly and disabled could join cause with younger paupers (as Dale Scott reported the "old codgers" playing cards with the prisoners), the institutional purpose of the poorhouse was caught in at least several contradictions. If, for example, the "worthy poor" should be excluded from the poorhouse, would this not leave the officials with only the vicious and immoral (not a promising prospect for ambitious officials)? On the other hand, if those often presumed to be malingering, such as the unemployed male, were excluded, how would the work of the farm or house get done, and what function would the institution be serving other than as a hospital or nursing home?

Although all agreed that some populations, such as children and the "insane," needed protection, it was hard for the overseers and superintendents to part with more "deserving" elements while keeping "undeserving" elements. Moreover, they had some good arguments against the growth of their sister institutions, the asylums and orphanages. Town and county overseers and superintendents of poorhouses, forced to respond to the reform movement of Dorothea Dix concerning the "insane" in almshouses and to later reformers aroused by the presence of children in poorhouses, agreed that these populations needed separation, but opposed sending them out of the poorhouse to state asylums and orphanages, respectively. They pointed out the great distance townspeople would be taken and their detachment from relatives (including, for children, their parents), in some cases never to see them again. Yet, of course, their arguments were not absent self-interest. The overseers of the poor in Worcester, Massachusetts, complained when a 1904 state law ordered the "insane" removed, both about the transfer of so many inmates out of their almshouse, and about the loss of workers: "There were some good workers among them and their going away necessitated the employment of extra paid labor to work on the farm," their annual report notes.[22]

But, oddly, if the overseers and superintendents protested the removal of some populations, there became a growing population that officials did *not* want, which contradicted both their self-interest in the number of almshouse inmates and the need for able-bodied workers. In the 1870s, America was overcome by a virtual panic over "tramps," unemployed men wandering for work, many displaced by the depression of 1873. Probably, the fear of tramps (which continued for decades) was, in retrospect, the old traditional antebellum image of America confronting the "reserve army" of capitalism, in which large numbers of men wandered about looking for work. Reports from virtually all the areas studied condemned tramps and demanded they not be a local responsibility:

> *Carroll County, N.H., Overseers, 1878*: This evil is assuming gigantic proportions throughout the country. Hardly a day passes in many of our towns but what the Selectman are called upon to entertain one or more of this class of vagabonds. They are almost entirely young men, banded together with a code of signals, and there is not one out of twenty of them who would work if they could have it furnished them. They follow the lines of railways throughout the country, and wherever night overtakes them they manage to be in the vicinity of an officer of the town, of whom they demand entertainment with as much assurance as through they were addressing a landlord, and had plenty with which to pay the bills.[23]

> *Lewiston, Maine, Overseers of the Poor, 1896*: [Our] expense . . . increases every year, and will continue to do so until some steps are taken in the way of legislation to prevent those people preying upon the public for support, and to make life and property safer than at present . . . the greater part of which [army of unemployed] are tramps claiming to be seeking employment, but would not work if they obtained it.[24]

By definition, tramps were always from out of town, having no settlement, and hence could be rejected from relief rolls under settlement laws. In the first decade of the twentieth century, all three states (Maine, Massachusetts, and New Hampshire) passed laws against vagrancy, forcing the traveling poor people who were already depending more on lodging in police stations to now face arrest rather than any relief. But the tramp fear went beyond the settlement issue because by the late nineteenth century and first decades of the twentieth century, repeated statements of the overseers and superintendents become negative toward the foreign-born immigrants and many able-bodied men seeking aid. "Tramp" had become shorthand for "undesirable." Worcester's overseers were typical in their 1900 complaint that "With the rapid growth of the city there come to us people of different nationalities, who live from hand to mouth, and when in want, by some natural instinct, or through friendly advice, find their way to the office of this board. Once they receive assistance they have an idea that they are on the list to be forever aided when their own efforts fail to furnish the necessities of living."[25]

While no city or county announced they would not accept the able-bodied or the foreigner, the change in tone clearly affected who would be accepted into the poorhouse.

In a contradictory fashion, then, the moralism of public officials contradicted the self-interest in maximizing both the numbers in almshouses and the availability of able-bodied (usually perceived as male) labor. Amos Warner, the leading thinker in social welfare (whose book *American Charities* became a must-read in the 1890–1920 period), provided a justification for the streamlined poorhouse. He noted if the almshouse could exclude children, the "insane," and "special populations" such as the blind and deaf, why not exclude the "pauper-delinquent" and send them "to work-houses or reformatories"? He argued for a "differentiation on the basis of character" that would "exclude habitual drunkards, prostitutes, and other misdemeanants." This process "would relieve the almshouse of many in-mates, and the worthy poor of a very considerable portion of the disgrace which attaches to going there."[26] Indeed, some poorhouses would move within several decades to being homes only for the respectable (primarily, the aged and physically disabled), ending the whole sorting process and the whole original aim of the poorhouse to contain those who were able-bodied enough to support the house and farm.[27]

ENFORCING WORK: HOW ARE YOU GOING TO KEEP THEM DOWN ON THE FARM?

Despite the widespread societal consensus that work was to be provided to able-bodied paupers and that this was a central purpose of institutions for the poor, it was quickly evident that work demands were primarily symbolic for social reformers, although not for superintendents who tried to run poor farms with inmate labor. Rothman quotes prison reformer Edward Livingston as advocating work (along with sobriety, instruction, and so on) to all inmates, as part of rehabilitation and character reform.[28] Historian Michael Katz quotes the nineteenth-century reformer William Letchworth as also demanding work as a moral value: "By failing to make paupers work, the poorhouse keeper was neglecting opportunities for both moral instruction and a reduction in the public funds necessary to run the institution. . . . [Inmates] sitting idly by . . . should be continually employed, if for no other reason than for the benefit of the moral influence inculcated by systematic labor."[29]

Because work was primarily symbolic, and able-bodied paupers quickly left the poorhouse in the warmer seasons to do manual, agricultural, or factory work, stories of "make-work" in poorhouses are legion. In some houses, men were seen digging holes and filling them up again, and in others, men carried wood from one place and stacked it, and then moved it back. In one of my interviews with those who remembered the twentieth-century poor farm, I found what was described as "work" seemed often to mean a division of household responsibilities. Former Carroll County almshouse workers all supported the ideology of work for the inmates, but generally what they described were a myriad of tasks assigned to inmates such as setting the table, cleaning a room, cutting potatoes for dinner, and sweeping a room. Not only were such tasks not very time-consuming but many of these tasks can be seen as a simple requirement of group living. Of course, by this time, many inmates were old, feeble, or disabled, and perhaps these were the only tasks inmates could do. Hence, at least the maintenance of the symbolism that inmates would not "get something for nothing" could remain.[30]

Yet farm superintendents, and quite often overseers, did require real work. Superintendents, matrons, and staff realized they would be judged by their agricultural productivity and efficiency, yet found themselves saddled with disabled and infirm people who could not work. Nor, of course, did they want the morally undisciplined who could not work. Beyond self-interest though, overseers and officials also had to run for political office; during the 1890s—which included mass depression, for example, in almost all cities studied—efforts were made to place able-bodied men in actual jobs or to create public works jobs. In fact, a too-negative view of overseers of the poor would contradict a number of instances, particularly in downturns, where they advocated public works jobs be financed by their governments.[31]

The issue of work, when looked at as a whole, becomes a rather incomprehensible mix of motives: the pauper should work for his keep, but except in depressions and cold winter months, most of the inmates who were left at the farm or house could not perform strenuous work. Political imperatives and economic interest drove both officials and inmates to secure real work on the outside, but the ideology of the institution still stressed labor on the farm.

There were no good remedies to these contradictions. As with the issue of classification, some institutions came to surrender the work imperative by the third or fourth decade of the twentieth century and to define themselves more and more as shelters for the infirm. Others—in our study, Lewiston, Rockingham, and Worcester—continued to have inmates perform major work roles, either farming or picking up the city's garbage, virtually until their demise. Still, many compromises were made to reality, deviating from the theory of the poorhouse. The "good" inmates often secured pay to continue to work or became full-time employees of the poor farm. Inmates were also allowed outside paid work or to scrape up income from other sources or through the underground economy to support themselves. None of these practices would have been looked on with favor by the originators of the house!

ENFORCING MORALITY: WAS BRINGING THE POOR TOGETHER A SOLUTION?

Throughout American history—and arguably to this day—poverty has been blamed on poor morals and poor habits. The leading thinkers of the late nineteenth century certainly felt poverty was linked to morality. Charles Hoyt, who delivered a famous report on pauperism to the New York Legislature in 1874, concluded confidently, "Most cases of pauperism are due to idleness, improvidence, drunkenness, or other forms of vicious indulgence, which are frequently, if not universally, hereditary in character."[32] When a reporter asked the superintendent of the Lewiston Poor Farm, George Bonney, what his experience taught him was the chief cause of this pauperism, he responded simply, "Rum in almost all cases."[33]

It is not my purpose here to analyze the actual influence of drinking or other behaviors on poverty and economic success. This complex issue is still very much debated today, as many Americans blame poverty and homelessness on drugs, alcohol, mental illness, and other behavioral factors, while most in the social welfare field would stress social stratification and economic inequality. What is most interesting here in terms of the poorhouse is how "collecting the poor," as it was called, could possibly help overcome intemperance, improvidence, and vicious indulgence.

Somehow, the reformers and political leaders of the nineteenth century believed the house would impart discipline and order, yet reformers such as Yates, Dix, Letchworth, Hoyt, and others never really spelled out how this was to occur. Can they conceivably have placed all their faith in Bible reading or did they believe inmates could be forcibly kept at the almshouse away from all liquor and from each other? One would think it logical that, by bringing together hundreds of poor people, many allegedly guilty of intemperance, immorality, and laziness, rather than the very few people in charge (initially in many poorhouses there was just a superintendent and matron) winning over the poor to hard work and temperance, "poor morals" would prevail.

As we have seen with the rounders in Worcester, and will see in succeeding instances, intemperance was a frequent occurrence in the house. Similar charges appear over and over again in all poorhouses I studied in each time period, despite the rules against "ardent spirits." Inmates, too, were found engaging in "sexual intermingling." In some cases, staff were clearly complicit in these acts as well.

Keeping in mind the almshouse/poorhouse/poor farm, as distinct from the workhouse, was voluntary and could be left at will, and that inmates vastly outnumbered their keepers (assuming for the moment the keepers were committed to temperance and proper morality), how exactly was the proper morality to be instilled? Certainly, the poorhouses employed chaplains who gave sermons and tendered to the flock. Many of these institutions provided written materials with temperance and moral themes. The Women's Christian Temperance Union (WCTU) developed relationships with several of the almshouses studied and were welcomed in to proselytize. And, of course, hard work on the farm was to have a therapeutic effect on inmates. All homes employed sanctions, including removal, for drinking or other acts of immorality.

Still, for those with any knowledge of alcoholism, to take one example, how would surrounding even a willing candidate for reform with so many inmates who were not amenable to temperance be conducive to what we today would call "recovery"? Nor were staff and superintendents committed to temperance. Not only do we know instances of staff bringing liquor to the almshouse but there is also no reason to believe that among the social classes and ethnic groups that tended to comprise the staff of these houses there was agreement with the moralistic precepts of officials. After all, temperance and prohibition were among the major issues of the latter nineteenth century and first three decades of the twentieth century, and split the nation apart along social class and ethnic and religious lines. Political officials, including overseers of the poor, were almost always Yankee men of middle class or higher, while poorhouse staff and inmates in New England were of lower classes, usually Irish, French Canadian, Italian, and Eastern European. These groups historically did not share the pro-prohibition sentiments of their Yankee "betters."

I suspect that grouping the poor and other inmates together was as likely to reinforce group norms of lower-class behavior as to reform them, hence serving as a constant frustration to the keepers. The modern institution has changed considerably in this regard from the poorhouse. Some institutions are sanctioned, of course, to resort at times to overt force, such as prison or mental hospitals. But most rely on a high ratio of professionals to counsel and "manage" their charges, as in many juvenile homes, group homes, halfway houses, and transitional settings where discipline is considered less desirable than change through individual or small group counseling. Here again, the homeless shelter most resembles the almshouse, since few large shelters have the staff to police the clientele, and alcohol, drugs, sexual liaisons, and other behavior is often reported to occur despite official rules.

4

✚

Undermining the Poorhouse: Long- and Short-Term Inmates in the Late Nineteenth Century

The almshouse [is] a winter resort for tramps, and a place where the drunkard and the prostitute can recuperate between debauches.

—Amos Warner, *American Charities*, 1894[1]

There is no known remedy to keep people out of the poorhouse. It is gladly accepted by the aged and infirm, the latter made so in far too many cases by intemperance, as a refuge where they are absolutely sure of receiving the care and attention that a beneficent municipality generously provides.

—Worcester, Mass., Overseers of the Poor, 1895[2]

I have suggested that the goals of the poorhouse, once framed in extremely lofty terms, contained numerous contradictions in practice. Yet neither the long persistence nor the gradual demise of the poorhouse can be explained by inexorable logic or by inevitable progress; nor, contrary to at least the implication in some social welfare literature, were changes brought about by the heroic actions of elite reformers. As with much history, those at the bottom of society are left out of this story far too frequently. Like all social institutions, the poorhouse required a clientele as well as a degree of legitimacy in the community. In response to both the unpopularity of the poorhouse, on the one hand, and what they saw as exploitation of the poorhouse resources, on the other, officials and elite observers voiced increasing dissatisfaction by the late nineteenth century. As the quotes at the chapter's start reflect, this dissatisfaction focused both on transient users of the house and long-term residents.

This dissatisfaction cannot be separated from poor people's use of the house. People in the millions passed through the poorhouses and used them in their own ways; the denizens included elderly people, young children, parents with children, able-bodied men and women, and physically and mentally disabled people alike. The partly successful reforms to move young children and the insane out of the almshouse did not drastically change the demographics of the poorhouse, which at the turn of century still included young and old, women delivering children, an array of disabled people including at least the "mildly insane" and the "feeble minded," and unemployed and transient men coming in and out.[3] While poor people were not conscious theorists changing an institution, they also were not "judgmental dupes," simply the victims of a system they knew nothing about. The fact that many poor people were not just pliable raw material but made use of the institution in their own ways helped undermine its goals as an agent of character rehabilitation, social control, and deterrence. This chapter, as well as chapters 5 and 6, moves beyond victimology to see how inmates shaped the poorhouse and the political and administrative battles that surrounded them.

One way in which the poorhouse stands out from today's institutions is the oddness of its being a long-term *home* for some (we find some inmates who spent as many as seventy years in an almshouse), and a short, even one-night, stopover for others. If a cheap motel room or homeless shelter seems combined with a long-term residence or with apartments in a housing project, this was not the intent of officials but of the poor themselves. This chapter focuses on these two populations—the "long-termers" who constituted a sort of "home guard" of the institution and the short-term transients—as a lens toward viewing how the poor used the institution of the poorhouse in the late nineteenth century. While overseers and other officials were driven to distraction by intermittent and seasonal use of the house by ostensibly able-bodied men, in many ways the use of the house by people for long-term residence also contradicted the character reform and deterrent purpose of the poorhouse. In neither case was a useful rehabilitative purpose served. Inmates who stayed for decades were neither being pressed into the workforce nor usually being made temperate or moral, but were simply being housed at taxpayer expense. But those who came to the house for only a few days or weeks and left were hardly being transformed either, and their evident lack of need for hard labor at the poorhouse belied their ability to obtain actual work when available in the warmer months.

THE CHANGING CONTEXT OF
NEW ENGLAND'S RELIEF SYSTEM

As historical background, it should be noted that well prior to the massive depression of 1893, poorhouses (as well as the outdoor relief rolls) were experiencing large increases in inmates. In the late nineteenth century, New England led the nation in manufacturing industries, attracting large numbers of mill workers in textiles, shoes and boots, small machine, and fabricated metal industries particularly.[4] Along with industrialization came a mass exodus from the small farms of New England and a large immigration from Canada and Europe. Most distressing to the Yankee elites, the millions of Irish in the Northeast were augmented by French Canadians, Italians, Poles, Russians, and Slovaks with limited English language and employment skills, many torn asunder from familial and other supports. The improved mortality rate combined with immigration to America and migration to pose a demographic threat to the poor-relief system.

According to overseers and officials in each area (even in prosperous ones), every year began with a higher number of people on relief and in the poorhouse than the year before. The new economy bred prosperity for some but with a large influx of people cut off from the land and from their ancestral support, there was little choice but public aid when layoffs, seasonal or long term, arrived. The aged, disabled, ill, widowed, and children once sustained by extended families remained on the rolls and in the poorhouse. Then, of course, came the devastating downturn of the 1890s, which lasted in New England for much of the decade, casting out of work hundreds of thousands of employees with nowhere to turn but relief. The combination of depression, increasing need among all segments of the poor, and the changed ethnic composition led to eugenic and Social Darwinist explanations, as well as considerable pessimism in heretofore civil New England. In the extreme, the overseers of the poor in Worcester expressed the anxiety of New England's decline from "the hard-fisted pioneer who broke and tilled the native soil of a once prosperous country town" to the "hereditary paupers" who left the area as one "known principally by its unoccupied workshops and abandoned farms."[5]

To give some idea of the growth of the almshouse population, new buildings in Haverhill and Worcester, Mass., were constructed and space expanded in at least two other poorhouses, Portland and Carroll County. Prior to 1894, Haverhill had a relatively small poorhouse with room for forty or forty-five residents at a time. Then it was forced to expand its poorhouse as its inmate population doubled, with about two hundred people spending some time there in a year, and ninety at any one time. Industrial Worcester added a new building in 1890 allowing room for sixty new inmates at a time, but it showed an even more dramatic increase, accommodating 228 in inmates in 1890 and 338 by 1899, a rise that would outlast the depression period. Portland in 1891 had only 106 inmates at the start of that fiscal year. Its one-time starting point went up by nearly 50 percent to 154 several years later, and further to 172 inmates by the decade's end. Total admissions soared from 228 to nearly double that amount in the midst of the depression, although total admissions would fall back some in the early 1900s.[6] In an effort to accommodate the increase, Portland added a structure for the insane, creating a separate wing for about thirty inmates.

Interestingly, the late nineteenth century reversed, in at least some areas of New England, the historic preference among elites for indoor relief or the poorhouse over outdoor relief or the dole. Each year as the 1890s went on, the overseers of the poor of Portland, Maine, grew defensive about the amount of outdoor relief they bestowed. But they reminded citizens that "It cannot be avoided unless we remove them [paupers] to the almshouse, which course would overcrowd that institution and gradually increase the cost of their support."[7] It seems three factors undermined the preference for indoor relief over outdoor. First, although the almshouse was sold to the public as a huge cost savings over outdoor aid, adequate care was not inexpensive. As the public and reform boards such as the state boards of charities and corrections pressed for improvements, almshouses in New England afforded medical care (including physicians, nurses, and attendants), improved buildings, food, sleeping accommodations, and so on, all of which raised the costs considerably. As would be true of debates in the twentieth century over mental health care and child welfare, good care in the community or an institution is not cheap. Second, outdoor relief, while still philosophically repugnant to some, was actually a more flexible or stoppable benefit than indoor relief. While at any given month many thousands were on relief, in all localities relief given at home—usually in the form of fuel or food—was a week-to-week or at most month-to-month process. The applicant had to apply to get relief and frequently was denied after a short period (such as a few weeks' aid). The almshouse did not quite allow such termination. Oddly, the more punitive form of relief had less of a cutoff point. Although, technically, rules existed that could potentially lead to an inmate expulsion, a person who chose to remain in the poorhouse was rarely ever expelled. In fact, a newspaper piece about the Portland almshouse in 1899 revealed some inmates living in rooms that they had been furnished with flowers and ornaments and even pets, clearly not intending to move on![8]

Thirdly, the poorhouse began to take on other critical functions beyond housing the poor. Most of the six almshouses actually handled orders for outdoor aid as well, collecting farm produce to deliver to the poor at their homes. Those poorhouses with particularly successful farms (such as Rockingham County and Worcester) came to be seen as valued public facilities whose staffing was important, both from healthy inmates and paid farm staff. Finally, the addition of refuse collection in Lewiston, Portland, and Worcester at the turn of the century provided still another critical role for the poorhouse and its inmates.

Although none of these developments made the almshouse a desired address or ended its stigma, it did mean that the rising population at the poorhouse was no longer subject to the kind of severe discipline or character reform that was the supposed purpose of the institution. Those who stayed there for years, it could be reasoned, might well (if they were old and infirm certainly) linger on outdoor aid anyway, while able-bodied inmates provided farm and other needed labor as quasi-public employees.

CHARACTERS OF THE POORHOUSE: THE LONG-TERM DENIZENS OF THE HOUSE

Because historical evidence is fragmentary, caution needs to be exercised in generalizing about the long-term residents of the poorhouse. While we have information based on inmate lists, such as the number of residents who were long-term, their ages, often their nationalities, and once in a while other facts such as their occupations or whether they were judged insane, we cannot recapture either their individual biographies or collective experience. It is quite interesting, however, to explore how some accounts describe the residents of the poorhouse; several provide us with graphic portraits that display both the fascination and repulsion of outside observers, and presumably the public, at these strange characters.

Reporters naturally focused, as now, on the more unusual, and seemed fascinated by the lengthier residents of the house. The long-term "home guard" of the poorhouse was considered to be either incredibly resourceful, even devious, souls who had carved out a living from the poorhouse or figures of pathos and ridicule who were so different from the norm that they could only be seen as "insane" or "vicious."

In Lewiston, Maine, the blind Grover brothers, Dean and Jonas, fascinated the local newspaper and may have been the stuff of local legend. The blind brothers were evidently the same brothers brought to the poor farm back in 1839 when it opened.[9] When a reporter visited the poorhouse in 1882, he described the Grovers as "almost a part of the farm itself." Jonas particularly impressed the reporter for both his intelligence and for his enterprising business.

Jonas is very smart and gets about the farm remarkably. He is the oracle of the place and can tell the dates when all the inmates came or left. Jonas has a speculative disposition. He occasionally gets a boy to lead him up town, where he peddles one thing and another. He has a little cupboard in his room, which he calls his "store." He has capital enough to keep on hand a barrel of apples and a few sticks of candy which he retails to the children, who come to him with the pennies they may be occasionally given. "Blind Jonas," in this way, accumulates a few dollars, and once in a while is able to make a visit to some of his friends "down east."[10]

Eleven years later, in 1893, a reporter assigned to cover the mayor and alderman's annual sojourn to the farm again found the "blind brothers." A sign reading "store" on a certain door of the almshouse had attracted the mayor's interest. This store was apparently the successor to Jonas's cupboard, now "under the back stairs of the house where they sell all kinds of trinkets, and where they [the brothers] place all their earthly treasures." The reporter was fascinated that no one had a key to the store except the Grovers. "For," said one of the Grovers to the reporter, "how do we know whether you will carry off our things or not—we can't see you do it."[11]

Another enterprising long-term almshouse resident was Jack Whalen of Portland. Referred to as the "oddest one" at the almshouse, he came into town often and was "sharp and shrewd," a reporter noted. He was apparently able to "fool the car conductors" into giving him a free ride from the poorhouse quite some miles from the downtown of Portland and back. "He has no money but that does not phase [*sic*] him," noted the reporter. "He tells everybody who asks him to pay for what he gets to send the bill to the overseers."[12] The ledger of inmates in Portland indicates Whalen had been at the almshouse since 1871, thirty-three years before. He was born in Ireland and had an occupation of laborer; Whalen was twenty-five when admitted, so was fifty-eight at the time of the report. We do not, of course, know how common these resourceful poor people were, but their great interest certainly suggests a public ambivalence about poverty, when we consider how little the reporter condemned him. While the description of the Grovers was ostensibly positive enough and at least grudgingly positive of Whalen, the deep ambivalence about pauperism and long-term poorhouse residents can also be gleaned from the papers. The Portland newspapers, particularly, seemed obsessed with longevity, and would state in its articles how long people had been at the house. But the residents, obviously fascinating in their ability to have lived so long away from respectable society, found themselves often slightly mocked for this or, if they deteriorated in demeanor, presented as insane. Lewiston's 1882 visitors gave a rather jaundiced view of many inmates:

Some [inmates] were smoking pipes of foreboding blackness, others were winding their shins around a cylinder stove, and some were stoically upright on a wooden bench. One man with no eyes and one leg put in a pathetic appeal for a pint of rum so soon as he heard strange voices. Another blind man instantly recognized and saluted "the Mayor of the City.". . . Going through the women's department, one finds a number of paralytics, with pitiful faces. One woman is said to suffer an almost living death from fear of being burned, and begs that no fire be kept in her room, even in the coldest weather. . . . Once in awhile there is a small rebellion in which bad blood is displayed. The women have been known to engage in eradication of each other's hair and to aim flat irons at one another. There is an occasional rumpus in the men's department also. . . . One of the veterans of the alms house is an old Scotchwoman, who takes a miff very easily, and who has been known to lie in bed for three weeks, out of pure spite.[13]

Seventeen years later, when Portland's *Sunday Times* visited that city's almshouse, they portrayed the home as an interesting collection of flotsam: "a crowded, floating population, they play cards or look aimlessly 'n'er do wells who come and go' particularly in [the] summer [while] others are the bummers and loafers, the able bodied men who could take care of themselves at any and all times if they were disposed and would forgive the temptation to spend their earnings in rum shops."[14]

Interestingly, when we revisit accounts of the same inmate, the presentation can change considerably. John "Rioux" (later "Raidix" and in the almshouse ledger spelled "Reidix"), an elderly resident of the Portland almshouse who had been there thirty-five years when described, was called "John Prussian" and praised for "doing his work with military exactness and precision" by the 1899 visitors. But five years later when another reporter went into the almshouse, John "Raidix" was described quite differently. Raidix had recently died after forty years in the almshouse. Raidix is now diagnosed as having "a malady . . . slight insanity and a mania for taking things." It is hard to interpret this but what follows would seem to indicate that, contrary to the 1899 news article, Raidix was kept confined: "Years ago he was taken from the dormitory and given a separate apartment. When he became violent, spasmodically, he was kept closely confined, a wooden cage having been built in the rear of his room. Here he was accustomed to gather all sorts of useless trash, old tin cans, buckets, baskets, torn garments, beddings, etc."[15]

The odd account is further confused even by the paragraph that follows the above: "He was the foremen [sic] of the wash day brigade. He superintended the clothes yard, hung out and took down the washings, three days a week, folded the clothes and also tended a small garden in the clothes yard. This kept him busy and he felt a sense of responsibility which the keeper humored."[16]

The strangeness of the description in combination with the earlier account leads us to wonder: Does the account mean that Raidix was well until some years before his death in 1904 (he was in his seventies) and hence able to be such an efficient worker? Was he in a separate room due to insanity or provided one as some "deserving poor" were in the Portland almshouse? What are we to make of his being "humored" by being given responsibility when the philosophy of the almshouse dictated that everyone should work and presumably would be rewarded? Even the collection of his odds and ends is a bit enticing to the observer. Did the Grovers in Lewiston perhaps also have only "useless trash" or did the fact that they ostensibly earned a few dollars mean they had more valuable goods? Or had Raidix (or Rioux or Reidix) himself sold goods?

Still another inmate who moves back and forth from a hostile to a bit more sympathetic treatment is Mary Belisle of Lewiston. In one April 1893 account, Belisle was described as "locked up for committing a grave offense to decency." The paper does not specify what acts she committed but speculated "it is hard to decide whether she is insane or vicious—but probably she is troubled with both diseases more or less." The paper further accounts that at the poor farm, Belisle "attacked Mr. McGillicuddy (then superintendent) once with a table knife and would probably have killed him, but for the help of the hired hand, who came to the superintendent's aid."[17]

Yet in another news piece, Belisle is covered more sympathetically. McGillicuddy affirmed Belisle was not insane, but "too cross." She is described as "unique" and "strange," not "insane" or "vicious." The paper notes, "when out of her head she is a dangerous woman . . . at other times she is peaceable and will work hard when kindly used." Again interpretation is a bit difficult. Are we witnessing a more nuanced treatment of mental illness? Or was Belisle "cross" at mistreatment of some kind, particularly since she was peaceful and a hard worker when well treated? Like Reidix being "peculiar" and Whalen "odd," we are left with Belisle being "unique" and "strange."[18] Lewiston records indicate Belisle was in and out of the poor farm between 1893 and 1902, and gave birth to a child named Willie during her first admission to the poorhouse. Willie is listed with her on subsequent admissions. One may speculate that her "offense to decency" may have been sexual in nature, but we cannot know for sure.

Perhaps almost humorous is the failure of the reporters to often appreciate the wry reactions inmates gave their higher-class visitors. Just as inmates saluted the "mayor" in 1882 or asked the higher-ups for rum, in 1893, the reporter is struck when arriving at the Lewiston City Farm by the greeting given them by inmate Felix Champagne when the mayor's entourage came to the farm: "I dunno whether to let you get out of your carriage or not. I like the looks of you but I own the farm and I ain't going to let you carry it off."[19]

It seems doubtful that Champagne thought he was the owner of the farm or did not recognize the mayor and the city's aldermen. More likely, inmates greeted the visits of powerful officials with wry humor and an attempt to exert some control over what they felt was, after all, their home being inspected by strangers. If nothing else, the various accounts of the poorhouse inmates of the time suggest "victimology" is not always an appropriate lens to view the inmates. Long-termers, in particular, seemed to have adapted to life in the almshouse, and older inmates, when not judged insane or idiotic, were sometimes looked up to by other inmates.

LONG-TERM RESIDENTS OF ONE POORHOUSE

We can gain some insight into how poor people came to use the almshouse by examining some of the homes where records are available to us. Carroll County's almshouse, both because the county published its record of inmates each year from 1872 to 1933 and because of the small population of the county, is a particularly fruitful venue for following inmates over time. Carroll County's almshouse, as was true of smaller and more rural homes, did contain a higher proportion of long-termers than larger urban facilities. For example, in 1899, Carroll County's home had twenty-four residents who had been there over ten years out of about fifty to fifty-five inmates on average (see table 4.1).[20]

There are a number of interesting pieces of information that can be gleaned from table 4.1. First, it is quickly evident how many inmates could truly call the almshouse "home" by the turn of the twentieth century. Not only had twenty-four inmates been there ten or more years but seven had been there since the records of the almshouse commenced. Another five had more than twenty years' seniority. Second, contrary to an association at least later with the elderly as being the prime inmates of the poorhouse, these inmates were not usually admitted when elderly. Only one inmate was admitted in his seventies and two in their sixties. Of the others, however, one was admitted as a child, one as a teenager, four in their twenties, two in their thirties, four in their forties, and nine in their fifties. Thirdly, most of these inmates would die at the almshouse; as the double stars indicate in table 4.1, twenty of the twenty-four died at the almshouse, and it is not clear whether the other four were transferred just prior to their deaths.[21]

Although we lack good information on the lives of our subjects, since Carroll County was an area with a very small population, it was possible to glean some information from the vital statistics of Ossipee, the site of the county farm. One interesting fact is that at least half of the inmates had family members who had either preceded them in the almshouse or who

Table 4.1. Long-Term Residents of Carroll County Almshouse, 1899

Name & Year	Age Admitted	Age in 1899	Town Settlement	Relatives in Almshouse
Olive Anderson** 25th yr.	57 or younger*	82	Conway	
Susan Brown** 17th yr.	41	58	Sandwich	
Julia Burleigh** 13th yr.	37	50	Tuftenboro	Father or grandfather?
John Copp** 11th yr.	50	61	Brookfield	Parents, brother?
Charles Emery 11th yr.	1	12	Freedom	Mother, 2 brothers
John Evans 10th yr.	78	88	Moultonboro	
Maria Fisk* 27th yr	58 or younger*	85	Moultonboro	
Ellen Foss** 11th yr.	50	61	Freedom	Children/grandchildren?
Charles Goldsmith** 17th yr.	29	46	Ossipee	Grandmother?
Belinda Hibbard 23rd yr.	57	80	Ossipee	Husband
Roxanna Jackson** 26th yr.	55 or younger*	81	Wakefield	
Mary Johnson** 22nd yr.	40	62	Conway	Three children

Name				
George Meserve** 24th yr.	43	67	Wolfeboro	Husband, wife, 3 children
Sarah Meserve 24th yr.	41	65	Wolfeboro	
Albert Pennell** 17th yr.	38	55	Hart's Landing	
Fanny Peavey** 27th yr.	17 or younger*	44	Tuftenboro	Brother, father?
Ellen Quimby** 13th yr.	27	40	Moultonboro	Husband; three children; mother-in-law?
Sarah Shaw** 10th yr.	52	62	Moultonboro	
Abbie Sinclair** 14th yr.	50	64	Bartlett	
Manuel Sias** 27th yr.	20 or younger*	47	Ossipee	
Samuel Sargent** 27th yr.	60 or younger*	87	Conway	
Eleazer Thompson** 14th yr.	66	80	Conway	Brother
Adelaide Walker** 27th yr.	20 or younger*	47	Albany	
Sarah Whitton** 24th yr.	59	83	Tuftenboro, later Wolfeboro	

*Present at the start of the county almshouse; may have been inmates of town almshouses prior to 1872
**Died in almshouse

were in the poorhouse with them.[22] A fair number of inmates had family with them either the entire time or for part of their stays: Charles Emery of Freedom entered with his mother and two brothers; Ellen Foss of Freedom entered with children or grandchildren; Belinda Hibbard of Ossipee entered with her husband, who died in 1890; Mary Johnson of Conway entered with her three children; the Meserves of Wolfeboro not only came together, but had three children there; Fannie Peavey of Tuftenboro had a brother and father also in the almshouse with her; Ellen Quimby of Moultenboro had her husband, three children (one who died as an infant), and at one point her mother-in-law in the almshouse; and Eleazer Thompson of Conway had a brother come into the almshouse in 1903.

Of course, it is not surprising that poor people had family members with no choice but to use the poorhouse; still, the poorhouse is not often described as a family affair in which some inmates had husbands or wives, brothers or sisters, fathers or mothers with them. It is also likely—given the comings and goings of some family members—that at least some of these inmates had relatives who continued to visit them after they themselves left, though obviously family estrangement, death and illness, and the demands of finding work all must have put strains on families. Moreover, as was evident from my interviews with former Carroll County staff who recalled a later period, almshouse staff in this rural area must have known many of these families personally from their own communities and particularly those who stayed there for a long time and who had other family members there.

It is also possible to situate almshouse use as a strategy for poor families. Some of this is obvious, as in going to the house to give birth or die, for which the almshouse was always acknowledged. In addition, husbands may have gone off on seasonal jobs or job searches while their wives were housed in the almshouse, fathers and mothers may have left their sons and daughters, and so on. Several possible examples emerge: Susan Brown was married and may have gone back and forth to her own home with her husband. She died at the house in 1903 of epileptic convulsions, and since epilepsy was often treated as insanity in this period, perhaps she was abandoned to the almshouse by her family.[23] Charles Emery, the boy in the almshouse since he was one year old, appears with his mother, Susan, who stayed in the almshouse from 1888 to 1897 and gave birth to Fred in the almshouse in 1892. Whether Charles had a special condition that forced him to stay in the almshouse we do not know (it was unusual by this time in New Hampshire for healthy children to stay so long), but from 1897 to 1900 Charles was left there on his own. In 1900, Charles left, so we do not know whether his mother secured sufficient resources to care for him or whether Charles went to another institution. The Quimby family presents what was surely a sad case. Ellen and her husband, George, a laborer, used the almshouse between 1886 and 1898, when George died. They had three children born in the almshouse, one of whom died. Shortly after George's death, Ellen died in 1900 with the cause of death listed in the vital records as "insanity."[24]

While unfortunately the full stories of most poor people and their families are lost to us, it is evident that the almshouse had come to serve a series of functions in people's lives. As is well known, no doubt, poor families needed to place incapacitated and elderly relatives in the poorhouse; they also used it for stays by husbands and wives, sibling groups, and whole families when necessary. Moreover, even long-term inmates had relatives outside the home to whom they might have returned at times. Like the later nursing and boarding home or chronic hospital that succeeded the poorhouse, already by this time, whatever the stigma and "specter" of the poorhouse, the need for a residence, and in some cases, medical and nursing assistance, took precedence.

THE POORHOUSE AS "WINTER RESORT"

As noted in chapter 2, few issues agitated officials and reformers for much of the history of the almshouse more than the intermittent users of the house. Although ledgers and records indicate the most common stay in *all* poorhouses throughout its history were short ones (a week, several weeks, several months), no doubt the cold New England winters led to a predictable seasonal increase, particularly of presumed able-bodied younger men. To gain some sense of the number of the winter residents, I explored the last available rosters of inmates at the Worcester almshouse (1896–1899). Additionally, since the Portland almshouse ledger is still extant and lasted until early in the twentieth century, I also studied a year of admissions at that institution, finding in fact that more inmates used the almshouse seasonally there than in Worcester.

In Worcester, there were twenty-nine men (excluding inmates who were children or elderly or who died in the almshouse) who had a winter pattern of admission in the years 1896–1899 (see table 4.2). Nine of these men had already (before the time that provoked the attacks in the overseers' reports) spent two or more winter stays at the Home Farm. I compared these men's names to entries in the city directories, since the overseers noted that in order to get a civil service job, an address was usually necessary and it would seem of interest to determine if these men were homeless or housed. This is a difficult record to reconstruct over a century later, since poorer people are not necessarily listed in the city directories, and common names provide for a great deal of uncertainty. Further, we cannot know whether the listed addresses were accurate.

Table 4.2.   Winter Pattern of Admissions to Poorhouse for Selected Adult Men in Worcester, Mass., 1896–1899 (Ends 11/99)

Name	Pattern of Admission
John J. Broderick	9/95–4/96, 11/97–5/99, 11/99– (57-year-old born in Ireland, likely wire drawer in directory)
Solomon H. Brooks	4/97–5/97, 11/97–5/98 (43-year-old born in England, no directory listing)
Alfred F. Buxton	1/97–1/98, 2–5/99 (51-year-old born in Rhode Island, in directory 1900 as a janitor, in 1901 as a painter)
Jeremiah Callahan	8/98–2/99, 4/99– (48-year-old born in Ireland, one tinsmith in directory)
Michael Conroy	1/99–4/99 (52-year-old born in Ireland, either a laborer or painter, by 1902 only laborer in directory)
John Cummings	11/97–1/98, 12/98–3/99 (40-year-old born in North Brookfield, Mass., too many in directory to identify)
George Dorman	9/97–4/98, 11/98–5/99, 10/99– (52-year-old born in New Jersey, wireworker)
Patrick Flannagan	11/98–4/99 (42-year-old born in Ireland, in directory as laborer)
William Foley	8/97–2/98 (62-year-old born in Ireland in 1900, a laborer in directory)
Edward Gallagher	1/99–3/99 (a 41-year-old born in Ireland, one laborer in directory)
Timothy Hartnett	2/97–7/97, 10/97–5/98, 12/98–7/99 (57-year-old born in Ireland, none in directory)
Owen Harvey	12/97–5/98, 11/98, 1/99–4/99 (45-year-old born in England, a hostler listed in 1900 directory)
Edward Kaveney	1/99–1/99, 2/99–2/99 (22-year-old born in Worcester, no directory listing)
Joseph Kerr	8/96–5/97, 12/98–3/99, 10/99– (48-year-old born in Ireland, no directory listing)
Peter Loughlin	12/98–4/99 (46-year-old born in Worcester, no directory listing)
Maurice Moran	1/97–4/97, 11/98–4/99 (61-year-old from Ireland, no directory listing)
Peter McCarthy	12/97–5/99, 11/99– (63-year-old born in Ireland, no directory listing)
James McDermott	2/96–3/96, 9/98–12/98, 1/99–4/99 (48-year-old born in Ireland, 4 listings, three of them laborers)
Daniel Mulcahy	1/98–5/98 (57-year-old born in Ireland, in 1902 one moulder)
James Murray	11/95–2/96, 4–5/96, 12/98–4/99 (51-year-old born in Ireland, laborer in directory)
Alfred C. Ranger	12/98–4/99 (38-year-old born in Holden, Mass. No entry in Worcester or Holden directory)
Patrick Ryan	9/97–3/98, 7–9/98 (60-year-old born in Ireland, too many in directory to tell)
Cornelius Shea	1/96–4/96, 7/96–4/97, 5/97–4/99, 6/99– (59-year-old born in Ireland, several laborers in the directory)
Lawrence Spellman	12/97–2/98 (45-year-old born in Medway, Mass., was one clerk in directory 1900, 1901, one packer in 1902)

Name	Pattern of Admission
John E. Simmons	2/99–4/99 (53-year-old born in Bolton, Mass., no directory listing)
Thomas Sproule	2/99–5/99 (20-year-old born in East Bridgewater, Mass., no directory listing)
Charles H. Spurr	1/99–6/99 (44-year-old born in Worcester; in 1901 he is listed as an attendant at Home Farm)
L. Sullivan	12/98–4/99 (59-year-old born in Ireland, only L in directory in 1902 as peddler)
Dennis Toner	12/97–5/98, 6/98–7/98, 1/99–5/99 (44-year-old born in Worcester, no directory listing)

Still, several interesting points can be made about this list in conjunction with my looking up another forty or some inmates who entered in the almshouse for short periods in 1898 and 1899. First, despite the rhetoric of almshouse, it did not stop them from hiring their own charges as workers. One noted in table 4.2 was Charles Spurr, an inmate, who was hired as an attendant sometime between 1899 and 1901; additionally so was Henry A. Maynard, an inmate between November 1897 and June 1899, later an attendant; and Hugh McCann, an inmate from July 1899 to September 1899, then hired as a painter at the Home Farm. Secondly, there is considerable evidence that the almshouse was likely a stopover point for workers, employed or unemployed, rather than some (imagined) permanent class of "poor." Table 4.2 notes which inmates we have some evidence of work for. They include wireworkers, a tinsmith, janitors, painters, many laborers, a hostler (or horse or carriage driver), a machinist, a peddler, a moulder, and a teamster. Although positions such as wireworker, screwmaker, and moulders were likely workers in the private sector of Worcester's large wire and machine shop industry, other titles could just as well be titles in Worcester's parks, streets, or water departments, particularly the laborers, janitors, and painters that Worcester's overseers were so exasperated about in the early years of the twentieth century.

Although Portland's overseers of the poor did not issue a public diatribe against "rounders," Portland is a good site to explore seasonal use by inmates since we have an almshouse ledger for this period and it is the only one of the six almshouses I studied that listed an occupation for each inmate.[25] Moreover, although to be treated with some caution, Portland's record lists reasons for admission.[26] During one of the same years I studied above, I actually found an even higher percentage of almshouse inmates in Portland who appeared to be winter users than in Worcester. Of the 174 adults in the almshouse on March 1, 84 (or 48 percent) had entered since September 30, 1898. Of this number, only sixteen would remain until September 1, 1899, including four inmates who left and returned in this period.

Of the sixty-eight inmates, occupations are available for fifty-five. The majority were, not surprisingly, low-skilled workers: twenty-three laborers, six domestics, five teamsters, a ragpicker, a cook, a seamstress, a hostler. Presumably higher in status (the vagueness of occupational titles leaves much to be desired) were one musician, one music teacher, one painter, one carpenter, one fish peddler, one cooper, one seaman, and one sailor. Certainly higher would be the one boilermaker, one harness maker, one bricklayer, two lathers, one tanner, and two masons. Elimination of the twenty admissions the almshouse staff wrote in as due to "sickness," one due to "insanity," and one due to "intoxication" (this was the only inmate in March 1899 to be court-ordered as a house-of-correction prisoner) does not alter the occupational mix dramatically. The occupations of inmates admitted due to poverty (only) are as follows:

Bricklayer (1)	Mason (1)
Carpenter (1)	Painter (1)
Domestic (4)	Ragpicker (1)
Fish peddler (1)	Seaman (1)
Harness maker (1)	Tanner (1)
Hostler (1)	Teamster (3)
Laborer (19)	Housewife (5)
Lather (2)	Traveler (1)

Because of the lack of record of almost any women in the available city directories, table 4.3 focuses on the information available from the Portland ledger (name, age, birthplace, occupation, and reason for admission) combined with the information available in the city directories for the male winter admissions to the almshouse only. While the information is scattered, it does suggest a fair number of the inmates (about seventeen to nineteen of the forty-four in table 4.3) seem to have had some stability as measured by their presence in the directory with a continued address.

Taken together, the data from Worcester and Portland suggest that reasons for stays in the almshouse were likely complex and varying. Illness or infirmity may have accounted for some not listed in the ledger in that way, but on the other hand, some listed as "sick" or "intemperate" or "feeble" may well have fallen into the poorhouse primarily because of economic adversity. In this coastal city, a large number of seaman, sailors, and related workers frequently sought refuge off ships. Some inmates may have been homeless between addresses even if they were listed in the

Table 4.3. Occupations and Reason for Admission of Adult Male Winter-Only Inmates, Portland, Maine (1898–1899)

Name	Age	Birthplace	Occupation	Reason for Admission
Walter Atus	21	USA	teamster	"poverty"
William Barnes	44	USA	bricklayer	"poverty"
Matthew Cady	60	Ireland	laborer	"poverty"
James Carey*	43	USA	teamster	"poverty" (consistently in directory)
Stephen Connolly	46	Ireland	laborer	"poverty"
William Colfar	53	Ireland	laborer	"poverty"
Jesse Coombs*	42	USA	painter	"poverty" (consistently in directory)
David Connolly	61	USA	laborer	"poverty"
Matthew Foley±	28	Ireland	laborer	"sick," a laborer and bookbinder in directory
Thomas Follan±	36	Ireland	laborer	"poverty" in 1902 directory
John Flynn	38	USA	stone mason	"poverty"
William Follett	65	USA	teamster	"sick"
George H. Gill*	unk	USA	clerk	"insanity," died May 1900
William Gormley*	76	Ireland	fish peddler	(died August 1899) listed at 3 Monroe Street
Thomas Griffin	28	USA	laborer	"sick"
Richard Hanlon*	26	USA	laborer	"poverty"
Thomas Herbert	43	USA	laborer	"poverty"
Bernard Hern	53	Ireland	carpenter	"poverty"
George Hudson*	46	USA	laborer	"poverty," likely given job as "keeper insane ward, almshouse"
Allen Jones*	37	USA	teamster	"sickness," listed consistently at different addresses
John Joyce	65	Ireland	laborer	"poverty"
Thomas Leaford	55	England	laborer	"poverty"
Walter Lee*	47	USA	laborer	"poverty," listed each year in directory

(continued)

Table 4.3. Occupations and Reason for Admission of Adult Male Winter-Only Inmates, Portland, Maine (1898–1899) *(continued)*

Name	Age	Birthplace	Occupation	Reason for Admission
Charles Leighton	50	USA	sailor	"sick"
Dennis Mahoney*	57	USA	laborer	"poverty" consistently listed, died February 1901
James Mannebenny	35	Ireland	laborer	"poverty"
Jeremiah Marr	65	USA	laborer	"poverty"
Otto Mathieson	28	Norway	laborer	"sick"
Patrick McDonnough	44	USA	lather	"poverty"
Henry McQuade	23	USA	tanner	"poverty"
Coleman Milan	26	Ireland	laborer	"poverty"
James Murphy*	65	USA	harness maker	"poverty"
John Murphy*	65	USA	cooper	"sick"
Thomas Murphy*	38	USA	laborer	"poverty"
Thomas Norton	30	Ireland	seaman	"poverty"
Daniel O'Brien	54	Ireland	laborer	"poverty"
William Powers	61	USA	traveler	"poverty"
Joseph Reed	52	USA	laborer	"poverty"
Timothy Relahan*	42	USA	lather	"poverty"
Thomas Riley*	35	Ireland	mason	"sickness"
Edward Roach	52	USA	hostler	"poverty"
John Sears*	48	Ireland	laborer	"poverty"
Daniel Skillings*	50	USA	musician	"sickness"
Daniel Small*	62	USA	cook	"sickness"
Charles Stafford	19	USA	teamster	"poverty"
George Stebbins	20	USA	laborer	"poverty"

*Appear housed per Portland directories in 1898–1902 period
±Possibly listed

directory and used the almshouse essentially as a homeless shelter. However, it should be remembered that in all three of these states, to secure city or town aid one had to have settlement; in Massachusetts, this required a five-year residence and taxes paid, while in Maine a five-year residency was required without having drawn pauper support.[27] Given these requirements, many inmates would differ from today's homeless population in being somewhat less marginalized from the working class. It is likely, given the settlement laws and presence of some inmates at addresses, that some poorer workers may have been saving on fuel and food while staying in the almshouse or having some family members there, as we found some inmates did in mid-twentieth-century Carroll County. Others may have given up their lodging for economic reasons to return to a room at winter's end. Many likely were transient workers, moving from place to place for work, particularly when April of the year came.

The seasonal use of the poorhouse was a creature of its times. While workers faced massive barriers to stability that were in some ways harsher than today—lack of Social Security and unemployment insurance, lack of health care and other benefits at work—they also faced in other ways a more flexible pattern of daily survival compared to the twenty-first century. Housing costs were not astronomical as in our current day; strangers as well as family took in lodgers and boarders; lack of enforced inspection and building codes meant far more units, albeit decrepit, of housing; and sharing of wood, food, clothes, and other provisions may have been more common among extended families and nonfamilies of the same ethnic group. In this sense, many seasonal inmates of the almshouse did not fit the stereotypes of tramps and rounders held by officials. Rather they went from a modicum of eking out an existence in the housing and employment market to the almshouse, which acted as supplement.

Overseers, however, could never really separate (try as they might) the tramps and vagrants (the poor with no legal settlement in their areas) from those people who were residents and wandered in and out of the house. To officials, the paupers, particularly the foreign born, often seemed "intemperate," "vicious," or a "rounder," whether from the area or not. This trend continues; even today, many cities continue to blame home-grown poverty and the homeless on those from out of town.[28]

FRUSTRATED OVERSEERS IN ONE CITY

The undermining of the poorhouse and poor relief system, however, was even greater than indicated by the dismay at "rounder" elements that came and went from the poorhouse or by the long-term residents who refused to leave, because (even then) Americans were mobile and moved from place to place to obtain work and better fortune. Under the poor-relief system (which to a great degree continued up until the 1960s when the Warren Court decisions made the use of residency laws more limited), one could only obtain assistance from a city or town in which one held residency (through voting and tax payments) regardless of where one currently lived or applied for aid. All towns and cities kept copious files of letters battling with other cities and towns as to settlement of paupers. Many settlement battles ended up in court, as each city or town tried to save some tax money by getting their neighbors to admit pauper settlements.

Deep in the vaults in the basement of the city hall in Haverhill, Massachusetts, are numerous files of letters sent by the clerk to the overseers of the poor in other towns and cities throughout New England and occasionally much farther afield, denying or acknowledging settlement.[29] What struck me was the hostility vented by the clerk of the overseers at many of the paupers who were the subject of letters. Unlike the idealistic days of the poorhouse, overseers seemed to be weary of some of the poor, about whom they claimed much knowledge, and expressed hostile advice to overseers in other cities. A sample of some of the letters follows:

[January 8, 1897] To Springfield, Massachusetts:

Gentleman: Your notice of December 30, 1896 notifying us of Robert D. Sleeper received. We refuse to aid him except at our almshouse.

[February 25, 1897] To South Kingston, New Hampshire:

The Board of Overseers of the Poor of Haverhill refuses to pay the board of Calvin Marble after Feb. 15, 1897, on which date we sent for him to remove him to our Almshouse and he refused to go.

[March 1, 1897] To Boston, Massachusetts:

In reply to yours of Feb. 26 regarding grandchild of S[unreadable] H. Estabrook would say: The mother is at our Work House on a six month sentence from the court for having no visible means of support. Knowing her well, we do not think she will ever take the care of the child.

[December 15, 1897] To Chester, New Hampshire:

In reply to yours of December 14th would say: Benj Kimball ran away from our Almshouse, and we refuse to aid him except at the Almshouse.

[December 17, 1897] To Boston, Massachusetts:

In reply to your notice of December 15th would say: we admit the set.[tlement] of Thos. Caffrey family. We know them well and would request that you aid them as little as possible. They do not try to help themselves, but prefer to live on charity. If their call becomes large let us know at once.

Much can be said about the letters above, certainly regarding the parsimony of the overseers and their anger toward those who refused to comply with their orders and decisions. What perhaps is less evident is the ability of individuals and families to simply move to other places, and then apply when necessary for aid in other cities. Obviously we have records only of those who either volunteered that they were from Haverhill or were somehow traced back to this city. Clearly, many people were not so traced. But even when they were traced, the city had little authority under the poor-relief system of this time except to reject payment or advise the new town of its thoughts. Absent a legal warrant, they could not force anyone to go to the almshouse. We cannot know how these individuals and families survived; some certainly made out poorly, and given the sharp inadequacies of poor relief, may have fallen even deeper into adversity. Yet others likely did not need to come to back to Haverhill where they were so unwanted because they found work, moved on, or somehow survived in spite of the hostility.

A CONFUSED STATE

As the twentieth century opened, the poor-relief system, including the poorhouse, stood in a confused state, one that would continue unabated until its demise. The huge economic decline of the 1890s tested the limits of the old system and threatened the traditional deserving/undeserving lines, particularly as ethnic immigrants constituted the bulk of the poor. Further, the tendency, on the one hand, for the poorhouse to be in the process of becoming a long-term institution (most developed in Carroll County, N.H.) rather than a place of work and reform, and on the other, a "winter stopover" for the poor, rather than a place of "industry," troubled the officials in charge. This confusion over the purposes of the poorhouse/poor farm continued for many decades into the twentieth century, ending in Portland and Haverhill only with conversion to health facilities in the 1930s, while continuing in ambiguity for decades more in New Hampshire; Lewiston, Maine; and Worcester, Massachusetts.

5

Inmates, Overseers, and the Politics of the Poorhouse

When the grievances of disgruntled ex-inmates are aired for the purpose of making an ex parte case against citizens whose characters are above reproach, it is time to call a halt.

—*Haverhill* (Mass.) *Evening Gazette*, editorial,
July 26, 1895[1]

When the conduct of public officials is such as to render them a laughing stock, their period of usefulness is pretty well over: this is the general rule.

—*Portland* (Maine) *Evening Express* on the overseers of the poor,
editorial, March 2, 1910[2]

Changes in the poorhouse were not only affected by the patterns of inmates' utilization that tended to undermine the original mission of the institution; change also occurred as inmates, citizens, and officials engaged in political conflict. Some conflicts inevitably pitted at least some inmates against their "betters." An important tool of inmates was the making of charges and calls for public investigation into conditions at the homes, rather than other forms of protest. In most jurisdictions I studied, inmate complaints (or those of ex-inmates or family members) became the subject of interest of news reporters, mayors or city councilors, overseers of the poor, or competing factions within the city, county, or town. Inmates clearly were aware of this power. In most jurisdictions studied, complainants were guaranteed some audience, not necessarily simply out of a sense of fairness but also likely from public interest in scandal and

from the interest of various local and state level officials in using contro-
versies to jockey for power.[3]

The local political system politicized conflict not only between inmates
and superintendent and the overseers of the poor, but among overseers
themselves, as well as city councillors, county commissioners, and within
factions of city, town, and county government. This had the effect of making these conflicts as common as the conflicts between inmates and those
who controlled their lives.

In choosing two moments in time to explore in this chapter, I develop
some particularly rich sources of unique historical material. The first example is an investigation of the city farm conditions in Haverhill, Massachusetts, in 1895, which was similar in many ways to other investigations
that occurred in other towns, cities, and counties about their poorhouses,
quite often provoked by complaints of inmates or ex-inmates who went to
local political officials to voice their views. Though many of the complaints were dismissed (as was true elsewhere), the weeks of testimony
and charges did produce a number of changes that benefited the inmates,
as was the case in other locales.[4]

The second example chosen was the ongoing, bitter conflict among the
overseers of the poor in Portland, Maine, which simmered for years in the
first decades of the twentieth century, and which we sample at a particular
time, 1909–1910. While not every town, city, or county had such conflicts,
internal conflicts were extremely common since not only was the care of the
poor and other groups in the poorhouse controversial but also because all
officials—including city or county physicians, some farm employees, superintendents and matrons, and most overseers—were elected (unlike today's bureaucratic and professionalized social welfare system, which generally relies on an appointed staff). This was an important opportunity for
inmates and their primarily ethnic supporters, who could make good use
of the political arena to effect change. In Portland, the years chosen show
not only overseer conflict but also how this conflict politicized relations
with the superintendent and other employees at the poorhouse.

A POOR-FARM INVESTIGATION

Sometime in late July of 1895, a sixty-one-year-old inmate named "Flint"
(Moses) Peaslee went to a Haverhill alderman and then to the mayor,
Samuel Jewett, with charges about the Haverhill City Farm. Peaslee, who
had been in the almshouse for several months, had been asked to care for
another inmate, John Doton, who was "paralytic," with open sores on his
body. Peaslee exhibited a "bottle partially filled with vermin which he

claimed to have picked from a sore on [Doton's] body, and allege[d] that the man's bed ha[d] been at times alive with them."[5] While Peaslee was referred to by the newspaper as "a well-known character" from the first, within days the mayor and the chair of the board of aldermen initiated a formal investigation of the city farm. To the dismay of the *Haverhill Evening Gazette* and certain other actors in the drama, such as city farm superintendent Louis Savage, the investigation, alternating between closed and public sessions, went on for a month and then lingered still another month before a report was made public.[6]

From a historical perspective, it is important to note how newsworthy the charges were. Poorhouses and the departments that ran them were among the most important departments under municipal jurisdiction, comparable to police forces today. Despite its editorial denunciations, the *Haverhill Evening Express* provided banner headlines beginning on July 25 ("Serious Charges Made") and July 26 ("City Fathers Will Investigate"). Moreover, it is interesting that, as in other cities studied, inmates were invited to meet with officials and then publicly testify, despite hostility expressed to this practice by others, including the newspaper editors. To some extent, the visibility of the city almshouses and farms tends to argue against the "out of sight, out of mind" argument made by many about the nature of indoor relief.

A joint committee was appointed, which included the mayor, city marshall, two aldermen, the city council president, and three councilmen. The inquiry quickly moved beyond the Doton case to include a wide range of opinions, charges, and defenses that occurred in private and public testimony.

On the Doton case itself, Peaslee testified, "While I was at the farm my work was mostly looking after patients in hospital [ward of almshouse]. I had personal charge of George Doton. His condition is terrible [with] nothing being done to cure the sores." Superintendent Savage and the city physician Dr. Clarke denied that Doton was in the care of Peaslee, and stated that they were aware of Doton's condition, although Peaslee had not reported the vermin to either of them. Savage and Clarke stated that a rubber blanket was placed beneath Doton and cleaned often, and that he was moved several times a day. Dr. Anthony testified:

> The man [Doton] was paralyzed. I saw maggots crawling in some of the sores and the odor was disagreeable. I wrote for a disenfecting [*sic*] and healing wash and ordered it to be thoroughly used twice a day. Mr. Savage asked me if much could be done to heal it and I told him "no"; bed sores are the frequent accompaniment of paralysis . . . at times even in hospitals, and with the best of care . . . the paralyzed part is affected and it is the constant pressure that aggravates the trouble.[7]

Doton was described as "demented" and died on July 29. According to Oliver Hubbard, the chair of Haverhill's overseers of the poor, Doton's family themselves had asked the city to care for him at the almshouse, and Hubbard had visited him weekly (the ledger book of the poorhouse indicates Doton was admitted on May 14). Moreover, ex-mayor and overseer Joseph Sheldon met Doton ("who knew him perfectly well") the day he came, despite his sometime "dementia," because "he had been in the clothing business" as had Sheldon. Doton told him "he was well used and cared for" at the almshouse.[8]

Despite the conflict over Doton, had medical care been the only issue, widespread conflict would probably not have existed. From the first, the newspaper and officials noted the need for a trained nurse at the almshouse, and an improved hospital ward. These changes would be recommended by the committee's report. More interesting is how the scandal provides a lens into the experience of many inmates as well as the officials of the poorhouse system.

In the weeks of the investigation, the committee interviewed a total of twenty-two inmates or former inmates, and fourteen others. The committee would count ten of the inmates as critical of the management, twelve as supportive, and the preponderance of the other fourteen witnesses as favorable to the poorhouse administration. Although my own review of the public testimony suggests there were at least several inmates and ex-inmates whose testimony was too ambiguous to be clearly labeled "pro" or "con," the characterization appears generally correct. Overwhelmingly, the critics besides Peaslee were women who had been sentenced to the house for drunkenness. Those who testified on behalf of the qualities of the poorhouse tended to be male, longer-term inmates, and voluntary poorhouse denizens. For example, Bessie Murphy, identified in the ledger as twenty-nine years old in 1895 and as "intemperate," had been an inmate since October 1892. She had earlier been sentenced to the house in 1891 by the court. Murphy testified:

> The first year both Mr. and Mrs. Savage were good to me; I worked hard as I was strong then; the inmates did the work while the prisoners looked on; I was obliged to do the heaviest part of the washing; at one time Mr. Savage knocked me down and put me down stairs for five days and kept me on bread and water; because I had some pieces of sheeting in my hand Mrs. Savage sent for a doctor to pronounce me crazy; Mrs. Savage told me not to go up to town and tell any stories about my treatment for while I was there I would have to put up with things the way they were; was kept one day on bread and a bowl of milk; the cell floor was flooded with water, the same having been turned with a line of hose by Mr. Savage. I have been sick since then from the effects of it. . . . When I was six months along in the family way I was taken down stairs and kept in cellar for five days; I was forced to work when I was not able to.[9]

Mary Hussey, identified in the ledger as forty-one years old in 1895, Irish, and "intemperate," had (like Murphy) been sentenced by the court to the house in 1890 and again in 1891, but had been at the almshouse—presumably not by court sentence—since January 1895. She too spoke of forced stays in the cells and conflict with the Savages:

> I was required to do all the washing for the inmates and some for Mrs. Savage and the help; I was sick at one time and I was unable to do the work; for this reason I was placed in the cell in the cellar and kept for five days on bread and water; Mr Savage nailed down the windows and had them painted, shutting out the light and air; it was in the winter time and it was bitterly cold and after the third day, the straw mattress was taken away and I had to sleep on a bare iron bedstead.[10]

Samuel Marble, identified in the ledger as a sixty-six-year-old man who had been at the almshouse since 1880, was one of the first inmates at the hearings to defend the management, and it was noted favorably by the press that he was "once a well-to-do stableman." As a number of other inmates testified, he stated he was "Never served poor or tainted food. . . . There is plenty of everything and it is clean and wholesome, and has always been so." He added he saw no uncleanliness, nor any cruelty. He said, "I have seen inmates punished, but humanely and I should say deservedly." Like other witnesses, he noted Peaslee did not mention the maggots found on Doton to other inmates nor had he reported them to the superintendent.[11]

A fair number of inmates who supported the Savages were highly critical of Mrs. Murphy and Mrs. Hussey. Margaret Towle (age unknown), though herself sentenced by the court in 1890, stated, "The only fault I have to find is with the inmates, particularly Mrs. Hussey and Mrs. Murphy, who had tried to get me into a scheme to oust Mr. and Mrs. Savage, and when [I] refused, [they] had ill treated me." The newspaper noted her testimony "created quite a stir" and when she was questioned, she stated further that Mrs. Murphy "had told the women that if they put their heads together they could rid of Mr. and Mrs. Savage." Perhaps as exciting a testimony was provided by a Lizzie Oakes, identified as a thirty-four-year-old woman, also "intemperate," and who (like Towle, Murphy, and Hussey) had also been at times sentenced by the court but was now at the almshouse voluntarily. She admitted she had been

> at the farm many times for drunkenness but always received good treatment. I never saw any undeserved treatment. . . . Mrs. Murphy is a bad, ill-spoken woman . . . who . . . tried to get her [Lena Forest, another inmate] to run away from the farm and go into a house of ill-fame, but I told her not to do that. Mrs. Murphy and Rosa Chase [another ex-inmate who testified against the Savages]

were a bad couple and often raised a racket. When Rosa Chase was sick I attended her and she had the best of care. She got dropped eggs and toast and such food and had no reason to complain.[12]

It is difficult to chronicle in a short space of time all the complaints and their responses, much less the veracity of each charge. Some complaints led to ridicule toward those complaining. For example, Peaslee charged that "the chairman of the board of overseers of the poor [Hubbard] has been served with roast chicken and the best meats at dinner, while the inmates were given crackers and cheese, and that too, on Sunday."[13] Not only was this favoritism denied but such charges also led the *Haverhill Evening Gazette* to write an editorial entitled "Please Burn a Rag":

> The burden of the song of the principal witnesses at Wednesday night's session of the almshouse investigating committee was to the effect that chicken is not served the inmates though officials occasionally partake of that delicacy. To the citizens of Haverhill who pay the taxes but do not eat chicken save upon occasions, this will hardly seem a heinous offence on the part of the official of that institution, yet it would seem to be of sufficient importance in the eyes of prosecutors in this case to be brought out with most dramatic expression by a witness who doubtless would only be satisfied if fed upon a diet of angel cake and humming birds, with side dishes of terrapin or canvas back duck, topped off with coffee and ices.[14]

Although the newspaper used sarcasm to continually attack both the inmates and the city administration for allowing such public testimony, the officials themselves responded seriously and calmly.[15] Savage, while denying certain charges, such as improper medical attention, any serving of "bad meat," and diversion of goods to family members, did admit he gave cider to the inmates "though never to the point of drunkenness" and noted he had now ceased the practice after it was questioned.[16] Recognizing the more important question of humane treatment, Savage admitted that "it was necessary to imprison [some inmates] at times for misconduct" and when asked to respond to the individuals who felt maltreated, he often expressed frustration: "I know Mrs. Murphy. Sometimes she was good and at other times she was unmanageable, and would swear, make trouble and do nothing she was asked and she was punished for offenses."[17]

Perhaps his biggest frustration was with a young girl named Lena Forrest (fourteen at the time of the hearings) who had given testimony against him, but was contradicted by numerous inmates who called her "a bad girl," "saucy," and a user of "foul language." Forrest, who was first admitted to the almshouse with her brother in 1892, had been readmitted in 1894 after evidently not working out in a foster care arrangement. Savage noted:

I have known [Lena Forrest] three or four years. I was always kind to her but she was untruthful, disobedient, and stubborn. Corporal punishment was never inflicted on her nor any punishment except confinement. She had medical treatment for her weakness, but a large part of her action was due to her own laziness. . . . [While in cells] she was told any time she wanted to come upstairs if she felt [her behavior] able to improve. The cell is dry, heated in winter, lighted and as good as any room. . . . [There was] no flood while she was there, [and] about [the alms]house she would go into the men's apartment every chance she got.[18]

Apparently key to this investigation were the attitudes of the mayor and the police chief. At least according to the newspaper, they were in favor of making significant reforms at the almshouse. In fact, early on, the *Haverhill Evening Gazette* took Mayor Jewett and Marshall Rand to task for meeting privately with Peaslee and other inmates. At the close of the hearing, the committee was divided 6–2, with the majority favoring a complete exoneration of all officials on all charges, but Jewett and Rand were insisting on a minority report. All agreed on the need for a "trained nurse" and better accommodations for "invalids," but disagreed on other issues.[19] Evidently, they agreed as well that, contrary to testimony of a few inmates, the cells were roomy and comfortable, and well ventilated, and no actual mistreatment had occurred. But the mayor in particular wished to get out of the business of admitting drunks to the almshouse, while others on the committee charged "the drunks in the summer are paupers in the winter."[20] In the course of almost another month, the mayor agreed to a compromise report, but Rand stood firm and refused to sign it.

The report, issued on September 19, unanimously exonerated the superintendent, matron, staff, and overseers.

The committee having heard and considered the evidence, deem it a simple act of justice to find and report that the poor department has been properly, capably and efficiently managed, and that they find no fault in the manner in which the duties of the superintendent of the almshouse, of the overseers of the poor and of the city physician have been performed. The inmates and prisoners [persons sentenced there for crime are termed prisoners] at the almshouse are supplied with an abundance of good and wholesome food. They are humanely treated. They are not subjected to unreasonable restraint or cruel or improper discipline. The cells are dry and comfortable and the house itself is cleanly kept and well managed.[21]

Not surprisingly, the committee managed to square its favorable report with the accusations by resting on the long tradition of the "deserving" and "undeserving poor," blaming some prisoners for the hubbub: "Our almshouse is not only a home for the poor and indigent, but it is also a place of detention. . . . In addition to the worthy poor, there are found the

lazy, the disorderly, the stubborn and the vicious, to whom work, neat-
ness, and restraint are distasteful."[22]

The committee issued six recommendations. As expected, it recommended to the overseers that a more formal hospital ward be created with
separate male and female accommodations under the supervision of a
trained nurse and the city physician. It endorsed earlier calls for one overseer to devote his entire time to city work and be compensated for it. Beyond other minor recommendations—staff at the almshouse should be
city residents, the almshouse should be screened in, and the clothing of inmates better marked—the major recommendation, in a concession to the
mayor and police chief, was an "experiment" for a year in having "persons . . . not be sent to the almshouse for drunkenness." It noted that they
had no authority to do this, as it was up to the courts and overseers. It also
recognized a large amount of opposition to this, as the majority of the
work at the almshouse was performed by prison labor. Still, it urged an
attempt to separate the prisoners "as such inmates are a constant source
of trouble and complaint."[23]

What are we to make of this investigation over a century later? There
are both local conditions that require comment and some broader generalizations that can be made.

Locally, it is interesting to note that the 1890s were a time of great turmoil and conflict in Haverhill, and that while the press did not relate such
conflicts to this investigation, the events probably cannot entirely be separated. In late 1894, the shoe manufacturers (the predominant industry) of
Haverhill locked out their employees and were able to force shoe workers
back to work in the spring without meeting any of their demands. In response to the defeat and the sentencing that year of local strikers as rabble-
rousers, a Socialist party was formed in Haverhill. According to a regional
history, the events of that year propelled the leaders, James Carey and John
C. Chase, into becoming the first elected Socialist city councilor (Carey in
1897) and Socialist mayor (Chase in 1898) in the nation.[24]

Whatever the exact relation (if any) between agitation among the inmates, labor, and political unrest in Haverhill, it is interesting that the opposition both of the earlier mayor and of Mayor Chase in 1898 to the
workhouse clearly prevailed in the city of Haverhill. A separate ledger
starting in 1895 was found by this author in the vault of the city hall.[25] The
"overseers of the workhouse" kept a ledger book that had only about
eight narrow pages filled, with most of the meetings devoted to voting to
release individuals and in some cases to pardoning them. In 1898, the
overseers of the workhouse voted themselves out of existence!

On the other hand, it could be noted that neither Mayor Chase nor another Socialist mayor (Parkman Flanders) did away with the almshouse
or changed it radically, though both advocated more public works jobs

and blamed poverty and unemployment on the capitalist system. Interestingly, Superintendent Savage stayed on in his job until his death in 1926 (an extremely long duration for a superintendent, as he had been hired in the 1880s! Mrs. Savage, the matron, stayed until 1929.). The 1900 census of the almshouse records several of the actors (on both sides of the testimony) were still present: Margaret Towle, for example, and Mary Hussey and Margaret Kelley, the latter two who testified against the management. "Flint" Peaslee, Lena Forrest, and Bessie Murphy, however, were not there.

Since obviously some of these issues were particular to the city, it is difficult to generalize about all of them. However, in addition to providing a lens into a poorhouse at one moment in time in one city, it does suggest some common themes. First, the cities, towns, and counties that I studied took their poorhouse conditions very seriously. All of them used phrases like "it is our pride," or claimed to be "the best in the state," or at least striving to "be the model." While neglect may have characterized some periods of time in poorhouse history or in some regions of the nation, it does not appear true in New England at this time. As Michael Katz notes about the battle between superintendents and the reformers who favored mental asylums and orphanages, the superintendents had a valid point that local communities had more interest and more power in monitoring conditions at poorhouses than they would ever have at observing mental hospitals, large orphanages, and other statewide institutions.[26] For a number of reasons (including physical remoteness), scandals about facilities such as mental hospitals, state schools for the retarded, and prisons would only come to light fifty or sixty years later.

Of course, while cities, towns, and counties were extremely concerned about the "worthy poor" (i.e., the elderly, ill, widowed, and other respectable individuals), they discounted the experience of others by the presentation of their characters. At the investigation, it was noted that "all witnesses have been investigated" and those complaining "were bad people to handle." The newspaper reported, "it was evident that the committee was not impressed by the appearance of the[se] witnesses."[27] Although this is not terribly surprising, it does indicate the willingness of towns and cities to discount information from people who were no longer "intemperate" or "criminal" simply based on their past labels, and their willingness to let those judged immoral be punished. There was obviously a wide consensus that punishment was needed for the recalcitrant and that inmate (or at least prisoner) labor was a natural thing.

The existence of the poorhouse as a combination hospital, old age home, homeless shelter, and local jail is illustrated by the 1895 Haverhill investigation. To modern eyes, of course, this appears strange and unwieldy; we feel it is natural that a more professional hospital be established and separated from a more secure jail. However, these notions would not completely take hold for many, many decades. Police stations were used for homeless lodgers well into the mid-twentieth century, and some courts sentenced people to houses of correction, and even regular poorhouses, for years to come. Medical facilities kept their identities as places for the poor since public institutions were often the only institutions to accept patients who couldn't afford private hospitals. Alms/poorhouses may have had their problems, but for the poor they held certain advantages. They were near to home and neighbors, could (except for prisoners) be entered or left at will, and allowed work to proceed both seasonally (stay there in the winter, leave in the summer) or daily (stay at almshouse at night, while work during day).[28] But most importantly, the investigation itself shows the power of inmates, and indirectly the poor and working-class people in general. In the August 9 *Evening Gazette*, the paper itself said the complainers "raised the ire of the committee as well as the audience *except the rabble whose applause was frequently waited for* [my emphasis]."[29] Despite the split among the inmates in their view of the Savages and the almshouse, public opinion among poorer people must have favored the investigation and the later decision to end the workhouse as well as the improvements in care that came about. Indeed, after the investigation closed, Peaslee was reported resuming a campaign against the poorhouse.[30]

THE BATTLE OF THE OVERSEERS

As the two quotes from the local newspapers that start the chapter suggest, in Haverhill, while the leading newspaper attacked the ungrateful poor, the overseers of the poor came to be a subject of ridicule up the New England coast in Portland, Maine. Although I focus mostly on one particular year, it appears that the board quarreled so much with one another and with each superintendent of the city home and hospital as to almost paralyze operations for at least a decade and a half in the first quarter of the twentieth century. In 1924, when the city as a whole moved from a mayoral to a city manager system, the overseers of the poor were abolished as a separate board and their duties passed onto the city council.

Although many issues caused conflict among the overseers of the poor in Portland, the constant turmoil at the home was certainly a catalyst. As inmates came and left the Portland almshouse as they wanted, were seen in intoxicated condition, and even gained payment for their work (a major contradiction for an institution based initially on the concept of forced labor), the overseers were drawn into conflicting sides. Generally speaking, the elected representatives of the more recent immigrant groups and the poorer parts of town supported more liberal treatment and backed the superintendents of the Portland home, in this period. The Republican Yankee faction was more critical of the superintendents and the direction that the Portland home seemed to be moving in.

The size of the Portland board of overseers and the close political competition in the city also made the board highly politicized. While in Haverhill there were three overseers of the poor in the period we observe, there were twelve overseers of the poor in Portland. This rather unwieldy board (composed of individuals elected to a three-year term, staggered so that four were elected each year), in a highly competitive environment between Democrats and Republicans, nearly always became equally divided by political party. Some notion of the difference between the Portland and the Haverhill systems can be seen by simple numbers: between 1905 and 1923, there were only six individuals who served as overseers in Haverhill, while in Portland, there were sixty-four (notwithstanding the mayor's successful drive to reduce the overseers to a board of ten in 1910).[31] Moreover, while from 1886 to 1927 the Haverhill City Farm had one superintendent (Savage), in Portland, there were six superintendents between 1905 and 1923.[32]

But probably most surprising to a modern reader was the level of formal democracy that existed in New England towns and cities. In 1909 Portland, for example, not only did each party nominate overseers of the poor for the upcoming vacancies, they did so as well for the city physician, consulting physicians, a truant officer, and host of positions, such as "superintendent of clocks" and "city weigher of hay." After the city elections held in Portland in December, at the first meeting of the overseers, the board elected not only a superintendent of the home and hospital but its matron (despite the fact that it was almost always the superintendent's wife), an assistant matron, an engineer, assistant engineer, baker, night watchman, chaplain, head teamster, keeper of pigs, keeper of the insane ward, drivers of offal teams (the city farm, as in Worcester and Lewiston, picked up the city's garbage and fed it to the pigs on the farm), and all the nurses! It also elected what would become the most powerful position, the board's secretary, a position that became a professional social worker, and in some cities emerged as the director of welfare or relief in the 1930s.[33] I trace below the election period of 1909, which led up to an embarrassing deadlock on the board. The board of overseers, prior to the election, was deeply split between a conservative faction led by real estate agent William Derrah and a more liberal group that included Lizzie French, one of the first female overseers and an activist who sat on the state board of charities and corrections,[34] and Samuel Rosenberg, probably the first Jewish overseer of the poor in Portland, who was a clothing store owner and later an active leader of Hebrew philanthropies. All four vacancies in the 1909 overseers board were for positions held by Democrats: Rosenberg's slot as well as those of James J. O'Brien (a boot and shoe store owner), William T. Howe (a grocer), and Harrison R. Waterhouse (a clerk). Although it is difficult to tell how closely the citizens of the day paid attention to political contests for overseers of the poor, considerable activity and controversy preceded the December election.

In October, Overseer Derrah led a campaign against "bums" staying at the Portland City Home. Derrah charged that "many able bodied men who work in the Summer and spend their earnings for liquor, apply for admission in the Winter." According to the *Portland Evening Express*, Derrah opined that "they should not have so easy a time" and recommended bringing back a blacklist (presumably a list of banned inmates considered abusers of the house's hospitality), bringing all cases for admission to the total board of overseers, and cutting the tobacco rations, which he claimed had reached "a ton" and the "greater part of which goes to bums."[35] Derrah's proposals were adamantly opposed by Rosenberg, who noted "it is difficult to obtain employment in the Winter months" and he "did not see how any person could be turned away who was cold and hungry." O'Brien quipped that if the blacklist was returned, it would "be very long and it might include two thirds of the inmates of the home." The blacklist itself was carried in an undisclosed vote, indicating in all probability that Derrah was waging his campaign for public political consumption. The board deadlocked 5–5 on the proposal to bring every case to the board, hence leading that motion to defeat. On the tobacco proposal, the motion was amended to make it weaker and eliminate the tobacco supply only to those sentenced to the almshouse. This motion passed by an undisclosed margin. [36]

Evidently feeling the Republicans would be the likely winners in the general election, two Democratic candidates—O'Brien and Rosenberg—sought bipartisan support. In one news piece, the paper reported "Republican friends" of O'Brien supporting him and praising his service, saying, "he was in close touch with the people of [his district] and knows the needs of the poor. Through his influence and efforts many persons have been kept out of the workhouse and prevented from becoming paupers."[37] The following day's newspaper contained prestigious endorsements: a statement by the Rt. Reverend Mgr. Edward F. Hurley, pastor of St. Dominic's Catholic Church, supporting O'Brien, and another from Captain of Police Hugh McDonough.[38] In a letter to the paper on another electoral bid, a Republican candidate for overseer of the poor, David Shwartz, took Dr. Elias Chaplin to task for writing in to support Samuel Rosenberg. Schwartz questioned Chaplin's supposed Republican credentials, claiming he supported the Democrat, Curtis, for mayor. He further called into question Chaplin's opinion that Rosenberg had the greater esteem of the Hebrew population than Shwartz.[39]

Despite the intense politicking, O'Brien and Rosenberg went down to defeat. On December 14, the vote for "subordinate city offices" was held in a joint convention of the aldermen and city council and they overwhelmingly elected Republicans Arthur M. Soule, William A. Holland, and Thomas H. Randall and returned William T. Howe as a Republican-endorsed minority party representative.[40] These candidates received twenty-seven votes to O'Brien, Rosenberg, and Daniel E. Bowen's five and John Brown's seven votes.[41]

Now the politics really began rather than ended! The newspaper reported the same day as the "subordinate elections" were held that Superintendent Frank J. Seeley, in that office since 1906, would be opposed for reelection. Though citing no reasons, it reported "a feeling of dissatisfaction among a few members of the board" and rumor had suggested Overseer Edward Chaplin would be a candidate. Chaplin denied this in a published statement.[42] Praising the superintendent for increasing the revenues at the city farm, the *Portland Evening Express* endorsed Seeley for reelection. They also slapped the overseer system by noting Seeley had done well "in spite of conditions which may not have been altogether favorable, owing to the system which places the superintendent under the control of the Board of Overseers of the Poor."[43] Seeley's opponents had no opposing candidate, but took the strategy of seeking to defer the vote. Derrah made a motion to postpone the vote of both superintendent and matron to the next meeting. Derrah stated that "there was an investigation in progress of certain things pertaining to the City Home management" that had not been resolved to his satisfaction. New Overseer Randall supported Derrah, stating he had nothing against Seeley but had not yet met him, so could not vote for him. Overseer Bibber, clearly miffed by this, remarked that many Americans had never met then-President Taft, yet had voted for him! Trying a different tack, Randall argued that the Seeleys were not residents of Portland. In still another line of argument, Overseer Howe said "it was common knowledge that . . . Seeley may not be able to work and that he has been on the couch the greater part of the time for the past few months." Overseer Soule, who earlier made clear he would not ally with his newly elected party colleagues by attacking their efforts to discredit Seeley, remarked that if Seeley could not work, why was he not being discharged. There was apparently no answer. The motion to vote was supported by seven overseers to four, with Chairman Ross (already reelected) not voting, and then the Seeleys were elected. Similar votes found Lizzie French winning vice chair (7–5) and incumbent John Foley winning reelection as farm teamster (7–5). For some reason, however, the most contested election would be for the position of assistant matron, which would continue as a deadlock for many months.[44] It is not totally clear what an assistant matron's job description was, as most almshouses did not seem to have this job title. The matron's tasks ranged in some poorhouses from essentially serving as the superintendent for female inmates to, in others, being the officer responsible for all inmates' actual conditions and personal needs while the superintendent focused on farming and the budget balancing for their cities and counties (see chapter 7).[45]

At the December 21 meeting, the overseers clashed again on reports that Superintendent Seeley was paying some inmates for work done at the home. Mrs. French thought this was fine, as the city would otherwise have had to pay an employee, but Overseers Randall and Ross objected strenuously, saying if some inmates were paid, others would demand it, and that if they could work to support themselves, inmates should be discharged.[46] On January 20, 1910, at another overseers' meeting, Chaplin complained of "inmates being allowed to leave the Home [in the] evening[s] and come to the City, sometimes returning to the Home in an intoxicated condition and carrying liquor with them into the Home." Mrs. French said this was a matter for the superintendent, but Chaplin and Randall wanted stronger action taken.[47] While inmates in Portland at this time had no visible representation at meetings or an actual voice in the newspapers, clearly the battles reflected the controversy over how much control should be exerted at the home over Portland's poor.

The "Seeleyites," as the newspaper came to nickname those who supported Superintendent Seeley, nominated a Mrs. Hattie Haskell for assistant matron, who had recently been placed in that position. Immediately, the "anti-Seeleyites" challenged her, saying she was a nonresident of the city. Overseers Harriet Barker, French, and Bibber spoke to the contrary, saying she had just moved to the city to take the job, while the latter two also cited other employees who were not residents. The anti-Seeleyites nominated a Miss Nellie Tarr, and a 6–6 tie ensued between Tarr and Haskell. Interestingly, to the chagrin of the press, the overseers remained deadlocked for months on the issue, taking dozens of ballots. Tarr, the home's cook, pulled out of the election in January 1910 to remain in that job, but the "antis" replaced her with a Mrs. Mary B. Tolman, and the deadlock continued.[48]

Overseer Harriet Barker made the logical and modern argument that "the system was wrong" and that the "keeper of the home should select the help over which he has charge" since he had that expertise.[49] This would likely be our view today, to have administration separate and professionalized, not subject to constant voting. But the *Express* was probably right that the issue was bitterly personal and partisan: "It has become almost an unwritten law in the Board that anything which is favored by the friends of Superintendent Seeley . . . must be opposed by the other faction, regardless of the merits of the case."[50]

Although efforts to reduce drastically the number of overseers of the poor failed in the short term,[51] conflicts would continue long after both Superintendent Seeley and his opponents left the scene.[52] The minutes of the overseers of the poor's meetings between 1913 and 1923 (which we shall return to in the next chapter) document conflict after conflict. Battles occurred with every superintendent of the home as the political makeup of the board changed annually. Inmates in Portland, in this period, tended to ally with the home's superintendents, perhaps because they tended to favor a policy paying inmates for work (see chapter 6). Occasional issues that likely would have been seen as scandalous by the public arose. In 1920, for example, it was revealed the overseers had voted themselves private gardens at Portland City Farm. An overseer, Fred Johnston, "stated he wished to go on record that he should protest against any overseer or any other person having a garden, as being a conversion of city property for private purposes." His motion failed, but a few weeks later, the board returned to this issue and voted that any member of public could have a garden plot on a first-come-first-served basis at the city farm, evidently hoping to assuage the political damage.[53] In 1920, the mayor (now Republican Charles B. Clarke) complained in his annual report that the city had "a most efficient secretary" of the overseers in Percy Horton but "[he] is much handicapped by squabbles among the members of the Board."[54]

A close reading of the minutes of the overseers shows Secretary Horton's gradual rise to power. In the early years of available minutes, overseers of the poor appear to be micromanaging the home, approving purchases of shoes, discharges of inmates, buying of uniforms, and so on. But as the years went by, most cases are referred to Horton to "investigate," as was becoming the case in other cities studied. Although not a professionally trained social worker, by 1919 Horton was securing approval to attend the National Conference of Social Work in Atlantic City.[55] Inevitably, this led to some clashes—such as when Superintendent George Pennell protested to the overseers that Horton was "encroach[ing] on his prerogatives by giving orders to his men and interfering in the management of the institution." Although the overseers seemed to have taken a middle ground at the time, within a year Pennell was gone, while Horton remained as secretary.[56] After nearly three decades of service, Horton was eventually appointed in the 1930s to be a supervisor of the new Old Age Assistance Office for Cumberland and York Counties, Maine.[57]

Just as the particular details of the Haverhill City Farm investigation differ from others, the overseers-of-the-poor battles in Portland certainly differ in specifics but not in general, at least with respect to public perceptions about the overseers of the poor. Looking from the hindsight of nearly a century later, I suggest that, on the one hand, the overseer system was paternalistic, and hence duly subject to criticism, while on the other hand, reformers were somewhat unfair in their criticism.

As the name itself suggests, the idea that individuals need an "overseer" and that the elites of towns could dispense aid and advice without expertise of any kind was paternalistic. For this reason alone, it is not surprising that citizens came to resent the overseers, particularly when they were perceived as ineffective, privileged, and out for their own gain. No doubt some citizens feared the overseers' power if they themselves ever had to go on relief, and ridicule was an excellent response.

Yet the view taken by reformers against the poorhouse system—that both the system and the overseers and superintendents were corrupt—is questionable. In a particularly scathing book attacking the poor farm in 1926, *The American Poorhouse and Its Inmates*, Harry Evans opined:

> [The poorhouse] . . . is in the hands of local politicians, rather than specialists and scientists. Members of local boards divide the spoils. One will appoint the supervisor, another the matron. . . . The poorfarms and their inmates are under the domination of a vicious political system that cannot be reformed. . . . The management must be taken out of politics. There are some things that democracy cannot do. There is no more reason for submitting the care of the poor to the electorate than there is for requiring school teachers to be elected by popular vote.[58]

Evans's criticisms were somewhat overblown. All levels of government at the time were subject to patronage, and, gradually, with the coming of civil service, came to be more regulated. This, too, was done with the poorhouse most notably in Massachusetts, where civil service law was applied to all employees from superintendent to farmhand by the 1910s. Further, Evans and others ignore the substance of what was being battled about. The Portland factions may have sought to influence who was superintendent or matron or farm teamster to reward their friends and political allies, though even the critical press did not allege patronage as the main reason. But the battles also had an idealistic and ideological divide. For example, the lines that separated some of the liberal overseers of the poor, such as French and Rosenberg, from conservatives Derrah and Chaplin are not all that different from the political conflicts over welfare and poverty today. Like the issue of the blacklist and the tobacco allotment, the issue of inmates receiving money for work at the almshouse split the factions, and the charge that inmates were getting drunk when going downtown brought forth predictable splits between liberals and conservatives. Evans and other critics of the poorhouse were explicit critics of more liberal treatment of inmates, and so mixed humanitarian-sounding indictments of poorhouses with often more repressive intent, such as embrace of eugenicist proposals.[59]

Evans's and other critics' attacks are in fact somewhat ironic. For all their many failures and at times even their comical nature, the officials of the poorhouse—from nurses and teamsters down to offal collectors—were elected. The poorhouse operated in a fish-bowl atmosphere of public meetings. The assumption that people like Percy Horton, who became "the specialists and scientists," would be better than the "vicious political system" is itself a very *political* view. It is rarely commented on that the growth of professionalism, in fact, came at the expense of a (on paper anyway) more democratic system. Once professionalization became dominant, the decisions about the poor were no longer for all to see. By being "referred" to social workers, people became "cases" beyond public scrutiny, except for aggregate statistics. It is clear even in the old overseers-of-the-poor minutes that once "cases" were delegated to Horton, it is more difficult to see what the treatment was like, even decades later. It is also very difficult to separate the modernist impulse of the reformers from their disdain for the ethnic minorities and their "political machines." It was, after all, this motive that promoted the city manager system and other reforms, which made urban government less subject to popular vote.[60]

Finally, the Portland example provides us with a glimpse into the conflicts of interests between superintendents of the more successful city or county farms, who became businessmen-farmers, and the overseers and other politicians. The agricultural focus of the superintendents and staff in fact led poor farms in New Hampshire to become centers of agricultural innovation and, in some counties, university extension work. Superintendents' chief concerns came to be how many crops could be turned out, and on how many pigs, cows, chickens, and so on were raised. The reports of each county and city are dominated by a list of produce and sales. Moreover, superintendents needed to accommodate inmates more than more distant officials to secure their help in working the farm and other chores, and also to minimize the type of resistance that we noted in Haverhill. But if the superintendent looked to farm business, overseers were torn by conflicting motives besides finances and the bottom line (though this was highly important to taxpayers). Overseers were also concerned for their own political futures, for political patronage offices, and for the ability of their party to do well, and were motivated to avoid scandal and impropriety. Finally, many officials did have humanitarian feelings, and most had strong beliefs. Overseers by this period were torn between the reform impulse of those like Lizzie French and the beliefs of William Derrahs and Edward Chaplins, who favored the original mission of the poorhouse to discipline the poor, at least the "unworthy." This review does not even mention the motives of matrons, physicians, other employees, and inmates, which made for a high level of complexity. Competing agendas, in most ways similar to current conflicts over poverty, welfare, and homelessness, for example, characterized the system more than did any particular "viciousness" not still present in the system today.

An idyllic nineteenth-century painting of Rockingham County Almshouse and Asylum. I found a large number of pastoral poor-farm scenes in print, postcard, or photograph. (Author photograph)

The Portland, Maine, almshouse, late nineteenth century. (Courtesy the City of Portland)

Haverhill, Massachusetts, almshouse (later Glynn Memorial Nursing Home), probably in the 1920s or 1930s. (Courtesy the Trustees of the Haverhill Library)

Carroll County, New Hampshire, Almshouse and Farm. The 1890s building still housed the jail prisoners in 2004. (Author photograph)

Lewiston, Maine, City Farm, 1930s. (Courtesy Gertrude Landry Mynahan)

Inmates and farm employees working at the Lewiston City Farm, 1930s. (Courtesy Gertrude Landry Mynahan)

An inmate, Worcester, Massachusetts, "Home Farm," 1904. (Courtesy Arthur S. Tirella)

Inmates in the Women's Ward, Worcester, Massachusetts, 1920s. (Courtesy Arthur S. Tirella)

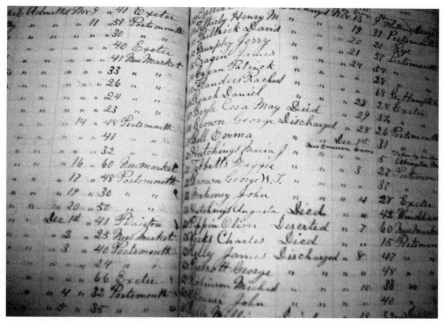

Typical ledger listing names of those admitted to the Almshouse. (Author photograph)

Old ledgers at Rockingham County Complex. The books of "Inmates," "Insane," and "Prisoners" capture the nature of the poorhouse as "one-stop shopping" for generations of poor people. (Author photograph)

Rockingham County Complex, twenty-first century. Particularly rich farm land still surrounds the area that houses a long-term care facility and county jail as well as other buildings. (Author photograph)

Barron Center (Portland, Maine), twenty-first century. The original Deering (Maine) poor farm, it became Portland's almshouse in 1904 when Deering became part of Portland. The center includes not only long-term care and an Alzheimer's program but also supported housing for low-income people. The gazebo was probably a 1930s addition. (Author photograph)

6

+

The Long End: Inmates in the Twentieth-Century Poorhouse

If you do not "snap out of it" and get to working and paying your rent, my next call on you will be with the police officer and will take your whole family to the county farm. The state of New Hampshire will place your children. A word to the wise is sufficient.

—Letter from a county commissioner to a relief recipient, Rockingham County, January 26, 1937[1]

She steals, makes whoppee with the male inmates. At the board meeting it was voted to discharge her.

—Meeting of the Farm Committee, Worcester Home Farm, May 6, 1949[2]

Despite the widespread sense among experts and professionals from the beginning of the twentieth century that the poorhouse/poor farm was becoming an archaic institution, such homes continued to exist for many decades. In fact, those homes studied held by far the largest number of inmates in their history during the period of the Great Depression. The poorhouse continued to serve multiple roles—including as a health care provider for low-income people, a maternity hospital, a holding area of orphaned children, and a homeless shelter. Given these roles, many views of the poorhouse coexisted in the twentieth century. A look at available historical evidence suggests some individuals and their families demanded admission to the houses (particularly in the case of the aged, disabled, ill, and children who could not be cared for at home) and others sought to leave the institutions, while still other poor people resisted any contact with poorhouses.

I was lucky to find three rather in-depth sources of information on inmates in the twentieth-century poorhouse that, while fragmentary, give some sense of the wide variability in poor people's attitudes toward the institution. In Portland, a book of minutes of the overseers of the poor from 1913 to 1923 presents cases that came before the officials and the constant confusion and division among them as to which groups to include and exclude in their home and hospital. The Portland documents suggest how the days of the poorhouse were not so far removed from the problems of modernity; by the 1910s, issues of bed utilization and triage were well known, with medical and moral issues competing. In Rockingham County, I happened upon several boxes of letters from the mid-1930s to early 1940s between the county commissioners who served as overseers of the poor and those who sought relief, both outdoor and indoor. Letters from the poor are often heartrending and painful. Some sought out the poor farm, some complained about relatives being sent there, and some were threatened by commissioners with being sent to the poor farm. In these selections, the specter and threat of the poor farm, so talked about in historical whispers, is made quite vivid by some of the commissioners' letters. Finally, in Worcester, I was able to go through a box of material kept at the Belmont Home, the city nursing home that succeeded the Worcester Home Farm. The box contained memos, minutes, talks, and notes from Ellery Royal, the last superintendent of the farm, from the 1930s to 1950s. These documents are very descriptive in general, and, in particular, contain much frustration voiced by the superintendent and other officials about inmates in the home who, like the "rounders" in the same city, tended to upset them by their use of the home. The Worcester documents, along with the Portland material, suggest the degree to which inmates—at least in these two areas—seem to have controlled events at the home as the century went on.

PORTLAND'S CONFUSED ADMISSIONS POLICIES

The minutes of the overseers of the poor in Portland, except for the annual election of officials, deal with cases and issues judged to be difficult or unusual. With the Portland Home and Hospital[3] admitting over four hundred inmates a year at that time (1913–1923), only a relatively small percentage of cases were discussed. For that reason, it is somewhat surprising that so much of their time concerned issues of admission or discharge from the home, and reached the full board of overseers. To name several cases at the beginning of the volume:

[March 13, 1913]: A Mrs. Medea McCoy addressed the Overseers and asked that she be given permission to leave the City Home and go to Augusta [Maine] to live, [she] said [her] mom needed no money to do so.

[April 2, 1913]: A William Maley, suffering from curvature of spine, [his] friends [were] anxious that he go to City Home so that he might overcome his temptation for strong drink.

[May 7, 1913]: A Margaret Woodward asked [the] Board to board her son of 8 years, she had been deserted by [her] husband and on account of ill health is unable to care for him properly.

[May 20, 1913]: In [the] case of William Dyer whose wife is old and helpless and without any one to take care of her. [He asked] that his wife be cared for [at Home].

[September 15, 1913]: A Mrs O'Neill living at 2 South St. appeared before Board asking that her husband, Michael, an aged man who has been at City Hospital about 8 months be allowed to go home. With assistance [she] could care for him at home.[4]

The cases provide us with some idea of the personal crises the home and hospital handled. In the cases of Mrs. Dyer and Mr. O'Neal, some combination of old age and illness was clearly at issue. With Mr. Maley, though, the facility is being used as an alcohol rehabilitation center. With Mrs. Woodward's son, the home is being asked to provide what today would be called "respite care" or perhaps longer-term foster care or adoption. With Mrs. McCoy, we do not know exactly why she had been at the home.

While in the above cases the overseers accommodated the requests (McCoy was allowed to leave; Mr. Maley was allowed entrance, but for no more than a month; Mrs. Woodward's son was boarded for four weeks; Mrs. Dyer was admitted to the home and hospital; and Mrs. O'Neal was granted a stipend to care for her husband at home), the fact that admissions and discharges had to come up so regularly to the entire board signaled ongoing conflicts. On the one hand, as with modern hospitals and other health care facilities, the home and hospital was becoming a valued commodity. Presumably the combination of increasing population and improved medical care made the home a more desirable place to stay. Yet over the years, the board kept reversing itself and seemed to reflect a number of conflicting priorities and interests. In 1914, seemingly consistent with the reported complaints of overcrowding at the Portland Home and Hospital, the overseers' annual report suggested a rationing of care at the home: "[Our] policy is to get applicants for relief to their homes rather than board them at the City Home, where it is more than likely many would be content to stay for several weeks."[5] As in a modern hospital concerned with bed utilization, the poorhouse's original raison d'être had been turned on its head: as people were overstaying their welcome, they needed to be moved along. This certainly seems consistent with the overseers' decisions in the Maley and Woodward cases above, in which the length of time was specified (a month and four weeks, respectively) rather than placing people in the home for an open-ended period.

Yet on July 1, 1914, following the board's vote to discharge three inmates from the city home, overseers also passed a motion that no more discharges be given except by vote of the full board, effectively restricting the superintendent and staff from the routine discharge process. Six weeks later, at the urging of Superintendent Anthony Frates, all discharges were suspended "because of all the work to be done at piggery" on the poor farm.[6] Clearly paralleling the crowding of the home and hospital was a need for labor at the home. At least four times in 1914, Frates clashed with members of the board over hiring inmates or ex-inmates to work, a situation we saw with Superintendent Frank Seeley and the overseers. For example, the board deadlocked in March on putting inmate Robert Walsh on the payroll, effectively defeating it. Frates did get an agreement in April to discharge an inmate (Frank Purcell) retroactively, as the man was already working at the cow barn, though Frates admitted he was still technically an inmate. In September clashes continued, and Overseer Reuben McLean asked to be placed on record as opposed to paying *any* wages to inmates.[7] Later in the minutes, in both 1916 and 1921, the board voted against paying inmates for work, although in between it was clear that superintendents had been making exceptions to this policy.[8]

But while the conflicts among overseers, and between overseers and superintendents, in Portland (such as those discussed in chapter 5) were certainly a reason for admission and discharge conflicts, they were hardly the only source. Over the years the minutes book was kept, no consistent standard could be discerned for the admission and discharge decisions of the overseers. At times, the overseers appeared to be practicing a form of triage, preferring to care for those at home who could be, while urging the more seriously impaired to reside at the city home and hospital. This appeared to be the case in two decisions in 1916. While two elderly former inmates (Mrs. Kleinbeck and Mrs. Simpson) wanted outdoor aid, Secretary Horton voiced his opinion that "they were entirely incapable of support [on their own]" so that only aid at the home should be given. Since we do not know if they took up the overseers' offer, it cannot be assessed how much this may have been an effort to provide a barrier to any assistance (e.g., the offer of the house was often a deterrent to accepting aid) as opposed to simply an offer of help. On the other hand, an inmate named Fred Getchell wanted to leave the home and support himself but needed a new artificial limb. The board voted to expend $75, and since the limb was later ordered from a Boston firm, one assumes that he did get to go to his own home.[9] In 1917, the overseers reached a similar conclusion about finances and the preferred place of care in relation to the case of George Warren. The board, after study, felt that the family would need complete support including rent if he were placed on outdoor relief. Since apparently they were unwilling to do this, they "voted that if the Warren family require[s] complete support that they be notified to go to the City Home."[10]

But there are many decisions that do not support the objective of either caring for people most cheaply or at the most appropriate setting (their own homes or the city home). Moral concerns continued to mark many of the actions of the board. Those who left the home without notice were the subject of great reproach, and in 1916 the overseers asked the city's corporation counsel "to give an opinion as to the power of the Overseers to have runaways from the City Home apprehended."[11] Since very few inmates were prisoners by this time in Portland, it appears that overseers wanted to know what they could do about inmates who simply skipped out of the home. This concern seems to contradict the objectives of reducing "overcrowding." In a case involving one Robert Armstrong, the overseers voted to deny him assistance at his own home, and cited the failure of his son to reimburse the city for previous bills.[12] Since the city was proceeding legally against the son, the board's decision seemed retaliatory, as the board instructed Armstrong that aid would be given only at the almshouse.[13]

An almost amusing serious of twists and turns occurred with an inmate named Cora Christiansen. This inmate is first mentioned in March 1916 when, along with two other inmates, she was seriously reprimanded for bringing liquor into the home. Somehow, Christiansen must have been seen as the prime culprit, as of the three inmates disciplined, she was the only one who was to be "discharged as soon as her physical condition permits."[14] A month later, the husband of Ms. Christiansen protested her discharge from home, saying he was unable to care for her.[15] Apparently, this kept her in the home and hospital, because her name again appears in the minutes four months later. She appeared personally before the board and pleaded "for a furlough from the Home," which overseers granted her at their September 20 meeting.[16] Somehow, though, in March 1917, Ms. Christiansen was an inmate again. We do not know when or why this occurred, but she was then "voted . . . a discharge with [the] provision [that] she would not be readmitted" ever again to the home.[17] It is again ironic, considering the origins of Portland's home in the workhouse of the eighteenth century and its forcible demand for character reform for many years (including only recently asking lawyers what power they had to chase down inmates), that this inmate was judged such a problem as to be expelled from the home rather than be the subject of any intensive reform. Christiansen's treatment is reminiscent of the old New England practice of "warning out" when undesirables were ordered by officials to leave town. It would appear by this historical period that faith in rehabilitation was considerably less than the optimistic hopes of the 1820s, which had claimed that the poorhouse would solve social problems.

As the years went on, issues such as the level of need, the need for labor power at the home, and morality were suddenly cast aside in the board's minutes for the sole issue of whether the applicants were in families or not. This policy is first noted in the minutes in a January 17, 1918, entry involving the case of Joseph White. White's friends made application for him to receive a stipend for outdoor relief, but the overseers refused, stating according to the notes that "as Joseph White is a single man, [he] should be cared for at the City Home."[18] Five years later, with almost no references to admissions policies or decisions in the interim, the board voted that "in [the] future no single persons would get aid without special approval of Board" outside of the city home and hospital.[19] Since there is no official explanation of this change in either the minutes of the overseers or the annual reports, we can only speculate. This new drive against outdoor relief may have been motivated by the renewed fear of tramps and vagrants following the First World War.

Single men had always been associated as drifters or tramps. Family status may have also served as a convenient divider between deserving and undeserving, and a politically expedient way of aiding families that had settlement and relatives who could vote as opposed to paupers who usually could not vote. While the number of the poor served in Portland in this period peaked in 1914 and remained stable for the next seven or so years, the cost of relief had doubled. Moreover, the home brought in some receipts to the department through crops, livestock, and garbage collection, while outdoor relief was more costly.[20]

The glimpse into a decade of the evolving combination hospital, almshouse, farm, and small insane asylum at the edge of Portland can be as confusing for the modern reader as it likely was for the people at the time. The differences in the type of need represented by the issues presented were certainly becoming recognized and specialized in this period. The overseers had special sessions with experts in the treatment of mental health issues, and the city physician began creating a pool of attending physicians and residents for the hospital. The blend of modernity and premodernity is sometimes startling in the minutes. One can certainly see clearly the seeds of movement of the Portland facility into a full city hospital, which it was later to become by World War II. Yet at the same time, overseers, superintendents, and the clientele refused to give up the old roles. Parents such as Mrs. Woodward asked the home to board their children; the friends of Mr. Maley wanted him helped to stop drinking; the Warren family wished what today would be long-term nursing home care; and clearly some individuals and families on the road wanted temporary shelter. In part, the institution sought to oblige clientele who did not have options of respite care, alcohol rehabilitation, nursing homes, and homeless shelters. But, in part, officials and staff also struggled with the moral authority to use taxpayer money to those they regarded as drifters or the undeserving poor.

LETTERS FROM ROCKINGHAM COUNTY IN THE 1930s

Unlike the system in Portland, where overseers were elected separately from other city officials, the county commissioners themselves served as overseers in New Hampshire. In Rockingham County, the three-person commission appears to have divided up the county, with each commissioner responsible for certain specific towns. I found (along with other public documents at the county offices) four old-style, large accordion envelopes from the 1930s to early 1940s containing several hundred applications for forms of relief. There were also letters back and forth from commissioners and applicants as well as outside parties such as employers, the state mental hospital and school for the feeble minded, various merchants and suppliers, local officials in the county, and a range of officials throughout the state. Many were routine exchanges and many were applications sent to social workers or "investigators," as they were called in this period. It is evident that the tasks of the overseers had gotten far more complex, as both the Old Age Assistance (OAA) and mothers' pension programs (in the process of changing to the federal Aid to Dependent Children program) had been put in place in New Hampshire, joining the traditional form of outdoor relief.

Given the modernizing features, what most surprised me was the number of harsh letters between county commissioners and poor citizens.[21] First, since the commissioners were not buffered by other intermediary officials, I expected that they would be "political" in orientation, with commissioners taking credit for positive actions such as providing relief. While this was the case in some communications, apparently those poor people who were judged undeserving or deviant were not seen as potential voters, but merely as miscreants. Second, since this was the Great Depression and more benefits were being put in place from the federal government, I imagined perhaps a greater acceptance of the vastly inflated numbers of poor. While commissioners did display compassion in some of their letters, many letters expressed anger and voiced the purpose of the poorhouse as one of punishment.

The harshest letters focused on control over drunken men who had allegedly shirked their duties, sexually "immoral" women who were judged in need of sterilization, or other women who were not coupled. One letter quoted in part at the opening of the chapter was from a county commissioner threatening a Mr. Green[22] with the poor farm and the removal of his children:

> I am informed that you are three months back on your rent. The understanding that I had in your case was that if the county furnished the food, you were to take care of your own rent. If this rent is not paid, you will get a notice to vacate. I am also informed that you are spending your money for liquor, and you do not work. This is the last warning that I am going to give you. If you do not "snap out of it" and get to working and paying your rent, my next call on you will be with the police officer and will take your whole family to the county farm. The state of N[ew] H[ampshire] will place your children. A word to the wise is sufficient.[23]

A similar letter went to a Mr. Edwards, charging him with alcohol and family abuse, and threatening him with the poor farm:

> If you are not willing to cooperate with the County in regard to buying liquor, getting drunk, and abusing your family, no more aid will be given you except at the county farm. The next time I know of your spending your money for liquor or being drunk, the County will serve a warrant on you for neglect and non-support of your family. Your family needs all the money you can earn, and I am giving you another chance to do the right thing by them.[24]

We cannot know all the circumstances that provoked the commissioner's letters, and the situations may well have been quite distressing ones. Yet what is striking is the degree to which the commissioner departed in private letters from the public presentation of the county home. After decades of trying to achieve positive publicity for the institution and insisting the home provided good medical, old age, child care, and, where warranted by the court, correctional care, the commissioner uses the threat of the poor farm in classic nineteenth-century rhetoric to attempt to correct individuals. In public, the commissioners, superintendents, and staff had already moved away from even referring to the county facilities as the "poor farm."

Moreover, there is a strong ambiguity as to whether the commissioner meant the county farm or the house of correction. If relief was misused, the usual remedy was simply cutting the person off. Recourse to criminal action could lead to the house of correction, but not the county home or farm. True, as I have mentioned, the borderline was vague, as some individuals charged with nonsupport, alcohol abuse, and vagrancy were indeed sentenced to the house of correction. But if actual legal action was the commissioner's intent, it is certainly disturbing that he was working from, at best, anecdotal knowledge. It is a bit scary to the modern reader to assume that on the word of the commissioner this information would actually secure a warrant and the placement out of the home not only for the miscreant but also for the families involved.

In four letters, sterilization of sexually active women was the subject of correspondence. Interestingly, here the commissioners did not suggest sterilization but the idea was recommended by social workers. Nor was this unusual for this period; poor women who gave birth to illegitimate children, engaged in extramarital relations, gave birth to mentally ill children, or who were considered retarded were fairly routinely sterilized. In the case of sixteen-year-old Brenda who came to the Rockingham facility to give birth to a daughter, the social worker talked about the difficulty of achieving a voluntary agreement for sterilization:

> I have discussed the case further with Miss K. . . . It was suggested that the girl and her baby remain in the hospital until the girl possibly could be sterilized. The original plan on this case was that the Children's Aid and Protective Society would plan to place the baby in a foster home, and the girl would be returned to the Industrial School where she has been committed by Judge G. . . . In thinking of the case from a County point of view and possible future support of more illegitimate children, the question of sterilization was raised, however to obtain sterilization we would have to have the consent of both the girl and her mother. It would then be a question of what could be done with the girl after she was sterilized, as it would not seem advisable to consider placing the girl back in the home with her mother whether she was sterilized or not, as the girl would still feel free to go around a great deal with C[ivilian] C[onservation] C[orps] men, with whom she originally got into difficulty. . . . Of course it is very difficult to separate a mother and her baby, but unless sterilization should be carried through quite quickly I would feel that probably the best arrangement would be for the girl to return to the Industrial School as soon as she is able to leave the hospital. It is my feeling that it would be quite difficult to obtain the girl's and her mother's consent to sterilization if she cannot be promised to return home after that.[25]

We have no letters following this one, though Brenda was in the county farm for six weeks in 1936 and three weeks in 1937. Her daughter was described in the records as "born at the farm," and stayed for twenty weeks (until presumably being placed out) while a man's name was listed as the father. There is a handwritten note on the letter of April 1937 (above) indicating Brenda was "sent back to industrial school."

The superintendent of the State School for the Feebleminded wrote to a county commissioner in reference to a former charge who had been brought to the Rockingham home. While we don't know whether she was sterilized, the letter mentions another woman who was her cousin and also an inmate at Laconia (the state school). "If you have data on her ancestry and family that would indicate that she was a transmitter you might wish to consider the performance of the sterilizing operation at your institution."[26] The "transmitting" is clearly from the context "mental retardation," which in these years was widely believed to be hereditary. All we know from the Rockingham Home roster is that the first woman spent twenty-one weeks as an inmate at Rockingham in 1935 and sixteen in 1936, and in 1936 gave birth to a daughter at the poor farm, who stayed ten weeks. The second woman, the cousin, was admitted in 1940 to Rockingham at the age of thirty-two, also from Laconia, and stayed thirty-four weeks at the home.

The lengthiest correspondence on the topic of sterilization shows both the use of the operation as a vehicle of sexual control and the strong amount of power exercised by the county commissioners. In October 1936, a "field worker" wrote to the commissioners of Rockingham County about a "woman who left her husband to live with another man and now has a child born." This woman was living at the Merrimack County Farm in New Hampshire. That county had received a letter from the woman's uncle and aunt offering to have the niece and her baby live at their home. Because the relatives lived in Rockingham, the field worker wondered whether that county "could investigate the home as to its suitability for [the inmate] and her baby, and kindly advise us the same."[27] The county commissioners must have replied quite negatively because a week later, the aunt wrote indignantly:

> I don't quite understand why you should think [inmate] and her child would be a burden. Of course I am not rich but I knew if I took [her] and the child that I could take care of them or I wouldn't have wanted them. I know I shouldn't expect help from the town. I wished you'd please call and see me again before this matter is closed. I am very much disappointed in your reply. Since you refuse permission for [inmate] and child to come here permanently, would you be kind enough to grant me permission to bring [her] and child here for Thanksgiving and stay on for Xmas and New Years. Then if you refuse to let her and the child stay she could go back.[28]

The county commissioner was unmoved and clarified that he was not concerned about the uncle and aunt's finances, but about the morality of the situation:

> I have your letter of October 20 with further reference to your having [inmate] in your home. . . . I do not doubt that you must be able to care for her financially as you are the best judge of your own circumstances, but it is not

that consideration which influenced my decision so much as the moral consideration. [Her] past record being what it is, it seems logical to suppose that such a thing could happen again. Should this happen, Rockingham County would have to be responsible for the care of her and her children. I think that, as pleasant as it might be for both of you to have [her] until the first of the year, you will agree that it does not seem wise either for you and your husband or for the County.[29]

In this case, the relatives persisted but did not contest a need for "a sterile operation."

Thank you for replying to my letter. I understand your attitude in this case. But [her] mother told me they were going to perform [the] sterile operation on her before she left Merrimack Co[unty] Farm. That is why I felt safe in having her come here. I know about the baby she has and I'd be responsible for her and this baby. I was hoping that I could get permission to have her come here and that [field worker] would see to her sterile operation, so everything would be settled so to have her here by Thanksgiving. . . . P.S. If [inmate] has a sterile operation, I don't see what objection you have to her and the child coming here.[30]

Indeed, the county commissioner, in a follow-up letter, stated he had no objection to the woman going to the family once she had the sterile operation: "If I am presented with definite proof from the Merrimack County Farm, that [she] has had a sterile operation, I have no objection to her going to live in your home. Of course you will have to sign papers taking the responsibility for her as my Investigator told you when she called on you."[31]

Although the family did not contest the sterile operation, it is certainly noteworthy that the commissioner could insist on this as a condition of a woman's living with her relatives *on the basis of her poverty and morality.* Since she was presumably a danger of becoming a public charge in Rockingham as well as having children who would be charges, the commissioner could pressure her relatives, although the woman was not even in the poor farm of their county.

Control over women's sexual affairs did not always involve sterilization. In March 1936, for example, the mother-in-law of a twenty-five-year-old woman who had spent half a year at the county farm in 1935 and ten weeks in 1936, along with a daughter born on the farm, wrote a county commissioner asking that her daughter-in-law not be released. She opined, "I don't think the last one [child] is his [her son's] and we know the other one [child] is not his. I don't see why you want to let her back here with him when he is not able to take care of himself. He has lived on us all winter if you let them out it only means you will have four to look after."[32] The commissioner quickly agreed, writing her that he "wish[ed] to inform you that I have no intention of letting [inmate] out of the County Farm at least until her husband has a job and a home of his own."[33]

The harsh tone of the above letters was not representative of all communications. For example, we have a letter from a social worker exploring inexpensive apartment rentals for an elderly man who would later die at the county home, a letter from a commissioner asking the state mental hospital to investigate the case of a patient who he believed may have been "railroaded to your institution by her husband," and an exchange between a family that wanted their relative returned to the county hospital because he left prematurely and was ill.[34] Interestingly, the negative reputation of the poor farm would come back to haunt the commissioners when they tried to do positive work. For example, in the case of Mr. Bush, an elderly man who came in as a paid boarder to the county home in 1935 and 1936, when a cousin in California heard about this, she was livid:

> I have just learned of the breaking up of the home in Hampton of Mr. B. He is my cousin. . . I am much disturbed at what I hear—and no particulars. He had a home and an income; the "caretakers" were his tenants; I received a letter from him saying that he was not well and was at times forgetful: *but the County Farm*! [emphasis original]. . . . I am greatly distressed that he should be in a public institution. It seems to me that there is something wrong in this affair.[35]

Clearly, the commissioner involved was angry at her stereotypic response:

> Your letter has been received, and in reply I would say that Mr. B. . . . requested of me, himself, that he go to the County Hospital. After investigation of the case, I allowed him to go. . . . As to any stigma being attached to Mr. B's name because of his being in our institution there is none for our institution is conducted for the best interests of all concerned, and has better conditions than the majority have in their own homes. We have the best of food, warm rooms, and graduated nurses to care for all who are ill. I only hope that the State of California can boast of as much.[36]

In another example of a positive action that met with surprise, a county commissioner in 1941 wrote to the New Hampshire Society for Crippled Children expressing hope that they could assist a child at the county home "born with complete paralysis of both legs" who was rejected for treatment at the Boston Children's Hospital. When the official expressed surprise at the personal attention being shown the boy, the commissioner lightly rebuked him, noting that "your general classification of county commissioners" should exempt not only himself but the other two in

Rockingham "as I am positive, through my associations with them, that they have a most thoughtful interest in all matters pertaining to the welfare of the children."[37]

Like the Portland Home and Hospital earlier in the century, the Rockingham County Home and Farm stood, even during the Great Depression, steeped in its contradictory heritage. It sought, on the one hand, to bring modern medicine and improved facilities for the elderly, ill, and children of the county but, on the other hand, officials still sought the power to control the poor, including using the threat of the poor farm. They then seem surprised when citizens and other officials associated their institution with harsh repression. Yet the very actions and letters of the commissioners confirmed the poor farm's role as a place to put people away, a place where involuntary surgery was performed, and a place of punishment for those deemed unworthy of outdoor aid.

WORCESTER'S HOME FARM IN THE 1940s AND 1950s

While some poorhouses/poor farms were transitioning into health care facilities by the end of World War II, Worcester proudly held out its home farm as a model facility, upholding its many functions of service. In a mimeographed history by its last superintendent, Ellery Royal, he described how the home farm had actually expanded in the 1930s and 1940s:

> It is very true that there have been many changes, but the type of people who require Institutional care, exists today in perhaps a greater degree than it ever did. Those are people who are unable to care for themselves because of many reasons, They are the crippled, the chronic sick, the bed-ridden, those who are addicted to liquor, and those who just do not have the ability to get along with their families and whom no one else will put up with them. It is interesting to note that the population of the Home Farm has been greater in the last ten years than at any time in its history, regardless of all the other forms of aid that have been supplied at the City's expense. Each year we house many emergency cases, many times taking in whole families or children who have no place to go. Often we take children to keep while a widow has a chance to find a job or otherwise get back on her feet, or while a mother is sick in the hospital.[38]

A series of cases from 1945 and 1946, typed onto a page (it was not clear if this was for publicity purposes or internal use), showed the range of personal and social issues that the home farm handled:

> [December 28, 1945]: Mrs.[C], with two children, 3 years and baby, admitted Dec. 19. Had no home and were staying at the Hotel Warren. Husband in Indiana. He called from Ind[iana] reversing the charges to see how wife was.

. . . He got job in Indiana, they are staying here, Baby got sick and placed in Memorial Hospital. They ran out of funds, and then were sent to the Home Farm.

[January 22, 1946]: [B], 3 years old, an imbecile, spastic and blind son of WWII veteran, was here two months previous to this time, but brought in again because mother could not stand the strain. To be kept here until admitted to feeble minded institution. No one would take this child which required almost constant care.

[March 20, 1946]: [Mr. J.] on OAA [Old Age Assistance] came back after two years on OAA, dirty, half starved, and very unkempt. Was living at Columbia Hotel. April 4—went down with G[ ] G[ ] and got his clothes out of hock for $13.50. The same PM he went down and hocked his clothes again for $3.00 (he said). Comes in every day asking for $1.00 for cigarettes. Was drinking on April 10, 1946.

[April 11, 1946]: Police Precint [*sic*] 1 bought in [Ms. L], age 80. Living at 121 Franklin Street. Had no food, no heat in house. She is blind. Son E[ ] works at the incinerator. Nice looking woman but covered with body lice.

[April 12, 1946]: [Mrs. B] sent down, very much pregnant and with two illegitimate children aged one and two years. She was put out of her rooming house.[39]

Although the majority of the cases presented were of elderly people, cases also include those such as the abandoned wife with a young child, the disabled young child, and the pregnant mother with two illegitimate children. These traditional populations of the almshouse/poorhouse/poor farm were not so different in Worcester than elsewhere. However, what began to set Worcester apart from some other homes was the large number of single men. In 1938, the city had taken over a barracks that had housed fifty men and had previously been run by the Salvation Army. The annual report of 1940 praised the "Gardenside Barracks," stating that 175 men were now housed there. A 1942 city memo headed "Duties of Barracks Attendant" suggests the men had to work for their keep, following the workhouse tradition: "Men in good physical condition are to be assigned to the Farm Foreman, to work under his direction, a total of six hours per day. They are to report at the Barn Office, Monday through Friday at 7:00 A.M. holidays excluded. They may be worked in busy periods more than six hours a day, and in quiet periods, less hours, so that the average will not be over six hours a day."[40]

Reading through the various papers, which form only a fragmentary picture of the home farm at the time, it becomes clear that things did not always go well at the barracks. I found sporadic notes for two years of the Farm Committee of the home, which included Royal and some of the officials of city's Welfare Department. In one memo, officials noted, "It is difficult to supervise or control their [barracks men] actions without some such device as punishment. It would be hard to find a man who would go and fight them continually, for the small pay of an attendant ($6.00 per week) and live in the same building with them." In a typed "Suggestions for Improvement," among other things, the memo suggested,

> discharge for drunkeness, rowdyism, stealing, etc. carry a penalty of no aid for two months at the Home Farm. That we have the Police Department send a cruiser car in the afternoon and at night to go with the attendant through all three barracks, and arrest and lock up all drunks or disturbers of the peace. These persons to be automatically discharged. That as soon as the beds are made in the morning, the three barracks be locked up, and kept locked until 7:00 P.M. in the winter and 8:00 P.M. in the summer. That refusal to work or work properly be sufficient reason for discharge, as well as stealing.[41]

Who wrote up the suggestions is not clear, but at the bottom of the page, in handwritten notes, the paper reads, "It was voted, to put more pressure on persons getting drunk, to discharge them and to keep them out permanently. Also to discharge those who refused to work."[42]

Like the "rounders" in Worcester's almshouse at the turn of the twentieth century, the problem must have gotten worse in the winter, since on January 5, 1949, the entire minutes were devoted to "the situation at the Gardenside Barracks," which had "reached a point where some definite changes in policy seem necessary." Pulling no punches, the Farm Committee attacked the men for drunkenness, laziness, stealing, working "off the books," and lack of discipline:

> *Drunkeness:* A certain group of these men are drunk or half drunk most of the time. They perhaps represent seventy or seventy-five persons, and keep the place disturbed for the rest of the decent persons who reside there. They go out for a "Red and White" store beyond the Frolic and buy wine. We are trying to stop this store keeper from selling to the inmates. They also buy liquor in down town Worcester.

> *Stealing:* This same group also are stealing everything they can get their hands on, from each other and from the institution, clothes, [unreadable], etc. in order to get money to buy liquor.

> *Laziness:* A large number of these men lay around most of the day on their beds reading, sleeping and disregarding the "No Smoking" rule signs. In order to get some of these men lined up and to go to work [unreadable] more work than they accomplish. It is necessary to stand right near them or they quit the job and beat it for down town and or other spots. . . .

Guests [not clear] *Without Permits:* Numerous persons who do not have permits, slip in and spend the night, get meals un-noticed and otherwise enjoy the hospitality of the city.

Work on the Side: A number of Barracks men undoubtedly get jobs down town, and let the city furnish them with board and room which allows them spending money for liquor. Others spend most of their time collecting junk and selling it.

Problem Is Discipline: Discipline is hard to obtain unless you have some leverage to enforce it by. At present we have no punishment with which to keep them in line. If we discharge them, they come back in a few days at the same old tricks as before and giving the horse laugh.[43]

While the barracks problem is not mentioned in the several weeks of minutes that remain for the first half of 1949, clearly men were not the only problem. At the May 6 meeting, the Farm Committee reopened a discussion of "the case of H[ ] H[ ]. She steals, makes whoppee with the male inmates." In handwritten notes, it is added, "At board meeting it was voted to discharge her."[44]

On June 7, 1949, the meeting "voted to have the Superintendent discharge the habitual drunks at the barracks, and those who are able to work and refuse to do so."[45] Evidently, this formal power did not resolve the problem, for a memo written in 1950 (since it includes data about admissions and discharges between January 1 and May 12, 1950) complains:

I would say that about 90% of these men use liquor to the extent of intoxication, and most of them have police records. We find that the drinking at the Barracks seems to become moderate when we use stern messages, such as discharging those who become intoxicated, or having them placed under arrest. Some of our inmates will go along for weeks without drinking if they keep away from the down-town area, but it seems that as soon as they find work and receive a little money, they break out again.[46]

Although it is hard to know if the barracks problem ever resolved itself, a series of "general policies" adopted sometime in 1950 bespeaks the compromises that the Home Farm had to make to the realities of the twentieth century. While some rules are straightforward—no "transients or so-called 'tramps' are to be allowed," "inmates from the Barracks are not to be allowed in the rooms, dormitories or recreation rooms of the main Infirmary," "all inmates shall be required to perform such work as is commensurable with their age and physical condition," and "the Superintendent has the authority to discharge any inmate who persistently breaks any of the above rules governing their behavior, and also for possessing intoxicating liquors, drunkeness [*sic*], distrubing [*sic*] the peace or otherwise breaking the general laws"—several are interesting in their compromises. For example, "Inmates who stay away from the institution two nights in succession, without permission, will be considered discharged." This rule, of course, not only allows inmates to be out a night at a time but also implies there were probably occasions where permission was granted to be out more nights. Certainly absent a legal charge, the home farm could not be a jail or prison. The inmates also gained some positive incentives:

> The Superintendent has the authority to pay deserving inmates who perform extraordinary or responsible duties pin money, not to exceed $2.00 per week.

> Inmates are to be supplied with two packages of smoking or cigarette tobacco and two boxes of matches each week and a plug of chewing tobacco and cigarette papers also, if they so desire. Once each month, on the corresponding date of their admission, they are also eligible to receive two bus tickets for the purpose of visiting the center of the city.[47]

As discussed earlier, the payment of inmates and the provision of tobacco to inmates were responses to the efforts by the institution to maintain their inmate population and also their work on the farms. What is interesting is that for all the many notes in the minutes that are critical of the barracks' inmates, they also reflect the necessary compromises that superintendents and overseers had to make to run an institution. In addition, "free professional entertainment for the inmates" was arranged, including "moving picture films"; a blind inmate was permitted to continue to sell candy and tobacco at the Home Farm and to keep his profits; and an inmate barber was allowed to keep his profits.[48] Policies appear a compromise between control over the institution, which obviously was an object of struggle, and the necessary payments and amenities to keep the farm up and running, and to presumably ensure the institution continued.

If many of the letters in Rockingham County between county commissioners and the poor and their families reinforce the continued elements of repression associated with the poor farm, records of the Worcester Home Farm in the late 1940s and early 1950s reinforce the earlier historical images of inmates "using" the house for their own benefit. By 1950, Worcester certainly had many hospitals, orphanages, and social service agencies. Some poor people may have come to the Home Farm because of its greater flexibility with temporary situations (respite care, for example, was not offered by service agencies until quite recently), others may have been rejected by both religious and public agencies for reasons of morality (one suspects this was the case with the mother of the illegitimate children), and still others may have found more potential benefit there than in whatever else was available (for example, for some adults the potential of pay for work at the farm as well as room and board may have exceeded the potential benefit of living in a single-occupancy room elsewhere).

In Worcester, as well as in Lewiston, the end of the city farm did not come without protest. The collection of documents from the Worcester Home Farm contains lengthy memos and appeals to keep the Home Farm open after a 1953 tornado had caused much damage to life and property. The City of Worcester moved to merge it with Belmont Home, originally the old "pest house" for the almshouse, then beginning a transition to a long-term care facility. Considerable political battle occurred before the merger with Belmont Home in 1955.[49] Interestingly, after the inmates were transferred to Belmont Home, the home itself took on the institutional memory and stigma of the poorhouse with a "Hilton Building" that tended to house males who drank or were without shelter.[50]

A LOSING BATTLE FOR CONTROL

Although the historical materials from the three areas differ greatly in their focus and in their levels of exasperation about the inmates and potential inmates of the poorhouse, all represent in different ways the frustration of superintendents, overseers, and other leaders about their lack of power over the poor. The Portland overseers showed confusion and division in the second and third decades of the century as to whether the home and hospital should be an old age residence, a shelter for single men, or a continued catch-all for the poor. Was outdoor aid "immoral" any longer or, in some cases, cheaper than indoor relief? In the fourth decade of the century, the Rockingham County commissioners often became angry and hostile to certain people on relief, threatening them with the poor farm. But the 1930s were not the 1830s, and many of the people either did not end up at the poor farm or were there for just a short time before moving on. Of course, there were those who wanted to be in the home (or had family who wanted them in the home). In Worcester, the constant new rules and plans to enforce them seem to have been ineffective when pitted against the efforts of large numbers of inmates who came and went from the Home Farm as they pleased.

To say the poorhouse failed in the eyes of the overseers and political officials, however, does not mean that it did so to other constituencies. As we explore in the next chapter, staff as well as superintendents fought to preserve their own institutions. Secondly, local labor market needs were probably being met in areas where the poorhouse persisted, particularly in housing men of working age. The two industrial labor markets in this study most cut off from easy, quick, regional travel routes were those poorhouses that lasted the longest—Worcester, Massachusetts, and

Lewiston, Maine. Notably, both of these cities were also industrial cities with large nonunion workforces.[51] Finally, while those receiving threats of being forced into the poor farm (as in Rockingham) may have been horrified, still there is no sign that poor people themselves abandoned use of the homes when they needed them. By the 1930s, the development of public works programs, Social Security pensions, old age assistance, Aid to Dependent Children, and unemployment insurance clearly altered the balance of power between some groups who had no cushion between them and the poorhouse, and public officials. Still, in an era when the majority of elderly people were not covered by Social Security pensions (then Old Age and Survivors Insurance), when the disabled were not yet covered by federal Social Security, and when no health care insurance existed, there were locales where plenty of poor people needed aid.

7

Matrons, Doctors, Staff, and the End of the Poorhouse

The well-to-do recompense us all in the present but the reward for what we do for the poor and the orphan we may safely await with faith and patience.

—A. W. Mitchell, Rockingham County physician[1]

Saw the rules I had written to show to new inmates and remarked, why I didnt [*sic*] practice them myself. I suppose that he was digging at me drinking.

—Diary of attendant, Worcester Home Farm[2]

When the poorhouse as an institution arose, little thought was paid to a staff. Like other early American institutions from the asylum to the school to the factory, a very simple patriarchal system of rule was established. A superintendent (initially simply labeled the "master" or "keeper" of the almshouse) was placed in charge of the poor and provided with the relevant building and material to put them to work or otherwise care for them. A "matron," almost always the wife of the superintendent, was very much an underling who had little or no authority within the town, city, or county government. No definition or early job descriptions of this role could be found. It is likely, however, since matrons played a role in the most of the other early institutions from schools to asylums, their role probably developed out of the same attempt to recreate the domestic sphere of women's role away from home. In particular, nineteenth-century gender ideals promoted women as bestowing virtue and humanitarianism to the civic family as well as the nuclear one. The superintendent was the farmer-businessman-official, while the matron's role was the cooking, cleaning, feeding, and nurturing of the inmates.

No early observer, of course, could anticipate how the growth of the staff of the poorhouses would change the nature of the institution. From the superintendent and matron plus (usually) several "farmhands" in the early to mid-nineteenth century, larger institutions such as Worcester's and Portland's almshouses came to have as many as seventy-five staff members by the third decade of the twentieth century. Although the exact organizational contours differed, the poorhouse's gradual specialization and professionalization led to the modern hospital, nursing home, old age home, and chronic care facilities.

Despite the vast differences in personalities, styles, and views of the hundreds of superintendents, matrons, doctors, chaplains, farmhands, attendants, nurses, and others who were employed by the poorhouses over the years, they (like the inmates) significantly undermined many of the early idealistic objectives of the poorhouse that we have discussed. For them, the poorhouse was not a means to an end but an end in itself—whether this was "repressing pauperism," putting the poor to work, or deterring others. Superintendents and staff developed a great vested interest in their institutions. For example, in hundreds of superintendents' reports in the six jurisdictions, almost yearly the superintendents made variants of these points: the poorhouse/poor farm needed better accommodations in building, furniture, safety, and general comfort; that the poorhouse/poor farm needed more land, better livestock, or other additions to succeed as an enterprise; or that the institution could benefit from more staff, both professional (such as medical, ministry, nursing, and later, social service) as well as more physical laborers to work the farm or aid the inmates. It is true that since superintendents were public officials on a budget, they also usually sang praises of their own frugality. Often they framed their case for expansion on the basis that with an investment in the farm or in labor, more receipts would come from the poor farm and replace tax dollars. Overall, however, the superintendents (and other staff) had little or no vested interest in the poorhouse being a "deterrent" to the "indolent and vicious." Their proximity, both in living with or near the inmates and in getting to personally know their charges, more often provoked sympathy than not.

Even more so than superintendents, it appears from the fragmentary information we have that matrons, physicians, and other employees were often advocates for improved conditions for the inmates. Matrons, physicians, farmhands, and attendants had little or no budgetary responsibility and were less directly "political" in their appointments than the superintendents; hence, they were freer to express their viewpoints. Staff was a heterogeneous lot, but on the limited evidence may have identified as much with the inmates as with the higher officials of the cities or counties.

A FEW NOTABLE MATRONS

It is clear from many reports that the matrons did much of the emotional work with inmates of the poorhouse as well as a considerable amount of the physical and nursing work. In Estelle Stewart's survey of almshouses in the 1920s, she noted, "often [the] superintendent puts most of [his] energy into farm maintenance, frequently leaving the management of the charitable institution itself to the matron, she is a public official 'by marriage.'" All the housekeeping duties, meal preparation, and (particularly in the smaller almshouses) much of the nursing was often performed by matrons.[3] A study of Minnesota's almshouses by that state's board of charities and corrections in the late nineteenth century expressed concerns about the "confining" nature of the matrons' roles, whose large workload was combined with living in the almshouse, often without ever being able to leave the home.[4]

Both the Landry sisters in Lewiston and Win Hilton in Rockingham County expressed some bitterness about the treatment of their mothers as matrons. Matrons were unsalaried even into the fourth and fifth decades of the twentieth century; the salary of the superintendent was supposed to cover him *and* his wife. Additionally, as Win Hilton remarked, this kept his mother off Social Security until, eventually in the 1950s, she was put on a state pension plan.[5] She retired with very little by way of her own pension even after the total of thirty years as matron. The Landry sisters described their mother as an extremely strong woman who played a management role in the institution, including keeping all the receipts and helping her husband navigate the political winds of that city's politics. Gertrude Landry Mynahan describes her mother as a hard worker who did not mind at all working, an inspiration to other workers at the farm and to inmates to work with her. Yet resentment crept into the sisters' voices often about the lack of reward for their mother's efforts. Making fun of the term "matron," Lorraine Comeau recited a memory: "I remember when a man came [to the farm] and he demanded very officially to see the matron [of the place]. He seemed stunned when my mother with her apron on and her hair tied back in a scarf answered the door." Evidently the man associated "matron" with a higher-class official.[6]

Still, two matrons achieved some local recognition in their home areas. Frances Jane Parkhurst, who served as matron of the Worcester almshouse for seventeen years (1876–1893) became quite locally celebrated. She was born in Vermont in 1834 and married Benjamin Parkhurst in the 1860s, later moving to Worcester. Her mother had died when she was four, a similarity to the background described by the Landry sisters about their mother, who grew up in an orphanage after her mother died when she was fourteen.[7] The Parkhursts became superintendent and matron in 1876. She was described as "exceedingly popular among the inmates" and "ministered to the poor and friendless . . . like a mother to them [inmates]; she has not regarded her own ease or pleasure in adding to their comfort; she has watched over them in sickness and excused their follies and their ingratitude in health."[8] At her death in 1893 at the age of fifty-nine, her funeral was attended by a large crowd, including mayors and former mayors, aldermen, commissioners, overseers of the poor, and poor-farm employees and inmates; many wreaths and memorials were described by the local paper.[9]

One reason why the work of Ms. Parkhurst was not lost to time was a booklet written about her by Albert Marble, the city physician at the time. The booklet captures the conditions in the almshouse at that time as well as her role. With two hundred rooms in the almshouse, "acres of floors and flights of stairs by the dozen, all [had] to be kept clean when two hundred people are tramping on them." She did have the aid of "about a dozen employees" in washing and ironing, sewing and mending, cooking and scrubbing, sweeping and making beds, and tending to the boiler. Still, Marble notes, "she could not leave the grounds except for rare occasions and had few visitors."[10] Marble further describes Parkhurst, "at the bedside of the dying, she would soothe and comfort the parting spirit . . . the next moment she might be called to the kitchen to send away an unworthy servant, or to the insane ward to quiet a disturbance; and the next half hour she would sit down to dinner with a cheerful face as if nothing had happened."[11]

A second matron who gained some notice was Margaret Bean in Rockingham County. Bean was actually the only woman I could find in the six locales who for a time served as a chief executive of a poorhouse. Initially, Mrs. Bean was appointed matron when her husband, Henry, became superintendent in 1897. Mr. Bean died in 1900, and the county turned to Mrs. Bean, along with her son, Norman, who was then twenty-four, to run the poorhouse. Even before the death of Mr. Bean, Margaret Bean received an unusual citation in the state board of charities and corrections report of 1900: "The management of this institution is first-class in every respect, and very much improved in the last three years. Mrs. Bean, the matron, is an intelligent woman, very much interested in her work, and very much beloved by the inmates, who call her 'mother.'"[12]

During some years of their joint command (1900–1907), a rare "and" joined the names of Margaret and her son Norman as co-runners of the county home (at other times, her son was listed as "superintendent" and she as "matron"). It is, of course, not possible at this date to reconstruct who did what at the Rockingham facility, but upon her resignation in 1907, A. W. Mitchell, the county physician, provided a rare tribute to her, again a major exception in the many pages of city and county reports that I read: "It is impossible in words to represent how able, devoted and self-forgetful that service was or how much aid, comfort and cheer she gave the unfortunates to whom she ministered and to us whose duty and pleasure it was to aid her."[13]

While, no doubt, both Parkhurst and Bean were exceptional people, in part they are also singled out only by historical accident. Matrons served undoubtedly as one of the humanizing elements of the almshouse, and as the years progressed, they more and more seem to have ventured into the human services. For example, the prodigious scrapbooks of Dorothy Hilton, the matron of Rockingham County Home for thirty years, include booklets from conferences she attended on gerontology and social services. Interestingly, although not co-executives, the Hiltons, George and Dorothy, did sign their annual reports (and some other institutional communiqués) jointly, which was unusual even in that period (the 1930s through 1960s).[14]

THE ROLE OF PHYSICIANS

Few roles were as important to the health and well-being of the inmates than the city or county physicians. These public officials, particularly in the many isolated county or town almshouses, were often the first, if not only, outside party to visit a home, especially in the early days of the almshouse. However, particularly in the nineteenth century, working as a county or city physician with low pay and low prestige did not necessarily draw the best of doctors. To top it off, they had vast caseloads, responsible for public charges in sometimes heavily populated areas, not to mention the health of the city or county employees as well. Roy Brown's very critical history of the North Carolina poorhouses provides an anecdote in which a county physician kept promising a particular inmate with "chronically sore feet" that he would come to the poor farm and see him, but never did. After his feet became badly infected, the superintendent "decided to amputate . . . with a butcher-knife and a handsaw."[15] A more balanced and, one hopes, more typical report, comes from Sophonisba Breckinridge about physicians in Illinois:

Medical care [is] similarly uneven and depended much on [the particular] doctor. In some cases county physicians had to furnish medicines at [their] own cost. In Shelby County in 1880, a public-spirited county physician

protested to the board against the kind of keepers the county employed, saying the county got people who were cheap, but who were often no more efficient than the poor themselves. . . . In Monroe County . . . at [physician's]
insistence, many improvements were made. He compelled attention to the
comfort of the inmates and made daily calls to see that his instructions were
carried out.[16]

No doubt physicians in New England varied as elsewhere. Since they
were often paid a small fee out of which came travel costs and costs of dis-
pensing medicine, they had some incentive to skimp on care or certainly
to worry more about the health of those of higher status (for example, city
officials) than poorhouse inmates. Yet several physicians in this study
clearly took their professionalism seriously, particularly during the Progressive Era period (1900–1914), as evidenced by critical reports by doctors about almshouses, superintendents, overseers, county budget limitations, and inadequate care generally.

Two physicians fought battles that changed parts of their almshouses
into medical facilities. Dr. William McFee of Haverhill, Massachusetts, led
a struggle that resulted in the conversion of part of the poor farm into a
city-run hospital, while Dr. A. W. Mitchell of Rockingham County, while
not necessarily planning to move in that direction, helped create a county
hospital. Both physicians clearly stood out—in the context of the usual
dry reports—in their willingness to go public with their complaints.

In 1904, the Haverhill almshouse, under the leadership of Dr. McFee, secured the assistance of "some of best doctors" in the area who "volunteered to help with a hospital right at [the] farm." McFee's actions were
apparently the result not just of poor conditions at the almshouse for the
ill and infirm and the growing concern of contagion such as TB but also
the failure of the one Haverhill hospital, Hale, to accommodate nonpay-
ing patients and some of the physicians of the area.[17] In addition to securing $1,500 for alterations and repairs to equip a portion of the farm as
a hospital, accommodating at first twenty-five patients in a male ward
and five in a female ward, McFee recruited eight "well known and com-
petent doctors who volunteered" and also developed a training school for
nurses. The same year, however, Roswell Wood was elected mayor of
Haverhill, and to put it mildly, Wood was no fan of the project. Wood argued in his 1905 address that Haverhill could not afford "two hospitals"
and that "the overseers should at once place the hospital back to its purpose and let Hale [Hospital] be the City Hospital . . . even if the noses of
several ambitious physicians are put out of joint."[18] In his 1906 address,
Wood denounced the Poor Department and overseers:

> The Poor Department is costing too much! Business in Haverhill has never
> been better . . . yet in the face of these facts, the expenses of this department

have increased to [an] alarming proportion. It is time to call a halt. . . . No one knows the cost of [this] hospital. I warned last year against it, I do not blame [the] Overseers or [the] Savages but [the] doctors who indiscriminately bring their own cases there, at large expense to [the] City.[19]

No doubt supported by the populist tradition in that city, McFee received sympathetic news coverage and said Haverhill's "citizens may point to pride [to a hospital] where all who wish may find relief in time of sickness and distress."[20] By 1908, he was able to state that "the city hospital, as now established, has demonstrated beyond question its position as one of the most important of city institutions . . . officials and staff handicapped though they were, by meagre allowance and restricted conveniences, have labored diligently to make this institution all that it should be."[21] By 1909, McFee and allies appeared to have won the battle, with a new mayor winning office. They were able to report that the city hospital at the farm cost $.96 a day compared with $2.55 per day at the Hale Hospital. The hospital had gone from an average of seventeen patients in 1905 to forty in 1908, and fifty by 1910.[22] In 1915, the new hospital was started at a different location, and the infirmary, as the hospital at the almshouse came to be known, emerged eventually as the Glynn Memorial Nursing Home, a public facility.[23]

In Rockingham County to the north, Dr. Mitchell served as county physician from 1887 to the 1930s and eventually came to have the county hospital, Mitchell Memorial Hospital (erected in the 1930s) named for him.[24] Whether it was purely courage or an independent base of support, Mitchell wrote some of the most critical reports of public management that I discovered in the various jurisdictions. Prone to sarcasm, in 1910, Mitchell began his report by noting the erection of a new horse barn at the poor farm "emphasizes afresh the equal need at least for better accommodations for the human inmates." Noting the prison was overcrowded with seventy-nine inmates in space for thirty cells, he declared the almshouse worse. Many of even the smallest rooms, noted Mitchell, were now double-bedded: "The poor and the feeble and the jail overflow. This does not allow a normal air space per capita and unavoidably mingles more and more prisoners, the children and the aged. There is a constant struggle with cold, dirt, vermin and rats in this the oldest and poorest almshouse in [the] state." Warning further that the building was "a veritable fire trap," he most unusually declared that the county had the funds to build a new almshouse that would adequately serve the people.[25]

Like McFee, Mitchell had an escalating battle with the county, which made decisions through a biannual county delegation at which each town in the county had an elected representative. Known for their frugality, the delegation only very gradually moved on these issues, expanding the jail

in 1913, and then voting money to improve the home by rebuilding the insane asylum and making it a combination nursery (for children) and hospital. Neither move resolved Mitchell's complaints.

Taking up the care of children at the home, Mitchell charged the care
was not consistent with "twentieth-century humanity." While children
had one small room, it was overcrowded and they ended up "scattered all
over the house with old people where ever they can be tucked in." It was
as bad for the "old and infirm," who were exposed to constant fire risk
and going up and down, "some of them four stories, to meals and fresh
air." After listing other complaints, he said, "Now the cows, the horses,
and the prisoners are so well cared for, the needs of the poor and the little children appeal to us more forcibly than ever before."[26]

It took until 1917 for a county delegation to vote to raise bonds for a
new male almshouse. Although praised by Mitchell when it opened in
1918, he continued to advocate for a more advanced and separate infirmary and separate areas for children, on the one hand, and the ill and infirm on the other. Mitchell's vision seemed to be more far-reaching than
McFee's in terms of his concerns for children, the aged, prisoners, and
other populations beyond the ill, and, at least on the face of it, less self-
serving in terms of the needs of physicians to have their own admitting
privileges. The county's ultimate response to Mitchell's advocacy, like
Haverhill's, was the opening of a county hospital in the 1930s, which was
not only clearly a response to medical need but also to the perceived "deserving" status of the ill among the population as opposed to those who
were simply poor, old, or disabled.

While physicians' advocacy is not surprising in terms of the drive for
specialization and professionalization that gained steam by the twentieth
century, the alliance of physicians and some superintendents and parts of
the community who favored change in the poorhouse was an important
element in humanizing the almshouse and in transforming its functions
in many areas.

FARMHANDS TO ATTENDANTS: HARD TO GET GOOD STAFF

For most of the nineteenth century, most poorhouses or poor farms relied
on relatively few staff. Staff tended to be farmhands, aiding with the crops
and livestock while directing inmates' work. By the late nineteenth century, however, in larger institutions like Worcester, Portland, and Rockingham, a cadre of attendants began to be needed for the insane and hospital units of the poorhouses and to assist in the maintenance, cooking,
and other chores often directed by the matron.

Some smaller poor farms, like Lewiston, never exceeded four or five employees, who were farmhands. Where this was the case, loyalty to both the superintendent and the general mission of the poor farm was probably more secure.[27] The growth of additional attendants and other staff, however, proved more problematic. Like the staffing of asylums and homes for the feeble-minded and prisons, a job at a poorhouse combined many negative features, and according to the complaints of superintendents, overseers, and reformers, did not draw "the best of people." Attendants usually lived on the grounds—so, in addition to the extremely poor salaries and working conditions, they were heavily restricted by the rules and regulations of the almshouse. Their board remained a part of their pay even into the 1950s in Worcester. If one can imagine being an employee subject generally to the same rules that the inmates were, one can imagine the low status of an attendant. For example, the prohibition against "ardent spirits" at the homes would have been imposed on the workers, as well as the hours of curfew and general behavior. In a set of rules for attendants at the Worcester city almshouse, several suggest other restrictive practices: "Attendants shall not loiter on the ground-floor, or in halls and stairways, longer than their work makes necessary. If attendants wish to invite friends into the house, they shall first ask permission of Superintendent or Matron."[28]

In the overseers' minutes at the Portland Home and Hospital, many entries relate to staff, although they obviously do not give us both sides of the story. The overseers complained frequently of their inability to secure good staff. There were frequent suspensions or other discipline for employees, sometimes including alleged mistreatment of inmates. Moreover, the overseers seemed to have a running battle with the employees as to where they could eat or congregate. It is not clear why this was such an issue at so many meetings during the 1913–1923 period, but it is clear that staff were generally not regarded as being in a much higher class than inmates.[29]

The dangers of employees subverting the rules of the institution and "going native," so to speak, with the inmates is illustrated by a two-page diary fragment of "George Paulson," an attendant at the Worcester Home Farm in the 1930s.[30] One entry in the attendant's diary suggests the complicity of staff around alcohol consumption and selling of city property:

12-27-27 [*sic*; from context, the entry is 1937] Broke open [an inmate's] box. Copied his notes on separate page with answers. Without G.G.'s orders. 1. On Sept. 22 and Oct 4, 1936, I brought liquor for him and drank in Cherry Hill barber shop with him. Got 25 cents each time.

2. Did you know about the eight bags of City rags and 2 bags of zinc and copper flashing stolen and sold to the junky.

3. Drunk Christmas time 3 days 25-26-27, Went to work on the 28 of December 1936.

4. Never in the dormitiry [*sic*] only when you are looking for trouble. Not fit for the job. No good.

5. You let men lay in bid [*sic*] sick. No care when he is ready to die hospital for him fine work.

6. Oct 15 & 16 1937 away from duty 5 hrs., each day beating the payroll.

7. How about the 2 bags of City rags sold on this day Oct 16 1937 by [an inmate] to Junky.

Although not all of the above is clear, and it is obviously subject to some interpretation, further entries indicate Paulson's willingness to work with inmates to evade the superintendent's orders: "[3-6-38] Sup[erin]t[endent] rang 9:30, said all drunks to be locked up. I went to smoke hole, told him everything quiet. He wanted [inmate] I told him not around, same with [inmate]. Told [inmate] to duck. [Inmate] was in bed asleep. [Staff member] had given [inmate] tickets so Sup[erin]t[endent] believed me I guess."

The attendant throughout the diary admits to heavy drinking and a relationship with another staff member, whose name frequently comes up: "[10-26-37] [Girlfriend] says [supervisor] saw the rules I had written to show to new inmates and remarked, why I didnt [*sic*] practice them myself. I suppose that he was digging at me drinking."

Paulson also voices his criticism at the hypocrisy of the management of the institution, with its political patronage and poor quality of employees: "[4-26-38] [Staff member] to go to Barracks. [Man to have charge of Barracks] [name] told me. Supt. is some swell guy. [Staff member] has no experience but his father is a politician so he gets the job. [Staff member] did 1 yr. for hit and run driving, worse than my record. [He] did yr. for hit and run, nice man for barracks."

Although we cannot generalize about staff and attendants from Paulson any more than about all county and city doctors from Mitchell or McFee, it is likely that low-paid staff, with frequent turnover, often recruited from inmates or from the ranks slightly above, did not embrace the "character reform" of either the nineteenth-century or twentieth-century poorhouses.

An interview with four elder residents of Carroll County who had a combined total of more than a hundred years as workers at that county home ranging from "turnkey" to farmhand to attendants suggested the continuity with the earlier days in some ways. While the workers' experience dates back only to the early 1940s, some generalizations about the roles can be made. First, the four were intertwined with the institution at various levels, one former worker was born there, and another saw his father die there. Their identification clearly was more with the poor than management. While all four knew the superintendents and would comment briefly about them ("he died of a heart attack," etc.), none of them seemed to know the superintendents they worked with very well. They described the area where the managers were as "frontside" and said "you stayed away from there . . . there was plenty of area to hide and do your own thing." This certainly was a contrast with the older idea of loyalty and the family-like organization of the original almshouse. Secondly, while all four were caring people who clearly loved many of their charges (one still volunteers at the nursing home daily), their jokes and anecdotes about some of the inmates and patients frequently ranged from the sexual or scatological to those connected to alcohol. One gets the distinct feeling that rather than be the guardians of the morality of their charges, many workers at the home facilitated drinking by the inmates, aided and abetted in some relationships of patients and inmates, and knew of many "off-the-books" small scams to make money.[31]

Not surprisingly, then, the high moral ideas that led to the creation of the almshouse in the nineteenth century fell into disrepute in the twentieth century as workers, closer in status and norms to the inmates than to the overseers of the poor (and, later, welfare officials or health officials), helped undermine what had been many of the original goals of the poorhouse. While some staff, such as matrons, helped humanize the home, others like physicians helped reform the home, but few staff at the poorhouse were really left to support the original mission of the almshouse.[32]

8

The Ironies of History:
The Return of the Poorhouse

Those ready to return to relief through incarceration will call the facility
a refurbished mental hospital or a shelter, but it will be an almshouse, a
catchall for the disconnected, with very few differences separating the
modern version from the nineteenth-century version.

—David Rothman, "The First Shelters," 1987[1]

The prison has become our first line of defense against the conse-
quences of social policies that have brought increasing deprivation and
demoralization to growing numbers of children, families, and communities.

—Elliot Currie, *Crime and Punishment in America*, 1998[2]

Those who write about history cannot escape their own context. Many
experts writing in the 1960s and early 1970s, for example, regarded the
poorhouse as a distant reminder of the inhumanity of America's past,
which, with a growing "welfare state" and expanding economy, was perceived (or presented, in any event) as a strange historical oddity. Writing
as I do in the early twenty-first century—when hundreds of thousands of
people sleep in homeless shelters each night (or on the streets or in vehicles); millions of people spend each night in the nation's jails and prisons;
and hundreds of thousands of disabled people are in nursing homes, jails,
prisons, and other institutions rather than deinstitutionalized—the history
of the poorhouse seems quite different. The poorhouse experience is alive
and well, taken over by a host of modern institutions that continue to play
a central role in housing and controlling the poor. The situation of many of

America's poorest people is arguably worse than it has been since the nine-teenth century. Hence, the "new poorhouse" is not metaphorical, as condi-tions in many facilities—and certainly in homeless shelters, prisons, and jails—are worse than in many poorhouses or poor farms.

This chapter reviews the economic, political, and social events that led to the end of the poorhouse/almshouse/poor farm in its old guise, link-ing these broader developments with those seen at the level of individual poorhouses in New England. I then turn to how conditions, after only a relatively short historical hiatus, have returned to resemble the days of the old Poor Laws, showing a renewed historical continuity with the past. Some comparisons are made between the New England poorhouse and its closest modern relatives, the homeless shelter, prison and jail, and the nursing home.

THE END OF THE ONE POORHOUSE ERA

I have noted throughout this book the lengthy period in which institu-tions for the poor (such as poorhouses and poor farms) lasted in Ameri-can history. Although box 1.1 showed the poorhouses, workhouses, and poor farms as lasting from 1660 to the 1960s, their most predominant role was between the third decade of the nineteenth century and the fourth decade of the twentieth century.

Most historians, social scientists, and other experts agree on the eco-nomic, social welfare, and political changes that led to the decline of the poorhouse. Put simply, the historical consensus has concluded that in-creased political power by working-class and poor people, combined with the political and social impact of the Great Depression and the consequent New Deal reforms, gradually ended the poorhouse. The great event in this history is the Social Security Act of 1935, which—through enactment of old age pensions, widows and survivors insurance, unemployment in-surance, and federal welfare programs (Aid to Dependent Children, Aid to the Blind, Aid to the Disabled, Old Age Assistance)—gradually re-placed much of local relief and finally provided outdoor aid to those who were poor. Indeed, in my several interviews with elderly people, they cited Social Security as putting an end to the poorhouse. For the Landry sisters of Lewiston and the former workers of the Carroll County almshouse, the question was an easy one: Social Security had rendered the poor farm obsolete.[3]

Still, considerable caveats are necessary. First, the Social Security Act ex-cluded large numbers of people. Whole occupational groups, including agricultural workers, domestic workers, and public employees, were left out. Moreover, since Social Security pensions were constructed as "insurance," based on ten years of contributory payments, a large number of elderly people were ineligible for Social Security. Only one-fifth of all workers were eligible when Social Security payments were started in 1940.[4] Disabled people, who had always made up a large part of the poorhouse population, were not covered by Social Security until 1956, and then only those who met the requirement of sufficient contributory payments. Although the Aid to Dependent Children (ADC) program provided some income supports for certain mothers, the reality was that relatively few mothers with children would be on this program until two decades later, as it was essentially a widow's pension for those not eligible for the Survivors Insurance of Social Security.[5] Unemployment insurance was also predicated on past employment, and although a far more accessible program than it is currently, it excluded many of the low-income workers who often were the inmates of the old poorhouse, from agricultural workers to transient workers to those who worked for very small employers to those who were not rehired after their six months of benefits expired.

Secondly, as important as the Social Security Act was, it was a feeble act compared with social protections in other nations, creating less than a "welfare state." Those who received Social Security pensions or unemployment insurance could barely get by; federally mandated welfare programs provided even less to live on. The insurance components of the act excluded large groups of those viewed historically as the undeserving poor: the disabled, the elderly without work experience, the long-term unemployed, the unemployed without sufficient work experience, unmarried mothers, and so on. From the 1940s through the 1960s, however, the weaknesses of the welfare state were obscured (at least to most social scientists and historians) by the relatively good economic performance of the nation. World War II finally ended the Great Depression and created close to a full-employment economy. Although the prosperity of the postwar period has been somewhat exaggerated, in comparison with the past three decades, the American economy was growing and the most prosperous in the world.[6] Wartime economies led to production booms during the Korean and Vietnam conflicts. The growth of trade unionism, which began in the 1930s, was also key to relative prosperity for blue-collar workers, who in major industries gained fringe benefits, seniority rights, and healthy pay increases, including cost of living raises. In contrast, however, were the secondary labor markets—small businesses and industries, largely nonunion—that did not partake in this prosperity. Nor were those in the rural poverty of the agricultural sector or in the nation's growing slums and ghettos much affected.

The discussion of the Worcester Home Farm revealed how many sectors of American society were left out of this prosperity. Additionally, reviews of the rosters of the county homes in New Hampshire in the 1940s and 1950s and the limited anecdotal information we have for the Lewiston City Farm in the postwar period reinforce these generalizations: all the homes had elderly people with insufficient income to support themselves, much less to pay for medical care; all the homes had people with a host of physical and mental disabilities regardless of age; and all the homes had at least short stays by women with children as well as abandoned children.[7] Where our information is more scattered is in the role of the poorhouse in sheltering able-bodied men. Clearly, the home farm in the industrial center of Worcester maintained a high number of men between jobs, earning insufficient money at their jobs, or needing support for other reasons. In the absence of clear information, it is hard to know whether the memories of some about the poor farms having housed primarily alcoholic or mentally ill people are true or reflect the same sort of generalizations we hear today about homeless people. It is true that, in general, those men who did not have serious disabilities were at certain points in the postwar period able to obtain jobs after only brief stays. My guess is that since memories rest on long-term exposure—that is, the longer-term inmates capture the most vivid and sustained memory—those who remember the poor farms may be thinking of those who spent long periods of time there, which in addition to the aged would be disabled people.

There is no doubt that, despite the weaknesses of the American social welfare system to provide anything near a bare minimum subsistence to its citizens, the poorhouse was discredited by the time of the Social Security Act. Long a specter and a threat to those who lived on its outside, the poorhouse came to be an increasingly useful symbol of reaction. For example, Lawrence Powell and colleagues' study of the rhetoric used to support the Social Security Act shows how newspaper cartoons and editorials relied on the poorhouse as a symbol for the maltreatment of the nation's elders, and to a lesser extent, the unemployed.[8] By this era (1930s), no one stepped forward to support the poorhouse, just as few today would suggest returning to orphanages for children. Poorhouses can be compared, in fact, to orphanages in the sense that the public tends to view them as archaic institutions from another era, replete with Dickensian conditions. The alternative to poorhouses was not just the provision of outdoor relief but also the growth of boarding and lodging homes in low-income areas of the nation's cities as well as nursing, old age, and other specialized institutions. As became clear in the 1980s and 1990s, poor people need housing; without adequate wages or social benefits, the poor have nowhere to live. The period between 1950 and 1975 had a low level of what experts now call "literal homelessness" (those actually living on the streets or in their cars or abandoned alleys). Instead, the poor lived in "skid rows" or other low-income areas, but they mostly had roofs over their heads.

BACK TO THE PAST

It is interesting historically how quickly the old days have come back. It was only yesterday (in historical time) that the Lewiston City Farm shut down (1967) or that the people living in the Carroll County Almshouse were removed (1979). By the 1980s, homelessness was a revived topic on everyone's lips, as were words and phrases such as *plant closings, downsizing, cutbacks, the underclass,* and *deindustrialization.* The United States had ceased to dominate the world economically as it once had; the deterioration of conditions for the poor and those most vulnerable to poverty also required political, social, and cultural conditions to change so rapidly that the growth in the welfare state in the 1960s and early 1970s would reverse itself by the early 1980s.

The recessions of the 1970s and early 1980s revealed just how fragile the American economy was, particularly when double-digit unemployment was combined with unprecedented inflation ("stagflation") and the associated crises such as the gas embargo of that era. The more long-term trend of loss of millions of manufacturing jobs, which has continued relatively unabated since the recession of 1973, showed how temporary prosperity was for the average American. As many new jobs appeared without adequate pay, fringe benefits, and union protection, the new "service economy" failed to provide the limited prosperity that blue-collar work had for the previous generation. For those without a high level of education, the new jobs in the "knowledge industry" or "high-technology" sector proved a chimera as well. Since the 1970s, the outlook for all but the most privileged and educated citizens has been bleak, with low pay or multiple jobs as prospects.

Secondly, for those who were vulnerable to economic downtown, the changed condition of America's housing stock was a critical issue. Those who, like Gertrude Mynahan, knew the poor farms and saw their decline realized that many "inmates" went from the farm to boarding homes. Crowded in the centers of cities throughout America were large and small skid rows, with low-cost housing units, including single-room occupancies (SROs), boarding, and lodging homes. These were not attractive places, but they served an important critical need for millions of Americans. Beginning with urban renewal in the 1950s, but accelerating in the 1970s as the baby boom generation returned to the cities and developers realized the value of old historic or renovated housing, the phenomenon of "gentrification" squeezed out the poor from their housing. Some were evicted; others found no place to go when they entered or reentered the housing market.

Thirdly, what in the late 1970s was already a decline in the real value of social welfare benefits became an attack on them under Ronald Reagan, and continued since, including Bill Clinton's "end[ing] welfare as we know it." The combination of deep cuts in housing assistance and the virtual end of public housing; the dismantling of public works programs (such as CETA); deep cuts in welfare and the later complete replacement of AFDC with TANF (Temporary Assistance to Needy Families), which ended the entitlement to assistance; cuts in food stamps; state cuts in unemployment insurance, Medicaid, and welfare (with many states abolishing their general assistance programs); and massive cuts to disability programs in the 1980s have been devastating for the last two decades. While other nations have seen huge jumps in their unemployment, most nations in Western Europe have buffeted their citizens from the degree of hardship found in America.

But, finally, to understand the return of the poorhouse, we also need to comment on the cultural milieu. In response to a period of rapid social change and experimentation in the 1960s and early 1970s, America (under a variety of national administrations) has appeared ready to wage war against those who are judged deviant. Most vividly reflected in the "war on drugs" declared in the 1980s, which has led to a harsh attack primarily on poor people and racial minorities, the new "zero-tolerance" mentality has lent moral credence to "tough" punishment for anyone deemed deviant. This can be seen now with a variety of issues: youthful deviance, for example, as witnessed by constant surveillance of kids; the Patriot Act and the overzealous war on terrorism; and attacks on panhandlers, loiterers, or perceived "mentally ill" people on the streets. Just as an apparent consensus supported putting Adeline Nott in the workhouse in 1834 because she loitered on the street, the drug war and the increasing suspicion of all the poor, racial minority group members, and young people have led to a dramatic soaring in the daily prison and jail population from 500,000 people in the mid-1970s to 2.2 million in the early twenty-first century.

Although less commented on and a good deal more complex than the rise in prisons, both the creation of homeless shelters in virtually all the places large enough to have had an almshouse a century ago, and the growth of for-profit nursing homes and other facilities to house many disabled nonelderly adults, are part of the same complex of political and economic changes of the last decades. What seemed in the 1970s to presage "decarceration"[9] became arguably not "deinstitutionalization" but a "transinstitutionalization" of various groups.[10] For example, prisons, jails, nursing homes, and other institutions have replaced the older mental hospitals, state schools for the retarded, and orphanages.

As we have seen in this book, the almshouse/poorhouse contained within it several traditional functions; the most prominent were those of workhouse or house of correction, the nursing home, and the homeless shelter. The workhouse was overtly an institution of discipline and punishment that, over time, became the city or county jail in most areas. The workhouse is gone, but has clearly been surpassed in number by today's jails and prisons, not to mention the harsher conditions they exact. A second function, as we have seen, was long-term succor to those who were the "deserving" poor, such as the elderly, disabled, children, and single mothers. Today, some poor, elderly, and disabled people find themselves in the nursing home, the most direct descendant of the poorhouse in terms of the actual number of old poorhouse buildings that turned into them. Fortunately, for the most part, children and mothers have thus far been spared institutionalization, although the number of homeless families in shelters grows, as well as the number of female prisoners. A third function of the poorhouse was the housing of the unemployed or poor adults who were homeless; today, the homeless shelter, in some communities with a variety of supplements such as day shelters and soup kitchens, has taken on this legacy.

Reformers of the nineteenth and early twentieth centuries might in one way at least be pleased by our situation, as "specialization" was their constant wish for the almshouse, and lack of "separation" was one of their deepest grievances with the institution. Men and women should be separate; adults, children, and elderly separate; the criminal separated from the noncriminal; the mentally ill from the "sane"; the "lame" and "crippled" from the able, and so on. But even assuming the desirability of separation, there is a downside. While the poorhouse contained people, old and young, respectable and not, relatively close by their communities, today these parts of the populations gain less attention and sympathy for reform or change. Our millions of prisoners are both "out of sight" from their home communities, often "shipped upstate," and their segregation as "criminals" makes them undeserving of sympathy. The disabled and poor elderly traditionally hold more sympathy but are now often cast away in closed facilities that do not gain public attention. Finally, the treatment of those who are homeless and must line up each night in our cities for a bed has returned the very public stigma and humiliation of having to "go over the hill to the poorhouse." In fact, the poorhouse was easier to enter and continue to stay in than today's homeless shelters, which resemble actually more closely the lodging of tramps in the police stations across the United States in the 1870s through early 1900s. In any event, the splintering and segregation of the large numbers of groups that constituted the poorhouse population has not helped the overall treatment or unity of the poor.

A TENTATIVE COMPARISON: THE POORHOUSE
AND THE HOMELESS SHELTER

It is a somewhat difficult and tricky proposition to compare institutions across historical eras. There were considerable historical changes in the poorhouse and much variation from place to place, depending on local politics and culture, the particular overseers and superintendents, and the actions of inmates. The same can be said to a lesser extent for the variety of today's homeless shelters. (Since the passage of the federal Stewart McKinney Homeless Assistance Act of 1987 there has been far more uniformity because of federal funding guidelines than could ever have happened under the old local poor laws.) A second problem for comparison is the set of social and cultural expectations of subsistence change over time. On the one hand, few inmates would ever expect to be searched at the almshouse door, yet today all our institutions have beefed up their surveillance and control. Hence, metal detectors at almost all shelters could be justified by some as normal to our contemporary society. On the other hand, in a society that lacked routine plumbing in the 1870s, one would not expect full showers and bathing facilities in almshouses; today, few shelters would not have showering facilities.

Despite these problems, I believe it is important to make such comparisons, as tricky as they are. If we do not, we are simply surmising that the past was either worse or better than today, and we gain little understanding and insight that can aid us with today's social issues. In the case of the poor, oddly, there is a widespread tendency to believe that the American past is always worse than the present. Such beliefs seem to cross ideological lines. Generally, we tend to think of conservatives as most happy with the present—but the treatment of the poor evinces widespread sentimentality about charity and social services, which runs rampant among liberals and radicals as well as conservative and moderate Americans. That is, while at least some Americans bemoan the past—whether the poorhouses, slavery, the internment of the Japanese during World War II, or the many other events that have, by virtue of time and controversy, been exposed as inhuman—people are rarely as critical of the social welfare institutions of contemporary times. In fact, since liberals often sponsor social services and homeless shelters, they are in some ways less likely to criticize their operations.

Why those who started the movement for the homeless in the late 1970s and early 1980s (at a time when the numbers of people crowding the streets became apparent) geared their movements toward the solution of homeless shelters is a question that requires a broader inquiry. In theory, the development of homeless shelters came at a time when some social movements continued to exist in the United States that were committed to advocacy for the poor. We could perhaps surmise that new types of innovations could be made for the newly constructed issue of homelessness. For complex political reasons analyzed well by Cynthia Bogard, neither the movements in Washington, D.C., nor in New York City, the two most prominent centers of contestation about how "homelessness" would be defined as a social problem, led to other than a reinvention of the almshouse.[11] In New York City, the Coalition for the Homeless sued the City of New York and obtained the "right to shelter." The right to shelter quickly came to mean not permanent actual housing but a cot in a homeless shelter. The net result was a series of horrifying large and dangerous homeless shelters, which became known for crime, overcrowding, and even disease and gang warfare. Perhaps the political environment in New York City at that time (which ascribed homelessness mostly to mental illness) prevented advocates from achieving more. In Washington, D.C., under the more radical leadership of Mitch Snyder and the Center for Creative Non-Violence (CCNV), the movement also failed to move beyond demands for homeless shelters. While the actions of Snyder and his followers were often militant (hunger strikes, arrests, protests), the emphasis seemed to be on the symbolic nature of homelessness and poverty and its reflection on the Reagan administration, rather than a program of economic and social change that would have *ended* homelessness. Perhaps everyone perceived homelessness in the early 1980s as being only temporary, or perhaps activists wanted no part of the specifics of a social policy response.[12] But following developments in these cities, other cities moved to construct shelters in almost the exact form as the New York and Washington models, in much the same way that the Yates and Quincey Reports of the 1820s set off an almshouse movement across other parts of the country.

The shelter approach became national with the passage in 1987 of the Stewart McKinney Act, which provided federal funding for shelter, emergency food, and certain homeless services. Although there is considerable variety in the sponsorship of programs—many shelters are privately run rather than public, particularly outside the Northeast—almost all large communities currently have homeless shelters, and most have soup kitchens, clothing and food pantries, day shelters, and other services. Some have created a web of case management, counseling, and job programs as well. However, very few have attacked the structural causes of homelessness, such as lack of permanent housing and lack of income, just as our forefathers built almshouses rather than provide housing or income to the poor.[13]

The following quick generalizations about current homeless shelters, at least in New England, suggests how we have moved backward through time to the poorhouse:[14]

1. *Virtually all homeless shelters, public and private, are defined as "tempo-rary," leading to a "transition" elsewhere. Compared to the almshouse, this re-tards the development of community within the shelters and, more importantly, leaves many "clients" homeless when they are unable to "transition."*

Because public monies were attached to a "transition" (presumably to permanent housing), it is usually impossible to stay in a shelter over a long-term period of time, unlike the old poorhouses. In Portland, Maine, for example, the city's "resident contract" begins with the explanation that its shelter is a "temporary" one.[15] The second sentence notes, "The case management staff are here to assist you in your transition from temporary shelter to permanent housing or to provide assistance relocating to another community." This may sound good, but later in the contract an ominous note is added: "Failure to meet with your case manager may result in restriction from the shelter, dayroom and/or grounds." In practice, while homeless people clearly want permanent housing, the commitment to planning for a transition prevents many homeless people from continuing to stay at the shelter even when there is *no* affordable housing available in the community or in situations when personal or social impediments prevent the clients from obtaining an apartment.

In larger cities, the temporary quality of shelter is even more stringent. At the Pine Street Inn, Boston's largest shelter, beds are assigned nightly by lottery. According to their brochure, names must be placed for the lottery between 2:30 and 3:45 P.M. and are drawn at 3:45. The brochure notes, "to obtain a bed for the night, place your name in the lottery at the front desk. . . . When your name is drawn, you will be called over the loud-speaker. . . . If you choose to leave . . . you must return to the Inn by 8:30 P.M. to claim your bed. There are sanctions for not claiming your bed."[16] The lottery system has many obvious drawbacks. Homeless people routinely must line up throughout the nation for long waits for beds and must work their life schedule around the chance of getting a bed. The process is not only stigmatizing, physically uncomfortable, and humiliating but it also interferes with time that could be spent looking for work and/or actual housing. Further, the daily uncertainty of having even a cot to sleep in prevents holding down jobs or maintaining relationships. All of this does not even explore the weakening of any prospect of community that could potentially form stronger ties through the longer patterns of association that, as we have seen, were present in the poorhouses. All shelters surveyed insisted on temporary status and used vehicles such as a case manager to press for a "move out of the shelter system and into permanent housing."

What "temporary" means, of course, is subject to interpretation and various practices in different shelters. Those who are judged to be "working on" their life may be allowed a several-month (or more) stay in many shelters. Some shelters (sometimes dependent on particular staff) might allow the person to stay longer or to come back in after a short break if things don't work out, just as the almshouse had people admitted over and over again. But in some shelters, clients have to use a pseudonym to get back in. Those who are judged as "undeserving" (in more modern parlance, to have "behavioral" problems, or be "unmotivated," "noncompliant," or "disruptive") will find themselves likely discontinued by the shelter or even permanently barred. This is quite a difference from the almshouse, which allowed people to become more long-term "residents." Clearly, most people, particularly the able-bodied, did not choose the almshouse or poorhouse as home. But once there, they were rarely shown the door. We have seen how some almshouses were used as seasonal shelters by housed residents, as stopping points for transitory workers, and as long-term homes for others.

2. *Most homeless shelters are not open in the day, but are open only evenings and nights. This arrangement is less humane than the poorhouses, where people could stay during the day.*

With rare exceptions, since shelters were conceptualized as only a place to sleep, no space or facility exists in them for homeless people to come in from the cold of winter or the heat of summer during the day. It is not a home, but a "cot" for the night. In Portland, the "shelter closes promptly at 7:45 A.M. and all clients must be out of bed by 7:30 A.M. The shelter curfew is 9:00 or 10:00 P.M. depending on the time of year." At the Pine Street Inn, "wake up" is 6:00 A.M. and the shelter closes at 8:30 A.M. (in summer) and 9:30 A.M. in winter. As we have seen, the client must be back sometime between 2:30 and 3:45 P.M. for the drawing, and assuming a bed is won at the lottery, the curfew is at 8:30 P.M.

Note how different the current situation is from the descriptions of the late nineteenth-century poorhouses. Then, reporters found people milling around during the day, playing cards, and greeting the visitors. Even the very large almshouses in New York City and Boston a century ago show pictures of rooms for activities and card playing during the day.[17] The almshouses may not have been a desirable place, but they were "home" for thousands of people. It is true, depending on time and place, that inmates who were able were expected to work, particularly at the poor farms, although it is hard to know whether this requirement is dramatically different from the "workfare" requirements being made of citizens now in homeless shelters. It is also true that more progressive cities have now added "day shelters," but they are often at different locations and run by different organizations from night shelters. This means still another trek—in some areas, even across town—to another institutional facility, and, although they may have lockers or showers, generally all goods the person owns must be carried along on his or her back or carted to and fro. In the poorhouse, in contrast, inmates often kept personal effects nearby, which is an extremely important difference.

3. *While generalizations about living conditions are difficult, almshouses and shelters are generally comparable, and the six studied are probably better than most homeless shelters in regard to sleeping areas, waiting lines, food, and so on.*

Large city shelters with their long waiting lines, crowded armories where people sleep next to each other, and the generally dismal physical surroundings and food are certainly not new; pictures of the New York City and Boston almshouses reflect this, as do the large number of police stations that served as lodging houses.[18]

Today, virtually all homeless shelters are composed of barracks-type sleeping arrangements, with the numbers of shelter residents so great that cots are lined up next to each other with as little as a foot or less of space between them. The intimacy (to put it delicately) of the surroundings has been one of the chief complaints of poor people, who suffer crime and poor health as a result. These conditions were not routine in the six almshouses studied, but in the same cities and areas today, they are.[19] We have reference to private rooms at the Worcester Home Farm and at the Portland Almshouse. Dr. Mitchell of the Rockingham Home complained when the rooms started to "double up." We know, of course, during economic depressions and some other periods, widespread overcrowding occurred at the almshouses, but usually the six poorhouses studied were arranged as a house-style institution with small dorm rooms that more resembled suites in today's homes for the aged, nursing homes, group homes, or college dorms where two or more people have separate areas of a larger room. The poorhouses were not transitional in either legal terms or in practice, and some inmates had clothes, pets, plants, books, and other belongings stored near their beds.

All records I saw, as well as interviews with elderly people who were knowledgeable about the poor farms and county homes, commented on the high quality of the food in these institutions. In almost every jurisdiction there were sumptuous dinners at the farm provided to visiting dignitaries. Of course, the poor farms had the advantage of fresh vegetables, meat, poultry, and other items, as well as dedicated matrons whose cooking was often a point of pride to them. Similarly, as we have seen in the case of Mrs. Landry, mending clothing was an important aspect of at least some poor farms. The poorhouse served a different symbolic role in New England society than does today's homeless shelter. While a few politicians may on occasion venture into a soup kitchen to campaign, in nineteenth- and early twentieth-century New England, the poorhouses were seen as an important part of the civic life for farmers, political leaders, and the community. The cities and towns even rhetorically competed with each other. If homeless shelters do not arouse much scandal, they do not arouse much attention today either, except perhaps at times of Thanksgiving and Christmas when human interest stories appear on the news.

Of course, these generalizations must be made cautiously. We have no eyewitnesses alive to the older poorhouse experience and, in some cases, no disinterested parties to the later ones. Although most homeless shelters are large concrete buildings with little individualized space and institutionalized food, some private shelters provide a more personalized atmosphere (usually these small shelters are for special populations, such as mothers with children or those judged especially capable of a quick "transition"). The culture of 1890 or 1900 did not have available the mass-produced meals or clothes or other items, and hence drew on more personally made sources for all goods, whether made by the matron, objects donated by local neighbors, or food or clothes worked on by inmates. This reliance on free labor in the person of the matron and the inmates themselves is not something we countenance today, although the constant call for volunteers for soup kitchens and shelters in some ways reflects the continued low value of this work.

4. *The rules and social control power of homeless shelters over clients, while certainly far less complex than the original poorhouse rules itemized in chapter 3, are comparable if not more stringent than how the poorhouses studied were conducted from the late nineteenth century onward.*

Shelters have similar types of control to those the old poorhouses had and sometimes exceed them. Of course, it is difficult to say without controversy whether this can be separated from the other changed conditions of life in America that place all of us under increased surveillance.

Some practices and policies parallel the old ways. Portland's shelter prohibits those "under the influence" from entering and presumably from staying at the shelter; at Pine Street, "use of or possession of drugs and alcohol and the abuse of medication" are prohibited.[20] While we have noted the failure of many poorhouses to effect such sobriety, their rules insisted on it. It is possible, with increased security and surveillance today, that the rules are policed more fully than in the earlier days (also see the attendant described in chapter 7). Today, clients are frequently searched at the door of the shelter and often must pass through electronic surveillance. The Portland shelter "reserves the right to conduct regular and spot inspections of all client lockers at any time without prior notice." It is likely that some poorhouses maintained some scrutiny of those entering and could go through possessions, though I did not find any reference to these practices. Work requirements too are not so different. Initially, perhaps the major difference between homeless shelters and the old poorhouses was the work ideology of the latter. The rush to construct massive shelters and the emphasis on overnight quarters overshadowed a focus on work. Further, politically, the locus of the work debate in much of the 1980s and early 1990s was on the "welfare recipient," constructed as often lazy but not as a homeless person. In fact, the homeless were initially seen as nonworkers, just flotsam and jetsam.

By the mid to late 1990s, led by politicians such as Rudolph Giuliani in New York City, homeless people (now deemed able-bodied) were forced to work for their shelter and other aid. I found these requirements routine in the three states studied. Such "workfare" requirements, in most places, as well as mandatory job search, case management, and twelve-step and other programs of change, make the shelters very comparable to the original idea of the workhouse and poorhouse in which character reform and rehabilitation from poverty were philosophically believed to flow from forced work and moral rehabilitation. Because of the variability in state welfare laws, it is hard to measure how many hours on average shelter residents work, much less do a comparison with the amount of labor on the poor farm.[21] Perhaps today's client works slightly less than some inmates did at the most productive poor farms, but equally likely, with both institutions being technically voluntary, the inmate may have preferred the farm work over the most common workfare tasks today such as raking leaves, folding laundry, and other relatively menial tasks usually assigned in today's workfare programs. The ideal of work on a farm, in fact, has even attracted contemporary projects to move homeless people to rural areas to work, and there is some evidence, as from the film mentioned in chapter 2, that a camaraderie and enjoyment of agricultural work did attract some people to poor farms.[22] Moreover, within American tradition, farming is a mark of citizenship and hard work, not punishment. This is not the case with many "workfare" assignments.

A list of "safety and security rules" at Pine Street Inn is extensive. With the backup of "detail officers from the Boston Police Department," the following are prohibited:

- Any act of violence that includes physical or verbal abuse of staff and other guests
- Loud, unruly, or intimidating behavior
- Use of or possession of drugs or alcohol and the abuse of medications
- Weapons, bottles, and drug paraphernalia
- Uncooperative or inappropriate behavior
- Gambling or stealing
- Taking food outside or keeping food in lockers or bags in the coat room
- Smoking in the building or front of the building
- Taking personal items or flammable items to the dorm
- Sexual conduct

The list ends with a note that "barring" procedures are "available in the counselor's office."[23]

While the list may not strike the twenty-first-century middle-class observer as surprising, in the context of managing poor people's lives (stressful to begin with, as they are often herded together for hours and have a culture different from the middle-class volunteers or professionals who staff the system), much misunderstanding occurs. Studies of shelters have found enormous variability by staff and shelter administrators in the enforcement of rules, and also a tendency to use rules against disfavored clients whose behavior is felt by staff to be morally reprehensible or simply not "therapeutic."[24] For example, "sexual conduct" could be flirting or revealing dress in which a disfavored client is sanctioned by a shelter worker who does not like her or him. Or a demonstrative client may grab another for a kiss or hug without being a serious aggressor and be "sanctioned" by staff. In my study of day-to-day life in Portland's streets and shelters, there were many times when people were boisterous, loud, sexual, or aggressive—many of the behaviors that would bring about the sanctions above—but often this behavior for those who knew the people involved was harmless teasing, horseplay, or testing.[25] Still, for those who do not know the behavioral codes and norms of the street culture or who dislike a particular client, the acts would likely lead to sanctions. Of course, the rules may or may not be invoked, but their broadness is disconcerting to street people who have nowhere to turn if barred from a shelter. A client who is angry and pushes a staff member, even if he or she has been waiting in line for hours or has a psychiatric or substance use problem, may well result in the client being banned permanently from a shelter or even a whole shelter system.

POORHOUSE TO JAILS, PRISONS, AND NURSING HOMES

Comparisons of the poorhouse with successor institutions such as jails, prisons, nursing homes and other institutions would be an important area to research. To me, it would appear to take little expertise to judge the conditions in the six almshouses studied (including those with a house of corrections) as being far gentler toward its inmates than today's crime complex. As we saw in chapter 2, low security prevailed at the Rockingham and Carroll County houses of correction. This was even truer of prisoners at the Haverhill poorhouse (see chapter 5) and in Portland's almshouse, where prisoners were totally integrated with inmates. Late nineteenth-century to mid-twentieth-century houses of correction used mandatory farm work as the standard punishment fare and barometer of how the prisoner was doing. Keeping in mind that we are not talking of serious felons, house of correction prisoners were understood to not require barbed wire, lockdowns, searches, and high walled fences. Those prisoners who did labor on the farm were rewarded with passes out of the almshouse and free mingling with the other inmates, and sometimes secured jobs at the house afterwards. Reformers, in fact, constantly complained about this intermingling. In the mid to late 1910s, the Maine State Board of Charities and Corrections continued to object to the lack of separation between Portland's prisoners and inmates. Only in 1918 did the overseers agree to take some measures to segregate sleeping quarters of the groups.[26] While the typical charges for house of correction prisoners (i.e., assault, drunkenness, vagrancy) are not all that different than the charges against most prisoners today, at least in New England (i.e., drug possession, driving while intoxicated, and assault), now the prisoner is often shipped far from home, placed in uniform, put on complete prison regimen, and treated not in an altogether dissimilar way from those who are charged with major felony crimes.[27] Even city and county jails have been beefed up with high-level security, although offenders sometimes have more opportunities for work release.

Clearly, for those who did not work or get along with the superintendents and matrons, such as some of the inmates of Haverhill in 1895, conditions were punitive and probably less predictable than today's jails and prisons. One example was the use of punishment cell, as we saw in the Haverhill almshouse. Today, more state regulations and rules governing guards, we hope, change some of the arbitrariness of lockdowns and isolation cells. The lack of predictability, along with our somewhat increased regulation of convict work, clearly leaves us less than nostalgic for the house of correction, but as the barbed-wire protected jails in rural New Hampshire counties suggest, we have not moved forward either. We claim advancement, while erecting huge bureaucratic enterprises of punishment, hidden away from middle-class society.

The most difficult comparison with the poorhouse is probably to the modern nursing home and other related care facilities, which often emerged on the same physical locations as the old poorhouse once stood. These populations (the elderly, the disabled) were often silent in the history of the poorhouse and have been understudied in our own day. We hope, and I suspect it is generally true, that better conditions of medical care, diet, hygiene, and recreation exist at these facilities than at the old almshouses. Still, the logic of separation on the one hand, the isolation of the aged, and also increasing numbers of physically and mentally disabled people, and on the other hand, the fact that the nursing home industry is almost entirely profit driven, provides some doubts as to our "progress." We know that elderly and disabled people for many reasons react to the need to go to a nursing home as older generations did to the poorhouse. There are many complex reasons for this, some perhaps un-avoidable. Still, do elderly and disabled people need to be cut off from in-tergenerational contact except with staff and occasional visitors, and do they need such high levels of segregation and control? The elderly women of Sarah Orne Jewett's story came in and out of the almshouse at will, as did some of the inmates in our six counties and cities. Today, while ex-cursions may be arranged for those physically well enough, bureaucratic and medical rules prevent much freedom; moreover, if patients demon-strate that they are able to perform too many activities, they may be dis-qualified from the "level of care" they are in—that is, they no longer need skilled nursing care facilities. On the other hand, nursing home patients today are generally far more ill than they were even a generation ago.[28] The non-elderly disabled find themselves paradoxically isolated at a time when new civil rights and acknowledgment of their personhood has fi-nally come. Yet a combination of lack of health insurance, poverty, lack of home aides, and difficult physical and emotional conditions forces many disabled people into nursing homes and chronic care facilities. Any study that compares conditions between poorhouses and nursing homes would have to isolate those private-pay patients in more upscale facilities from the vast majority of patients paid for by Medicaid, who constitute the bulk of the nursing home population.

INDOOR RELIEF, OLD AND NEW

Much of this book has described how poor people, and to some extent lo-cal officials and staff, resisted the original goals of the poorhouse and in various ways subverted them. Clearly, every human institution allows for such resistance, and poor people undermine shelter and even prison goals daily. Yet those institutions that sociologists describe as "total institu-tions" are far harder to resist. While the term *indoor relief* is a useful one, both linking institutions in which people lose aspects of their freedom and reminding us of their common origin, the term has its limitations in this regard. First, true "total institutions" such as prisons and nursing homes need to be distinguished from semi-total institutions like poorhouses or homeless shelters. Second, each type of institution develops its role in re-lation to the noninstitutionalized world, particularly the labor market. There is reason to worry that the new trends of the twenty-first century may surpass the past American history of mistreatment of the poor, as bad as it often was.

"Total institutions" like prisons, jails, nursing homes, and mental hospi-tals are truly places of confinement in which inmates are, around the clock, held to a regime in which they are cut off from the outside world except for visitors at regulated times. As we saw in this book, whatever the initial goals of the poorhouse, they did *not* become total institutions. Certainly, like homeless shelters, they had aspects of total institutions in the way officials defined the inmates, the rules they enforced, the terminology, and the limitations that inmates, particularly the more feeble, had in their mobility. County homes, in particular, were more geographically distant from inmates' own towns and hence were often isolating in a way that total institutions are. Several almshouses on islands, such as Boston's Long Island, also appear to have come close to being total institutions. But generally, as we have seen, most inmates could go into town and city centers during the day and many worked there. Some inmates were constantly irritating superintendents or overseers by going downtown and getting drunk. Other inmates, as with homeless shelters, came and went after a few days. What is ominous today is the long-term steady growth of the prison and jail populations—true total institutions—that cut off their occupants completely from the outside world and limit convicts' ability to maintain many aspects of individuality or group and collective life.

Paradoxically, total institutions, though growing out of the poorhouse experience, contradicted the labor market functions of the poorhouse. In a growing economy, which characterized much of earlier American history, relief was punitive and an intentional deterrent so that work (on the outside) would seem attractive and any type of work accepted as an alternative. True, a competing idea held to some extent that the poorhouse and poor farm could be made into a successful enterprise to provide work. There exist prison labor, mental asylum labor, and sheltered workshops even today. Institutionalized labor is a tempting source of cheap labor! But generally in a society that required agricultural and then industrial labor, not only were employers unlikely to accept widespread incarceration, but inmates themselves found easy escapes from the poorhouse, since a trip downtown or to the next city would often lead to work. In this light, the decline in the need for labor is also an ominous sign. As Nils Christie notes in his opening to *Crime Control as Industry: Towards Gulags, Western Style*, Western societies now confront the problem everywhere of inequality and of lack of paid work. The "crime control industry," as he calls it, is seductive in its very ability to provide profits while removing sources of unrest from society.[29] When large segments of society are now expendable, even as unskilled labor, our prospects for the future are daunting.

Not only are total institutions far harder to resist or change than are the semi-total ones, but the world of the twenty-first century has significant labor market differences from the "old days" that make even today's semi-total institutions more limiting. In the days of the poorhouse, when first agricultural and then industrial work was prevalent, no great transition separated those able-bodied from the "world of work." When work was available, appearance and social skills were not much of a barrier. But today, people who are very poor face more insurmountable barriers. While officials (and the public) tell homeless people, for example, to "get a job," there are not only few unskilled jobs around but, lacking an address, decent appearance, proper demeanor, and a willingness to serve people with a smile (such as at the pizza place or the hardware store), the applicant does not get far. In that sense, the poorhouse was less limiting, at least to the able-bodied, since they could literally take off (or "abscond," as the overseers put it) and end up working somewhere. Even the absence of a decent set of clothes or poor smell would not have kept them from a job. In an age with few jobs, and the dominance among them of "service" jobs with a premium on looks, many able-bodied people are not considered "appropriate." People who are experiencing extreme poverty have many barriers to ever being hired.

Perhaps the most positive changes have come, at least to a degree, to those not able-bodied. Some, if not all, of those previously viewed as "crippled," "lame," "idiotic," or "insane" are now legally and culturally viewed as more human as a result of the rights movements in America. Nor does America allow its growing number of elders to reside in situations exactly resembling poorhouses. Yet here too ambiguities abound; the poorest elders and disabled live with choices of eating or taking their medications, and with age and poverty, many elders are forced into institutions or quasi institutions. The stigma of serious disabilities prevents many from a full life or from the job market, and often leads as well to institutions. Some advocate building more mental hospitals and other institutions in response to perceived crises of violence by the mentally ill or by mentally ill homeless people. We see once again those who advocate institutions and claim to do so "for the good" of the potential inmate. Another deep danger of a society without work is that more and more people will be defined as "disabled" or "unproductive" and moved to the sides, whether they wish to work or not. Hence, we can at least see the possibility of not only continued prison and homeless shelter growth but also growth in other institutional facilities.

We in America are not far from the days of the poorhouse and, in fact, probably much closer than we were fifty or sixty years ago. With the economic, political, and social trends as they currently are, it is hard to envision positive changes in America's treatment of the poor.

Notes

AHF: Androscoggin County Historical Society, Auburn, Maine

BCF: Files at the Barron Center, Portland, Maine, the successor institution to the old Portland Almshouse, now a skilled nursing home, Alzheimer's center, and a housing complex

BHF: Belmont Home Files, Worcester, Mass. A box containing assorted memos, meeting minutes, budgets, and letters from Ellery Royal, the last superintendent of Worcester's Home Farm. Also contained material from Belmont Home itself, the city nursing home, which closed in 1996.

CCCO: Carroll County Commissioners office, primarily scrapbook file maintained at Ossipee, N.H., headquarters

HCHV: Haverhill, Mass., City Hall Vault

LCHV: Lewiston, Maine, City Hall Vault

MHS: Maine Historical Society, Portland, Maine

NHSL: New Hampshire State Library, Concord, N.H.

PHF: Papers of the Hilton family; scrapbooks and other items from George and Dorothy Hilton, the last superintendent and matron of the Rockingham County Farm, Brentwood, N.H.

PRPPL: Portland Room of the Portland Public Library, Portland, Maine

RCCF: Files at the Rockingham County Commissioners Office, Brentwood, N.H.

SCHPL: Files at the Special Collections of the Haverhill, Mass., Public Library

WHM: Worcester Historical Museum, Worcester, Mass.

WPL: Worcester, Mass., Public Library

CHAPTER 1

1. Frances Fox Piven and Richard Cloward, *Regulating the Poor: The Functions of Public Welfare* (New York: Vintage, 1971), 33.

2. Sarah Orne Jewett, *Betsey's Flight: The Country of Pointed Firs and Other Stories* (Garden City: Doubleday, 1956), 172.

3. The first American workhouse was erected in Boston in 1660 and my research has found poor farms that existed in Maine and New Hampshire through the early 1970s. Clearly, however, these early and late examples affected a relatively small number of people. The predominant use of poorhouses/almshouses for the poor and other populations was between the 1820s and the winding down of the Great Depression in the late 1930s. It should be kept in mind, however, that outdoor relief (or aid given outside of an institution, today's equivalents of welfare, Social Security, unemployment insurance, and food stamps) usually remained the most frequent method of relief despite constant efforts by reformers to end aid outside the institutions.

4. There is, of course, a critical academic literature that arose in both history and social welfare in the 1970s; three works are particularly important: David Rothman's seminal *The Discovery of the Asylum* (Boston: Little, Brown, 1971; new editions, 1980, 1990), which filled a large gap by tracing the development of most "total institutions" in America to their origin in the almshouse/poorhouse experience. The same year, Piven and Cloward's *Regulating the Poor: The Functions of Public Welfare* (1971) was published and began with a powerful chapter on the European workhouse and used this history as a continued metaphor for the social control function of relief. Finally, the most comprehensive historical work about the poorhouse came with Michael Katz's *In the Shadow of the Poorhouse: A Social History of Welfare in America* (New York: Basic Books, 1986; second edition, 1996), although much of his book after the early chapters is a history that uses the poorhouse as a metaphor. Katz provides the most complete and nuanced view, but since much of the work is about the entire history of the United States' social welfare system until the end of the twentieth century, it is limited in its attention to some issues.

There are, as well, excellent sources of the history on the disabled. See, for example, Joseph Shapiro, *No Pity: People with Disabilities Forging a New Civil Rights Movement* (New York: Times Books, 1994), and on the elderly, D. H. Fisher, *Growing Old in America* (New York: Oxford University Press, 1978), which do mention poorhouses. It may well be two factors—the lack of sales for books about depressing subjects such as the poor, and the attempt in treating other groups such as the elderly or disabled as less stigmatized to distance them from the poverty history—that account for the relative lack of material.

5. For information on Bellevue Hospital and its start as an almshouse, see Harry E. Dowling, *City Hospitals: The Undercare of the Underprivileged* (Cambridge: Harvard University Press, 1982), and John Starr, *Hospital City* (New York: Crown Publishers, 1957). A good historical source for the Long Island almshouse is William Cole, "Boston's Pauper Institutions," *New England Magazine* (orig. 1898), reproduced by Cornell University's *Making of America* at http://cdl.library. cornell.edu/cgi-bin/moa/pageviewer?coll=moa&root=%2Fmoa%2Fnewe. Roth-

man's *Discovery of Asylum* includes a picture of the almshouse on Deer Island, later moved to Long Island. Oscar Handlin's well-known *Boston's Immigrants* (New York: Atheneum, 1977) includes several references to Deer Island's House of Industry.

6. The first is occurring in Lewiston, Maine, the second-largest city in the state, where the old city farm was ended in 1967 and the last building burned down in 1998. To the dismay of the children of a past superintendent of the city farm, the city is selling the land to Wal-Mart. In Carroll County, New Hampshire, in Ossipee, the county farm still operates and is staffed with prison labor.

7. Annual reports of Haverhill and Worcester in Massachusetts and from Carroll and Rockingham Counties, New Hampshire, in particular. These statements were a little more muted in the two Maine cities I studied (Portland and Lewiston).

8. This is not true in *all* cases of institutional development. Some charitable hospitals, usually of a sectarian nature, began in eighteenth-century America, and the Quakers experimented with asylums and other forms of institutional care. Reformers, both religious and secular, saw the need for prisons and orphanages early on. However, as Rothman points out, the major institutional imperative in U.S. history began in the 1820s and 1830s and was a development out of the poorhouse as different "special populations" were subdivided out.

9. Personal conversation, Arthur Tirella, June 2003.

10. No issue was more central to the social welfare system of America until relatively recently than settlement. The Laws of Settlement arose in England in the fourteenth century after the Black Plague to tie the working population to their local area. In both England and the United States, the settlement laws became an obsession of local officials, as no one would be admitted into colonial and early American towns without proof of property. Even ship manifests were checked for paupers. Most communication by overseers of the poor in the eighteenth and nineteenth centuries and even the first half of the twentieth was about establishing settlements of paupers. In fact, in some towns, more money was spent on court cases about pauper settlements than in aiding the poor. The Warren Court finally overturned the principle of settlement in the 1960s, which ruled extensive residency laws for the purpose of welfare and other benefits violated the Constitution. For hundreds of years, nonlocals were regarded as "vagrants," "tramps," and "drifters."

11. From a document entitled "An Historical Sketch of the Worcester Home Farm," p. 2, BHF.

12. L. Smith, "Caring for the Poor," *Collected Articles*, vol. 4, 566, 1932, SCHPL.

13. D. Hodgkin, *Managing the Poor in Lewiston, Maine, 1795–1863*. Paper presented at Washburn Humanities Conference, Northern New England in the Nineteenth Century, Norland, Livermore, Maine, June 8, 2001, 10–11.

14. Cited in Rothman, *Discovery of the Asylum*, 166–67.

15. Katz, *In the Shadow of the Poorhouse*, chapters 1 and 2.

16. Social welfare texts are one indication of how history is portrayed. The poorhouse generally receives little attention. A review of six frequently used textbooks in social welfare courses (J. Axinn and H. Levin, *Social Welfare: A History of the American Response to Need*, 3rd ed. [New York: Longman, 1992]; P. Day, *A New History of Social Welfare*, 3rd ed. [Boston: Allyn and Bacon, 2000]; D. M. DiNitto, *Social Welfare:*

Politics and Public Policy [Englewood Cliffs: Prentice Hall, 1995]; B. Jansson, *The Reluctant Welfare State*, 4th ed. [Belmont, Calif.: Brooks-Cole, 2000]; P. Popple and L. Leighninger, *Social Work, Social Welfare, and American Society*, 3rd ed. [Needham Heights, Mass.: Allyn and Bacon, 1996]; and W. Trattner, *From Poor Law to Welfare State: A History of Social Welfare in America*, 4th ed. [New York: Free Press, 1989]) finds that they stress only the early nineteenth-century background with the Yates and Quincey Reports, and most texts return for a sentence or two on Dorothea Dix, and, finally, on the reformers' bid to move children out of the almshouses. Trattner's text is the only one that has as much as a paragraph on the twentieth-century poor farm and its gradual transformation.

Another body of literature—mostly forgotten—is from a wide array of social welfare specialists in the 1890–1940 period who reflected the new elite opinion of the poorhouse: that it was backward and would be remedied primarily by specialized institutions and more professionalized social work. See, for example, Amos Warner, *American Charities: A Study in Philanthropy and Economics* (New Brunswick, N.J.: Transaction, 1989, orig. 1894); A. Johnson, *The Almshouse: Construction and Management* (New York: Charities Publication Committee, 1911); Robert Kelso, *Public Poor Relief in Massachusetts 1620–1920* (Boston: Houghton-Mifflin, 1922); Roy Brown, *Public Poor Relief in North Carolina* (New York: Arno Press, 1976, orig. 1928); Estelle Stewart, *The Cost of American Almshouses* (Washington, D.C.: Government Printing Office, 1925); Harry Evans, *The American Poorhouse and Its Inmates* (Des Moines, Iowa: 1926); A. Kennedy, *The Ohio Poor Laws and Its Administration* (Chicago: University of Chicago Press, 1934); Sophonisba Breckinridge, *The Illinois Poor Law and Its Administration* (Chicago: University of Chicago Press, 1939); G. Brown, *The Development of Poor Relief in Kansas* (Chicago: University of Chicago Press, 1935); J. Brown, *Public Relief, 1929–1939* (New York: Bureau of Research, 1940); and I. Bruce, and E. Eickhoff, *The Michigan Poor Law* (Chicago: University of Chicago Press, 1936).

17. In addition to the city farm of Lewiston, Maine, which lasted until 1967, four out of the other five institutions studied retained aspects of their poorhouse origins for many years. When the Worcester Home Farm inmates were moved to Belmont Home (which eventually became a long-term care facility), many residents continued to be homeless, alcoholic, or non-elderly disabled men, particularly those at the Hilton Building. This building eventually became an alcoholic treatment facility in the 1980s. In Rockingham and Carroll Counties, New Hampshire, despite the renaming of the institutions as "County Home and Hospital," not only were active poor farms maintained but many groups from children, poor women giving birth, homeless people, and other poor continued to be admitted. The rosters of names at Rockingham in the mid-1950s include more non-elderly than elderly people despite the common reference to Rockingham as an "old people's home." In Portland, Maine, in 1946, the prior institutions were renamed as the City Hospital, but according to hospital consultants Neergaard and Craig (Portland Hospital Survey, May 1949, PRPPL), the hospital included both "patients" (131 at the time) and inmates (175 at the time). Neergaard and Craig further criticized the hospital, stating that "a considerable portion of the work is done by inmates or residents, (for example) there is only one paid employee in the laundry" (p. 7). In the four decades that it took the hospital to transition to a long-term

care facility, the Barron Center, a large number of indigent people were admitted who were not elderly. Today, in addition to the nursing home and Alzheimer's center, housing for low-income people exists at the Loring Building.

18. New social historians of the late 1960s and 1970s criticized the assumptions of the "progressiveness" of history. I first ran across the term "Whig version of history" in Marvin Gettleman, "The Whig Interpretation of American History," *Smith College Studies of Social Work* 44, no. 3 (June 1974): 149–57. This term was initially coined by Asa Briggs, "The Welfare State in Historical Perspective," *Archives européennes de sociologie* (1961): 222.

19. The best histories of the poorhouses (see Katz, for example) do stress the complexity of their role. However, since few books or other studies have focused entirely on the history of the almshouse, as opposed to a variety of other topics, these other roles are usually overshadowed by the repressive functions.

20. The U.S. Census started in 1880 counting paupers in a periodic "Paupers in Almshouses" series. The last report issued was in 1923. These are highly imperfect measures, comparable to recent efforts at counting the homeless. They tend to vastly understate paupers by greatly reflecting one-time counts of those housed in poorhouses at a particular time. Additionally, "tramps" or transients, which in some areas were the majority of inmates, were excluded. Other poorhouses did not count single mothers coming to give birth and certain other populations. It is also very unclear what the Census Bureau regarded as an almshouse, particularly in its twentieth-century counts where some were now titled infirmaries and some contained houses of correction and workhouses. Nevertheless, they do provide valuable information on the regional differences in almshouses, and the race, ethnicity, sex, age, and disability status of paupers in almshouses.

In terms of region, the New England states appear to have the most paupers in poorhouses per capita in their population. For example, in 1890, Maine had the eighth-highest per capita rate; New Hampshire, the first; Vermont, eleventh; Massachusetts, third; Rhode Island, fourteenth; and Connecticut, fifth; in 1903, Maine remained eighth; New Hampshire was second; Vermont thirteenth; Massachusetts, fifth; Rhode Island seventh; and Connecticut, fourth (U.S. Census, *Paupers in Almshouses* [Washington, D.C.: Government Printing Office, 1890, 1903]). Although New England had a slightly lower number of people of color than national averages (they were a minimal population of almshouses except in the South), New England had by far the highest number of foreign-born paupers.

Some observers suggested Massachusetts "and perhaps other New England states" along with Wisconsin "should be excluded from the universal criticism of the almshouse" (Franklin Sanborn in his 1884 survey cited in Frank J. Bruno, *Trends in Social Work 1874–1956* [New York: Columbia, 1957], 80). I could find no real confirmation of this opinion, however, and any statement would be fairly anecdotal. Noted social scientist Amos Warner, *American Charities: A Study in Philanthropy and Economics* (New Brunswick, N.J.: Transaction, 1989; orig. 1894), 211–12, praises Massachusetts in the 1890s, and Estelle Stewart's 1925 study has a number of positive things to say about Massachusetts but was silent on the other New England states (*The Cost of American Almshouses* [Washington, D.C.: Government Printing Office, 1925]).

It should be noted, on the other hand, that the large per capita number of paupers in almshouses in New England should not be used to argue mistreatment of the poor. It appears that some regions, such as the Southern states, provided little or no social welfare of any type (indoor or outdoor relief).

21. Rothman's *Discovery of the Asylum* and Katz's work in *In the Shadow of the Poorhouse* as well as Katz's *Poverty and Policy in American History* (New York: Academic Press, 1983) provide good overviews of the early poorhouses. Even in the limited number of dissertations and single-city studies I have read, the origins of the houses draw more attention than the later periods. It is possible this is due to the fact that name changes (county home, poor farm) that occurred later made the subject matter more diffuse or that the almshouse and workhouse are perceived as being a more central part of American history in the early to middle nineteenth century than later on.

22. See Stewart, *The Cost of American Almshouses.* There were only sixteen almshouses in the nation with 501–2,000 inmates and only five with over 2,000 inmates.

23. One caveat to my earlier distinction of poorhouse versus workhouse is that most of those sentenced to workhouses and houses of correction were not only for minor infractions but also poverty-related ones such as vagrancy, begging, and nonsupport of family. The vast majority of offenses were for drunkenness. In Rockingham County, which has among the best records of its inmates in both facilities (poorhouse and workhouse), I found some, but only a little, overlap in inmates (about five to seven of the workhouse inmates each year were usually also known to the poorhouse). Given the relatively small size of the area's population, it may be that known "drunks" were placed in the workhouse, while the law rarely bothered those perceived as more "deserving." There were some cases, however, in all areas in which poor people got themselves arrested to be brought to a warm place in the winter.

CHAPTER 2

1. Charles Francis, "Homelessness in Portland's History: The Case of Adeline Nott," *Discover Maine* (1997): 1, 27–28.

2. Interview with Lorraine Comeau, Merita Fournier, and Gertrude Mynahan on April 5, 2003.

3. Considerable misunderstanding exists between those authors, mostly on the political left, and those historians and social scientists of liberal or centrist persuasion. See, for example, Walter Trattner, editor, *Social Welfare or Social Control* (Knoxville: University of Tennessee Press, 1983), which strongly attacks the Piven and Cloward thesis about "regulating the poor." First, I have never read the social control theorists to suggest that other functions, such as altruism, were not at all part of social welfare institutions. But, second, it may be true that a sole emphasis on social control and repression suggests too much an intentionality and clear purpose, which is not always demonstrable. For example, some poor farms began simply as a way to "group the poor" and seemed aimed at financial efficiency or even as a reform from auctioning and boarding out. As I read the social control

analysis, critics of American society and social welfare are indicating how the system inevitably works as a secondary institution in support of a capitalist society. Where critics often get confused is that this macro-level analysis does not explain (nor do I think it was meant to explain) how groups, towns, and other actors acted on a micro level.

4. David Rothman, *The Discovery of the Asylum* (Boston: Little, Brown, 1971; new editions, 1980, 1990).

5. The rejection of the workhouse in the late eighteenth century is cited in J. Lenane, "Haverhill: The Town and City," *Haverhill Gazette*, December 19, 1987, SCHPL.

6. Untitled document found in uncatalogued material from 1820s courtesy of the SCHPL. This document, complete with statistics from the first two years of the poorhouse and careful comparison with previous year's budget, is clearly from 1821.

7. Untitled document, 1820, SCHPL.

8. Untitled document, 1821, SCHPL.

9. This date is claimed in an unpublished manuscript by Malon Clark, "The House at the Edge of Town: The Portland Almshouse to 1850," 1985, BCF, and has been incorporated into various documents at the Barron Center. However, I found no independent verification of this date.

10. Francis, "Homelessness in Portland's History."

11. Francis, "Homelessness in Portland's History."

12. Francis, "Homelessness in Portland's History."

13. Robert Kelso, *Public Poor Relief In Massachusetts 1620–1920* (Boston: Houghton Mifflin, 1922), 118–19.

14. Annual Report of the Overseers of the Poor, Worcester, Mass., 1901.

15. Annual Report of the Overseers of the Poor, Worcester, Mass., 1901.

16. See, for example, the film *The Saint of Fort Washington* (1995) based on the Fort Washington Armory in Upper Manhattan; see also Gwendolyn Dordick's account in her book *Something Left to Lose* (Philadelphia: Temple University Press, 1997, chapter 3).

17. Interview with Comeau, Fournier, and Mynahan, April 5, 2003.

18. Annette Glasscock, "Lewiston Poor Farm 1882–1967." Unpublished paper at AHS, Auburn, Maine. Glasscock interviewed a farmhand (who remained anonymous) and Yvette Brochu, the last matron of the Lewiston City Farm (1942–1967), both of whom had similar views of the city farm as the Landrys. See also accounts of Rockingham and Carroll County homes throughout.

19. The sisters habitually refused with derision the label "poor farm," although they acknowledged the Lewiston City Farm was a part of the national phenomenon of poorhouses and poor farms.

20. Earlier interview with Mynahan, Fournier, and Friedman from A. Williams, ed., *The Experience of the Great Depression in Lewiston-Auburn, Maine*, vol. 2 (1998), 92. The French Canadian community is often stereotyped as being conservative. Certainly they were hard workers and, no doubt, the community would have supported the general trade-off between work and public assistance.

21. Williams, *The Experience of the Great Depression.*

22. Glasscock, "Lewiston Poor Farm."

23. See "Charge Breen Toured City in the Poor Farm Probe," *Lewiston Daily Sun*, May 21, 1929, for Louis Philippe Gagne's charges against Alderman Breen. These charges were also made in "Landry's Friends Blame Breen for Farm Exposé," *Lewiston Daily Sun*, June 4, 1929.

24. See my argument in David Wagner, *Checkerboard Square: Culture and Resistance in a Homeless Community* (Boulder, Colo.: Westview, 1993), particularly chapters 6–8.

25. County Commissioners' Annual Report, Rockingham County, N.H., 1908.

26. Catalogue (undated), "Catalogue of Poor Farm Library, Rockingham County," NHSL. The annual reports from the 1890s on cite the contributions of charitable groups in the neighboring towns of Exeter and Epping to the library and other donations.

27. I asked the families of the superintendents in Rockingham County and Lewiston (Win Hilton and the Landry sisters) about the distinction, as well as the employees of the Rockingham and Carroll County homes (Northrup and Jacobson, Moody, and the Haneys), and none of them had much awareness of the distinction between "inmates" and "boarders." The newspapers in Rockingham County, however, did publicize the private-pay inmates who wanted to stay at the county home. Why there was no record of boarders at the Worcester Home Farm or the Haverhill City Farm is not known. Perhaps those who could afford to do so went elsewhere or perhaps the homes had policies different from those in the other two states or simply didn't record boarders in the same way.

28. The house of correction only housed people with misdemeanor offenses of up to one year, with most being sentenced for only a few weeks, the vast majority for drunkenness. Some prisoners, though, were "vagrants," again making the "prisoner/inmate" distinction a bit tough.

29. The similarity in the popular culture is noticeable in that inmates named a rather decrepit building at Worcester's Belmont Home the "Hilton" in an effort at satire; the name stuck, and the building was known for years as the Hilton Building.

30. Interview by author with Win Hilton, November 26, 2002.

31. Letter of May 14, 1941, RCCF.

32. The scrapbooks (PHF) contain written permission from Mr. Hilton for the ex-prisoner to publish the piece, but it is unclear if it was ever published or if Dale Scott was a real name or pseudonym.

33. Michael Katz, *In the Shadow of the Poorhouse: A Social History of Welfare in America* (New York: Basic Books, 1986; second edition, 1996).

34. Interview by author June 17, 2003, with Lawrence and Becky Haney, Anne Jacobsen, and Ginny Moody, all former staff members of the Carroll County Home. The Haneys' adoptive father died there and Moody was born there.

35. "Will Close County Home Annex," *Granite State News*, May 31, 1979, from scrapbooks at CCCO.

36. "Days May Be Numbered at Old Carroll County Complex," *Granite State News*, June 27, 1979, CCCO.

37. "Days May Be Numbered."

38. Interestingly, a slightly different poorhouse episode occurred in the early 1990s in Maine. The Town of Sanford in southwestern Maine, population approximately 20,000, had seen its poorhouse turn into an old age home/nursing home.

Suffering a loss in income from low reimbursement, the town proposed selling the home, creating a great deal of controversy, particularly from the point of view of some residents who had lived in the home for decades. The town eventually passed in referendum a proposal to sell the home and the residents were all moved to a new facility.

CHAPTER 3

1. Superintendent's Report, Annual Report, Rockingham County, N.H., 1910.

2. Overseers of the Poor Report, Worcester, Massachusetts, 1901.

3. David Wagner, *What's Love Got to Do with It? A Critical Look at American Charity* (New York: New Press, 2001).

4. Yet again, in suggesting this, I do not mean to suggest that many officials, and certainly most workers at the poorhouse, were not often themselves compassionate people

5. David Schneider, *The History of Public Welfare in New York* (New York: New York State, 1939), 74.

6. The rules and regulations of the Portland Alms-House were found between the annual reports of the city of 1838 and 1845 with no explanation, MHS.

7. David Rothman, *Discovery of the Asylum* (Boston: Little, Brown, 1971; new editions, 1980, 1990).

8. Inmates were used as nurses at almshouses, and then city hospitals, for at least another six or seven decades; see, for example, Harry E. Dowling, *City Hospitals: The Undercare of the Underprivileged* (Cambridge: Harvard University Press, 1982). See also chapter 5 where an inmate assigned as a nurse to another inmate in the 1895 Haverhill almshouse provoked an investigation of the poorhouse by lodging a complaint.

9. Worcester's 1867 rules and regulations were reproduced in J. Weninger, *Do Much Honor: The Story of Belmont Home* (Worcester, Mass., 1987), 7.

10. Untitled document found in uncatalogued material from 1820s courtesy of the SCHPL. This document, complete with statistics from the first two years of the poorhouse and careful comparison with previous year's budget, was clearly from 1821.

11. D. Hodgkin, *Managing the Poor in Lewiston, Maine, 1795–1863*. Paper presented at Washburn Humanities Conference, Northern New England in the Nineteenth Century, Norland, Livermore, Maine, June 8, 2001, 10–11.

12. Esther McClure, *More Than a Roof: The Development of Minnesota Poor Farms and Homes for the Aged* (St. Paul: Minnesota Historical Society, 1968), 20–22. McClure is focusing in these pages on the relatively early history of the Minnesota poor farms in the 1850–1870s.

13. Both Haverhill and Worcester reports mention the use of woodlots during depressions to allow the poor to cut wood, a commodity often more expensive than food in New England.

14. Portland Committee to Investigate the Almshouse, originally published in *The Advertiser*, quoted from pp. 23–25 of unpublished manuscript of Malon Clark, "The House at the Edge of Town: The Portland Almshouse to 1850," 1985, BCF.

15. Report of Overseers of the Poor, City of Lewiston, Maine, 1888, 93.

16. Report of County Commissioners, Carroll County, N.H., 1879.

17. Report of County Commissioners, Rockingham County, N.H., 1896.

18. Frances Fox Piven and Richard Cloward, *Regulating the Poor: The Functions of Social Welfare* (New York: Vintage, 1971).

19. Clark, "The House," BCF.

20. Cited in Roy Brown, *Public Poor Relief in North Carolina* (New York: Arno Press, 1976, orig. 1928), 70.

21. Evans quoted in Michael Katz, *In the Shadow of the Poorhouse* (New York: Basic Books, 1986; second edition, 1996), 30.

22. Report of Overseers of the Poor, Worcester, Mass., 1905.

23. Carroll County Commissioners Annual Report, 1878

24. Report of the Overseers of the Poor, Lewiston 1896.

25. Report of the Overseers of the Poor, Worcester, 1900

26. Amos Warner, *American Charities: A Study in Philanthropy and Economics* (New Brunswick, N.J.: Transaction, 1989, orig. 1894), 205.

27. By the third decade of the twentieth century, Haverhill and Portland, on one side, and Lewiston and Worcester, on the other, most differ, with the New Hampshire homes falling in between. Whether intentional or influenced more by their particular demographics, Haverhill and Portland took Warner's advice and became more and more homes for the aged, ill, and disabled, while Lewiston and Worcester, by aiding unemployed men, seemed more of a labor repository. The New Hampshire almshouses also came to include a larger percentage of the aged and ill, but still included a fair number of people of all ages, including working-age males.

28. Livingston quoted in Rothman, *Discovery of the Asylum*, 188–89.

29. Letchworth quoted in Katz, *Poverty and Policy in American History*, 68.

30. I am not arguing against work or tasks as a way of keeping one's mind occupied, learning skills, or even sharing the household chores. I am suggesting only the irony in the mission of the almshouse/poorhouse in teaching the discipline of work to working-class and poor people, who knew a great deal about work.

31. All cities provided work during depressions, but there are some interesting examples of overseers actually serving as job placers; for example, in the Lewiston's 1890 Annual Report of the Overseers of the Poor, the overseers state, "we have procured employment, in many cases, for those who were able to work, but were unemployed." In 1896, they reported communicating with the public works department to secure jobs (the Minutes of the Overseers of the Poor, Lewiston, Maine, 4/20/1896, LCHV); in 1921, in response to a downturn, the Portland overseers called for jobs to be created in the parks and public works departments (minutes of Portland Overseers of the Poor, 9/21/1921, MHS); and Haverhill annual reports make frequent mention of provision of public works jobs, particularly in 1898, 1899, and 1921.

32. Hoyt quoted in Schneider, *The History of Public Welfare in New York*, 27.

33. Quote of Superintendent Bonney from "Over the Hill to the Poorhouse," *Lewiston Weekly*, February 11, 1882, 2.

CHAPTER 4

1. Amos Warner, *American Charities: A Study in Philanthropy and Economics* (New Brunswick, N.J.: Transaction, 1989, orig. 1894), 220.

2. Annual Report of the Overseers of the Poor, Worcester, Mass., 1895.

3. In response to demands of reformers, and in some areas, local officials themselves, states moved to bring the "insane" to asylums. However, there was never enough room for all the "insane" to be institutionalized. Hence, they left responsibility for those who were "mildly insane" (never very defined) to local officials.

4. Peter Temin, ed., *Engines of Enterprise: An Economic History of New England*, (Cambridge, Mass.: Harvard University Press, 2000), 156.

5. Annual Report of the Overseers of the Poor, Worcester, Mass., 1898.

6. An important caveat to all numbers was the considerable presence of transients. Carroll County recorded, for example, several hundred "transients" without name after its annual list of residents of its poorhouse. The greatest percentage of transients served per long-term residents I found was in Deering, Maine, which merged with Portland in 1899. In 1898, they served 1,430 "transients and tramps" while only thirty-two residents were ever inmates (City of Deering Annual Report, 1898). The large number of transients and tramps, even though the numbers are probably not distinct individuals but the number of times a tramp was aided, supports comments made in chapter 1, note 20.

7. Portland, Maine, Overseers of the Poor, 1897–1898, 130.

8. "Poor Farm Scenes," *Sunday Times* (Portland), April 2, 1899, MHS.

9. "Over the Hill to the Poorhouse," *Lewiston Weekly*, February 11, 1882, 2; D. Hodgkin, "Managing the Poor in Lewiston, Maine, 1795–1863," 12–17. Hodgkin notes the moving of the two blind brothers to the poor farm in 1839.

10. "Over the Hill to the Poorhouse."

11. "Praised the Wood Pile," *Lewiston Evening Journal*, April 5, 1893.

12. "After One Hundred Years of Continuous Usefulness Old Almshouse on Portland Street to Be Abandoned" (Portland) *Sunday Telegram*, October 23, 1904, MHS.

13. "Over the Hill to the Poorhouse."

14. "Poor Farm Scenes," *Sunday Times* (Portland), April 2, 1899, MHS.

15. "Poor Farm Scenes."

16. "Poor Farm Scenes."

17. "Poor Mary Belisle," *Lewiston Evening Journal*, April 13, 1893.

18. "Mary Has Left Us," *Lewiston Evening Journal*, April 21, 1893.

19. Champagne is listed in the Lewiston annual reports (which listed names, ages, and nationalities of city farm inmates until 1907) as French (Canadian) and as having been at the almshouse since 1890 (and he was there when records of names ceased). His age changed a bit in the reports but he appears to have been in his thirties or forties when admitted.

20. In the case of Carroll County, information was arrived at by copying the annual reports' list of inmates each year (sometimes necessitating decisions on similar names and ages).

21. I indicated "died in almshouse" only where the report itself indicates this. Hence, the other four simply disappear from the list and could have died at someone's home or at a hospital or other facility.

22. Two inmates, Samuel Sargent and Sarah Whitton, could not be positively ruled in or out, as their last names were quite common on the relief rolls (both outdoor and indoor), so likely had some relations, but I cannot be sure.

23. Susan's husband may have been Jessie Brown, who had a settlement in Ossipee and received aid there prior to going himself to the almshouse in 1901 and dying there in 1903. Brown is such a common name, however, that I cannot tell for sure.

24. Sally Quimby of Moultenboro, who died in the almshouse in 1887 after receiving outdoor aid two years prior, was almost certainly George's mother.

25. We do not, however, know whether this was a self-reported occupation or secured by other means or whether it meant the person was working just prior to admission and, if so, how recently she or he was working prior to being admitted to the almshouse. Because of the statement of occupation by so many inmates, even in depression times, it probably reflects not current employment but the stated trade of the inmate.

26. Not only should 1899 assessments of "insanity" and other "diagnoses" be suspect, but my own experience in contemporary shelters and other facilities suggests a considerable amount of pragmatic and retrospective analysis goes on. There is a strong tendency today because of ideology and funding to find many poor people mentally ill or substance users, as there was back then. It appears in at least some poorhouses that labeled the inmates, that all Irish inmates were labeled "intemperate" and few of the native born. Also inmates themselves may present themselves in a way that influences causation. Some that were identified as "sick," for example, may well have needed housing or aid but found illness a less stigmatizing label.

27. These laws did change from time to time. A good compendium of the state laws as of 1904 appears as an appendix in the U.S. Census's *Paupers in Almshouses*; see pages 43–45 for Maine, Massachusetts, and New Hampshire. Those who did not have town or city settlement became "state paupers" in Maine and Massachusetts and were funded by the state, usually being sent to state poorhouses in Massachusetts, while in New Hampshire, each county was forced to support those who were not town paupers.

28. In my hometown of Portland, city officials and others are always talking of "transients" filling the shelters, and it is my impression that almost every city continues to believe a version of this myth. Sometimes it is true that particularly noticeable homeless people are travelers from afar, but most studies suggest the vast majority of homeless people are from local areas.

29. Letters are numbered in a book of "Correspondence 1896–98," HCHV.

CHAPTER 5

1. "Suspend Judgment," editorial, *Haverhill Evening* Gazette, July 26, 1895, p. 4.
2. Editorial (untitled), *Portland Evening Express*, March 2, 1910, p. 4

3. Almost all published material written on the poorhouse mentions investigations, often discussed on the state level. I found some cities held almost constant investigations—for example, the city of Lewiston, Maine, where generally a continuing political conflict was occurring—and any complaint was fodder for investigation. In a sense, the 1850–1925 period paralleled the post–World War II period in its treatment of the mental hospital. Poorhouses were known as a place where scandal could occur, and a variety of actors, including the press, sought stories that reflected this possibility.

4. Cities, towns, and counties differ in their degree of frankness in records. Since none of the local press is indexed prior to the 1990s, it was impossible to check all time periods thoroughly. As far as can be told, the county system in New Hampshire seemed less subject either to scandal or to investigation and/or to internecine warfare that several of the cities of Massachusetts and Maine had. But it is hard to tell if this had to do with the style of press reportage or with the lack of political heterogeneity in that state compared with the other two states. (New Hampshire for most of this time was completely Republican except in the Manchester area, while political competition characterized the other two states, and compared with Portland, Lewiston, Haverhill, and Worcester, all heavily immigrant cities, New Hampshire was less ethnically and politically heterogenous.)

5. "A Sensational Charge," *Haverhill Evening Gazette*, July 25, 1895, p. 1.

6. The *Haverhill Evening Gazette* from the start protested against the wide attention to the case despite its own banner headlines. It declared "all efforts to put the city physician in an unfavorable light are unjust" and that "state officials had declared the Haverhill almshouse as one of the best in the state" (editorial, July 26, 1895). Savage, in a July 27th article ("In Secret") expressed anger against being "unable to defend himself" and promised to call "for another investigation" if this was not remedied. Some time shortly after, however, he was allowed legal representation, and he did not protest further in the press.

7. "Dr. Anthony Talks" in article "City Fathers Will Investigate," *Haverhill Evening Gazette*, July 26, 1895, p. 4.

8. Sheldon testimony in "All Hearsay," *Haverhill Evening Gazette*, July 29, 1895, p. 6. Interestingly, Doton, unlike many paupers, was listed in Haverhill city directories as a "heel cutter" and may indeed have known Sheldon, who is listed as in the clothing business as "Sheldon and Sargent."

9. Testimony in "Told Stories in Public," *Haverhill Evening Gazette*, August 6, 1895, p. 4.

10. Testimony in "Drawing to a Close," *Haverhill Evening Gazette*, August 8, 1895, p. 1.

11. "What Inmates Say," in "City Fathers Will Investigate," *Haverhill Evening Gazette*, July 26, 1895, p. 4.

12. "What Inmates Say."

13. "Some Other Charges," in "City Fathers Will Investigate," *Haverhill Evening Gazette*, July 26, 1895, p. 5.

14. "Please Burn a Rag," editorial, *Haverhill Evening Gazette*, August 9, 1895, p. 4.

15. "A Causeless Scandal," editorial, *Haverhill Evening Gazette*, August 10, 1895, p. 4.

16. "A Dull Sickening Thud," *Haverhill Evening Gazette*, August 9, 1895, p. 1.

17. "A Dull Sickening Thud."

18. "A Dull Sickening Thud."

19. *Haverhill Evening Gazette* reported as early as July 27th that the committee felt none of the charges were serious and that the farm's officials would be exonerated. On August 5th, it first reported the 6–2 vote "Complete." See also "Can't Agree," *Haverhill Evening Gazette,* August 21, 1895, p. 6 and "Next Time," p. 8.

20. "Can't Agree," August 21, 1895.

21. "Complete Exoneration," *Haverhill Evening Gazette,* September 19, 1895, p. 6.

22. "Complete Exoneration."

23. "Complete Exoneration."

24. P. Hudon, *An Illustrated History of the Lower Merrimack* (Woodland Hills, Calif.: Windsor Publications, 1977), 74–75.

25. "Overseers of the Workhouse," HCHV.

26. Michael Katz makes this point both in his 1983 book, *Poverty and Policy in American History,* and in his 1986 book (revised, 1996), *In the Shadow of the Poorhouse.*

27. The *Haverhill Evening Gazette* reported the "personal investigations" of the inmates in "Complete," August 5, 1895, and "Told Stories in Public," August 6. Quote from "Told Stories."

28. This was admittedly more tricky, as presumably if one could work, one could work on the farm for one's keep. Yet all poorhouses admitted this was often the case. One example from the farm minutes of the Worcester Home Farm in January 5, 1949, under the label "Work on the Side" states, "a number of the men undoubtedly get jobs downtown and let the city furnish them with board and room which allows them spending money," BHF.

29. "A Dull Sickening Thud."

30. See "Can't Agree" and "Editorial: The Almshouse Report," *Evening Gazette,* September 19, 1895.

31. In addition to its smaller size, the overseers of the poor in Haverhill showed remarkable stability. The length of service in this period was nine years for Albert Gale (1903–1912); Oliver Hubbard, four years (he was overseer chair in the 1890s and returned briefly between 1913 and 1917); ten years for John Lane (1917 until his death in 1927); fourteen for Robert Richardson (also interrupted by death, 1899–1913); thirty-four years for James Roche (1903–1937); and twenty-four for Fred West (1913–1937). Both Roche and West survived to be part of the renamed Board of Public Welfare in 1927, such name change coming later to Portland, Worcester, and Lewiston.

32. It should be acknowledged that while Portland was not that much larger a city than Haverhill at the time, its home and hospital was far larger and more complex than Haverhill's.

33. The list is taken from news articles of the *Portland Evening Express,* "Subordinate City Office Nominees," December 13, 1909, and "Seeley Re-elected," December 16, 1909. At the time, the other cities studied had similar systems; they appear at this point to differ only to the degree that the "election" was more or less pro forma in terms of the superintendents, matrons, engineers, nurses, and other positions in the other three cities.

34. The state boards of charities and corrections began in Massachusetts in 1863 and followed later by other states. Reformers succeeded in getting boards appointed to oversee—or at least visit—the "institutions for the poor and infirm." While these were state-appointed boards with a range of members, French appeared frequently in the newspapers promoting a liberal philanthropic approach to these populations.

35. Derrah, quoted in "Too Many Bums in the City Home," *Portland Evening Express*, October 7, 1909, p. 8.

36. "Too Many Bums."

37. "O'Brien's Friends Want Him Again on Board," *Evening Express*, December 9, 1909, p. 12. Note how when political battles surrounded the poorhouse, its identity as the "workhouse" again became prominent. Clearly, O'Brien, with his support of the church, represented the Irish community, who were still far more likely to be poor and sent to the home.

38. "Strong Endorsement for O'Brien's Candidacy," *Evening Express*, December 10, 1909, p. 12.

39. "Letter from David Shwartz," *Evening Express*, December 11, 1909, p. 12.

40. Apparently part of the system in Portland was to ensure one minority party seat. Interestingly, this had been the seat the "Republican friends" of O'Brien sought for him, but instead went to Howe.

41. "Subordinate City Offices Elected," *Evening Express*, December 13, 1909, p. 6. Bowen was a Democrat, and Brown evidently an independent.

42. "Seeley May Be Opposed," *Evening Express*, December 14, 1909, p. 6.

43. Editorial (untitled), *Evening Express*, December 14, 1909, p. 4.

44. "Seeley Re-elected," *Evening Express*, December 16, 1909, p. 6.

45. See Estelle Stewart, *The Cost of American Almshouses* (Washington, D.C.: Government Printing Office, 1925), 39–40.

46. "Overseers Can't Agree," *Evening Express*, December 21, 1909.

47. "Fail to Break Deadlock," *Evening Express*, January 20, 1910.

48. "Fail to Break Deadlock."

49. "Poor Overseers Are No Nearer an Agreement," *Evening Express*, February 10, 1910, p. 9

50. "Seeleyites and Antis Stand Pat," *Evening Express*, January 6, 1910, p. 6.

51. "Seeley's Report Was Amended," *Evening Express*, April 7, 1910, p. 8.

52. "To Abolish Overseers," *Evening Express*, March 17, 1910, p. 1. Legislation was proposed to change the overseers to a three-member appointed board. An even more drastic measure was proposed the year before, to replace the overseers with just one appointed official ("Remove City's Poor Overseers," *Evening Express*, February 17, 1909). Proposals of this sort did not pass until the board was abolished in Portland in 1924.

53. Minutes of the Overseers of the Poor, Portland, Maine, May 18, 1920, and June 1, 1920, MHS Archive.

54. Mayor's Address, Annual Report, City of Portland, Maine, 1920, 6.

55. Minutes of the Overseers of the Poor, Portland, Maine, MHS, May 6, 1919, for approval of Horton's trip to Atlantic City.

56. MHS, May 18, 1920.

57. Obituary of Percy Horton, August 24, 1944, obituary file, MHS.

58. Harry Evans, *The American Poor Farm and Its Inmates* (Des Moines, Iowa: 1926), 6.

59. Evans, as well as Brown, Stewart, and other contemporaries, believed the poorhouses were serving as a major breeding ground for illegitimate children, and particularly for feeble-minded and insane offspring. Many of the critics noted from the 1890–1930 period also objected to interracial liaisons in poorhouses. Although these facts do not undermine their humanitarian motives, it does suggest that some of the concerns of reformers had to do with the lives of poor people themselves, which would agitate them in the slums or at workplaces as much as in a poorhouse.

60. The vote for a city manager system in Portland was supported by two large rallies of the Ku Klux Klan and was opposed by ethnic minorities, though the "Committee of 100," who spearheaded the effort, disowned the KKK support. See A. Barnes, editor, *Greater Portland Celebration 350* (Portland: Guy Gannett Publishing, 1984), 146.

CHAPTER 6

1. Letter of January 26, 1937, RCCF.

2. Report of the meeting of the Farm Committee of the Board of Public Welfare held May 6, 1949, BHF.

3. Formerly the city's almshouse; I was unable to establish the exact date of the name change. The move of the Portland poorhouse in 1904 to the Deering Farm may have initiated the name change. It is difficult to determine as well what the change actually meant, as the annual reports of the overseers continue to discuss the "almshouse" and "town farm" separately from the hospital, and these terms seem to coexist for three more decades.

4. Minutes of the Overseers of the Poor, Portland, Maine, MHS, 1913–1923, entries of March 13, 1913; April 2, 1913; May 7, 1913; May 20, 1913; September 15, 1913.

5. Annual Report of the Overseers of the Poor, Portland, Maine, 1914.

6. Minutes of the Overseers of the Poor, Portland, Maine, 1913–1923, MHS, August 20, 1914.

7. Minutes, March 4, 1914; April 10, 1914; September 2, 1914.

8. Minutes, September 20, 1916, and October 5, 1921.

9. Minutes, May 3, 1916.

10. Minutes, October 15, 1917.

11. Minutes, July 5, 1916.

12. Throughout the history of the colonies and United States, local relief laws held family members responsible for the cost of care of relatives. This was obviously impossible if the family had insufficient resources. However, there were cases, such as presumably Armstrong's, where relatives had some assets and were sued by cities and towns.

13. Minutes of the Overseers of the Poor, Portland, Maine, MHS, January 3, 1917.

14. Minutes, March 20, 1916.
15. Minutes, April 20, 1916.
16. Minutes, September 15, September 20, 1916.
17. Minutes, March 6, 1917.
18. Minutes, January 17, 1918.
19. Minutes, March 6, 1923.

20. The number of paupers given aid in Portland peaked with 1,988 in 1914. It never went as high in the years after, with a low of 1,302 in 1920 and a high of 1,769 in 1916. However, costs of the department went steadily up from $61,623 in 1913 to $144,399 in 1923. Some of this more than doubling was accounted for by Maine's mother's aid program going into effect in 1917. Revenue brought in by the farm varied between $7,500 and $11,000 a year in this period. Annual Reports of the Overseers of the Poor, City of Portland, years 1913–1923.

21. I cross-referenced the many hundreds of letters and applications for relief at RCCF with a list of inmates of the Rockingham Home between the mid-1930s and early 1940s. Although I looked at hundreds of letters, only about four dozen were both substantive enough to record and involved the county home/poorhouse as opposed to unrelated issues. Of the letters, about three-quarters seemed punitive to this observer, with threats to remove people to the "poor farm" or efforts to implement sterilization. Others were humanitarian in nature, and some were, of course, ambiguous.

22. All names of people (inmates and officials) after 1920 have been changed in the interest of confidentiality except where I am quoting from news reports, as opposed to letters or notes.

23. Letter of January 26,1937, RCCF.
24. Letter of June 29, 1936, RCCF.
25. Letter of April 1, 1937, RCCF.
26. Letter of September 2, 1936, RCCF.
27. Letter of October 13, 1936, RCCF.
28. Letter of October 20, 1936, RCCF.
29. Letter of October 22, 1936, RCCF.
30. Letter of October 23, 1936, RCCF.
31. Letter of October 26, 1936, RCCF.
32. Letter of March 3, 1936, RCCF.
33. Letter of March 5, 1936, RCCF.

34. Letters of November 1, 1937, regarding visitor assisting elderly man; letter of June 24, 1935, regarding the mental hospitalization of a man's wife; and letters of June 20 and 22 and July 8, 1937, regarding the positive response to an evidently ill man seeking a return to the county home for medical care, RCCF.

35. Letter of January 9, 1936, RCCF.
36. Letter of January 16, 1936, RCCF.
37. Letters of October 24, 1941, and November 15, 1941, RCCF.

38. Mimeographed six-page document entitled "The Worcester Home Farm," 1946, WHM.

39. Untitled document, papers of BHF.
40. City of Worcester, "Duties of Barracks Attendant," November 25, 1942, BHF.
41. Farm Committee meeting, Thursday April 8, 1948, papers of BHF.

42. Farm Committee, April 8.

43. Farm Committee meeting, January 5, 1949, BHF.

44. Report of the meeting of the Farm Committee of the Board of Public Welfare held May 6, 1949, BHF.

45. Meeting of the Farm Committee, June 7, 1949, BHF.

46. Memo "Re: Gardenside Barracks," undated, BHF.

47. "General Policies to Be Carried Out at the Worcester Home Farm," undated memo, but after January 1, 1950, WHM.

48. See notes from April 8, 1948, Farm Committee meeting on entertainment; July 9, 1948, on the inmate barber; and February 9, 1949, on the blind inmate, BHF.

49. The 1953 tornado completely destroyed the Gardenside Barracks, and ripped off the roof of the infirmary and the chimney of the power plant. Seven residents were killed and thirty-five injured; see the report of the superintendent of Brookside Home, year ending December 31, 1953. For some of the strife accompanying the decision to move, see "Belmont-Brookside Plans Take Shape," *Worcester Telegram*, April 12, 1955, and "Worcester's Home Farm Marks End of an Era" in *Sunday Telegram*, December 18, 1955. For some of the political battles around the closure of the Lewiston City Farm, see "Tug of War Looms on Lewiston Move to Close Farm," *Lewiston Sun Journal*, November 1, 1964.

50. See Weninger, *Do Much Honor: The Story of Belmont Home*, 1987.

51. While clearly more study is needed to generalize, it appears that the longevity of the city farms can be related to the need to maintain a local labor force in Worcester and Lewiston. Both were not only major industrial centers but also nonunionized centers (unlike the shoe shops of Haverhill, Mass., for example) and additionally were somewhat cut off from major routes of travel, unlike Haverhill or Portland. Rockingham County occupies a middle ground since it included rural and small urban areas, with some factories and mills. The county home continued to have a high number of men of working age according to its lists of inmates into the 1940s and 1950s. Unlike the situation in Lewiston where city farm inmates picked up the garbage through the 1960s and the discussion of the "barracks" men in Worcester doing manual work, it is not clear by the 1940s how many of these inmates were able-bodied, as informants remember the home as "pretty much an old age home" by this time.

CHAPTER 7

1. Physician's Report, County Commissioners Annual Report, Rockingham County, 1912.

2. "Excerpts from Diary written by [name] while he was employed as an attendant at the Worcester Home Farm," 1936–1938, BHF.

3. Estelle Stewart, *The Cost of American Almshouses* (Washington, D.C.: Government Printing Office, 1925), 39–40.

4. Esther McClure, *More Than a Roof: The Development of Minnesota Poor Farms and Homes for the Aged* (St. Paul: Minnesota Historical Society, 1968), 95.

5. Interview with Win Hilton, November 26, 2002.

6. Interview with Comeau, Fournier, and Mynahan on April 5, 2003.

7. For Landry background, see interview with Comeau, Fournier, and Myna-han on April 5, 2003; for Parkhurst background, see "Matron Many Years," *Worcester Telegram*, November 7, 1893 (obituary).

8. See "Matron Many Years" and "Tribute to the Matron," *Worcester Telegram*, November 7, 1893.

9. "City Officials Attended," *Worcester Telegram*, November 9, 1893.

10. Citations to the Marble booklet are all from Weninger, *Do Much Honor: The Story of Belmont Home*, 1987, 20–22. I was unable to locate the booklet itself.

11. Weninger, *Do Much Honor*, 22.

12. New Hampshire State Board of Charities and Corrections Annual Report, 1900, 60.

13. County Commissioners Annual Report, Rockingham County, 1907.

14. PHF.

15. Brown, *Public Poor Relief in North Carolina*, 129.

16. Sophonisba Breckinridge, *Illinois Poor Law and Its Administration* (Chicago: University of Chicago Press, 1939), 89–90.

17. See annual reports of the City of Haverhill, 1904–1909, particularly the mayor's address and the physician's reports.

18. Mayor's Address, City of Haverhill Annual Report, 1905.

19. Mayor's Address, City of Haverhill Annual Report, 1906.

20. "Replies to Critics," *Haverhill Evening Gazette*, February 24, 1906, SCHPL.

21. Annual Report of Physician, City of Haverhill, 1908.

22. Annual Report of Physician, City of Haverhill, 1909, 1910.

23. "The Alms House: An Interesting, Gradual Metamorphosis," *Haverhill Evening Gazette*, September 30, 1975, SCHPL; B. Gallagher, "Glynn Has Changed since Grazing-Cow Days," *Eagle Tribune*, February 25, 1999, SCHPL.

24. The Mitchell Memorial Hospital, as a county hospital, had a short life and was closed down by the county in the 1960s. However, the Mitchell building remains today in Brentwood, N.H., as the central administrative unit of the Rockingham County Nursing Home.

25. Physician Report, County Commissioners Annual Report, Rockingham County, 1910.

26. Physician Report, Rockingham County Annual Report, 1912.

27. See, for example, interview of a farmhand in Lewiston done by Annette Glasscock, "Lewiston Poor Farm 1882–1967," unpublished paper at AHS, Auburn, Maine.

28. Although the rules are titled "Worcester City Almshouse," dated February 18, 1890, I believe the rules were related to the insane or hospital unit since the word "patient" is always used at a time when "inmate" was the name for non-medical cases, WPL collection.

29. Minutes of the Overseers of the Poor, 1913–1923, Portland, Maine, MHS.

30. All of the quotes are from a document entitled "Excerpts from Diary written by [name] while he was employed as an attendant at the Worcester Home Farm," BHF. The diary was clearly retyped by someone. It is not clear how the two-page, single-spaced diary written by the attendant got into the files of Ellery Royal, the last superintendent, and what happened to the attendant.

31. Interview June 17, 2003, with Lawrence and Becky Haney, Anne Jacobsen, and Ginny Moody.

32. Chaplains were probably the closest to this role. Annual reports of the Carroll and Rockingham County, N.H., chaplains (although all the homes had religious services, the other four did not have extensive reports by clergy) spoke of sin and redemption and setting the proper standards of Christianity for the inmates, at least through the third decade of the twentieth century.

CHAPTER 8

1. David Rothman, "The First Shelters," *On Being Homeless: Historical Perspectives,* edited by Rick Beard (New York: Museum of the City of New York, 1987), 19.

2. Elliot Currie, *Crime and Punishment in America* (New York: Henry Holt, 1998), 10.

3. Interview with Landry daughters Comeau, Fournier, and Mynahan, April 5, 2003; with Carroll County former staff members Haneys, Jacobsen, and Moody, June 17, 2003.

4. Cited in Philip Popple and Leslie Leighninger, *Social Work, Social Welfare, and American Society,* 5th ed. (Boston, Mass.: Allyn and Bacon, 2002), 589.

5. For two important discussions of how unmarried women were treated differently from married women by the Social Security Act, see Mimi Abramovitz, *Regulating the Lives of Women* (Boston: South End Press, 1996) and Gwendolyn Mink, *Welfare's End* (Ithaca, N.Y.: Cornell University Press, 1998).

6. Michael Harrington's classic *The Other America* (New York: Macmillan, 1962) was as powerful as it was at the time due to the lack of politicization of poverty. The poverty rate stood at nearly one-fifth of the nation as late at 1959; see Sar Levitan, *Programs in Aid of the Poor,* 6th ed. (Baltimore: Johns Hopkins University Press, 1990), 5–6.

7. We lack a great deal of data for the later occupants of the poorhouse. No ledgers now exist in Worcester or Lewiston, though we know from material retrieved in Worcester (see chapter 6) about the large number of working-age males. In Lewiston, as with Carroll and Rockingham Counties (which have ledgers going into the 1950s, but do not identify inmates who are disabled), we can only speculate. Former staff at Carroll County, the Landry sisters, the Glasscock work on Lewiston, and Win Hilton's discussion of Rockingham give the impression of mostly elderly and disabled inmates by the 1950s, but able-bodied people may have come and gone quickly, therefore leaving less of a lasting impression on living witnesses.

8. Lawrence Powell, John Williamson, and Kenneth Branco, *The Senior Rights Movement* (New York: Twayne, 1996), chapter 3.

9. See, for example, Andrew Scull, *Decarceration,* 2nd ed. (New Brunswick, N.J.: Rutgers University Press, 1984).

10. I first became aware of the term *transinstitutionalization* in the very detailed and cogent analysis of James Trent, who proves that most developmentally disabled people moved not out "into the community" from the state schools for the retarded but to nursing homes and other institutions. See James Trent, *Inventing the Feeble Mind* (Berkeley: University of California Press, 1994). The term is now widely used.

11. Cynthia Bogard, *Seasons Such as These: How Homelessness Took Shape in America* (New York: Aldine de Gruyter, 2003). See also Joel Blau, *The Visible Poor: Homelessness in the United States* (New York: Oxford University Press, 1992), chapters 7–10.

12. Lipsky and Smith's article makes a cogent analysis of how social problems that are defined as "temporary emergencies" lead to quick surface political solutions. See Michael Lipsky and John Smith, "When Social Problems Are Treated as Emergencies," *Social Service Review* 53 (1989): 5–25.

13. It was not until the mid-1980s and after that grassroots activism such as efforts to form a National Union of the Homeless and a large number of "tent-city"-style protests had become common that more radical activists and scholars turned to addressing poverty and homelessness at its root causes. Some areas do attempt a more radical approach; for example, in York County in southern Maine, a housing approach, as opposed to a service approach, dominates, and activists have stressed building homes for the homeless rather than counseling or charity.

14. In addition to the author's experience with homeless shelters, mostly in New York City and Maine, research assistants Angela Desrochers and Sheila Foley contacted New England shelters located in the approximate areas as the almshouses discussed.

15. City of Portland, Department of Health and Human Services, Division of Social Services–Oxford Street Shelter, "Resident Contract" undated.

16. "Guest Brochure," Pine Street Inn, Boston, Mass., undated.

17. See a wonderful set of pictures, including the "loafers hall" in Cole, "Boston's Pauper Institutions," and numerous pictures in *On Being Homeless: Historical Perspectives*, edited by Rick Beard (New York: Museum of the City of New York, 1987), particularly of the Blackwell's Island almshouses.

18. See Beard, *On Being Homeless*. Also for views of Blackwell's Island, New York almshouse, see www.nyc1044.com courtsey of the Roosevelt Island Historical Society.

During approximately 1880 to 1905, all the cities studied had housing for transients and tramps at their police stations. Each year under the city marshal or chief of police reports, the numbers were listed and reached as high as 11,462 in Worcester in 1898 (the counts include obviously repeat users, as small cities such as Haverhill reported as many as 4,000 for a year). The famous author and photographer Jacob Riis shot quite a few photos of the police lodging houses in the 1890s New York; see *How the Other Half Lives: Studies among the Tenements of New York* (New York: Hill and Wang, 1957).

19. Neither population growth nor poverty rate growth can be blamed for poorer conditions in today's shelters. New England has been stable in population, and several of the cities studied—Haverhill, Lewiston, and Worcester—have actually declined in population in the last four decades. Although we do not have good measures of poverty rates for each year before the last four decades, generally there was far more poverty in America and New England in the pre-1946 period than since. Differences are more likely structural and political. Land values have risen enormously, and buildings like homeless shelters are among the last places large expenditures will be made. Perhaps most important, though, is the low political priority of the poor. One hundred years ago, the inclusion of the "respectable" elder, widowed, and crippled may have led to the poorhouses being

seen as more of a priority. Further, while some transients and illiterate paupers could not vote, political machines did depend on the poor for their success. Poor voters have very little importance today in general and in the local areas studied.

20. There are such institutions euphemistically called "wet shelters" in which alcoholic clients are let in, but they have become few and far between.

21. In Maine and New Hampshire, most able-bodied clients must put in twenty hours of workfare or community service.

22. One example is a group called "Bring the People Back Home," led by a man named Winston Gordon who developed a program in the early 1990s to bring homeless New Yorkers to a farm in Dutchess County. There is also a project in Maine that takes homeless people to work in a farm; see Eric Brandt-Meyer and Sandra Butler, "Food for People, Not for Profit: Meanings of a Farm Project for Homeless and Very Poor Participants," *Journal of Progressive Human Services* 10, no. 1 (1999): 53–66. Although these programs certainly do not entail the same disenfranchisement that went along with the poor-farm model, I have found it interesting how much the appeal of farm work and growing crops has, at least in New England, for homeless activists. Many do not seem aware of the long history of poor farms!

23. "Guest Brochure," Pine Street Inn, 8 (pages are unnumbered).

24. The two best studies I have seen of how people are treated day to day at shelters are Gwendolyn Dordick, *Something Left to Lose* (Philadelphia: Temple University Press, 1997), particularly chapters 2 and 3; and Amir B. Marvasti, *Being Homeless* (Lanham, Md.: Lexington Books, 2003), particularly chapters 5–9.

25. David Wagner, *Checkerboard Square: Culture and Resistance in a Homeless Community* (Boulder, Colo.: Westview Press, 1993).

26. Maine State Board of Charities and Corrections, 1914–1918. In 1916, the overseers agreed to a separate eating table for prisoners and in 1918 to separate sleeping quarters. See minutes of Overseers of the Poor in Portland, May 19, 1916, and July 17, 1918, MHS.

27. There, of course, will be many who protest either that today's world is so much more violent than fifty or one hundred years ago and, hence, much more security is needed, or that somehow drug possession or drunk driving is far worse than the typical charges of years ago. My view is that it is very debatable that today's world is really more violent than American society has been throughout its history. Nor does it seem to me that the drug war and other behavioral wars are apprehending at all a different type of criminal from years past. Drinking, for example, was the major offense punished in the workhouse and house of correction, and certainly this included inmates who engaged in behavior dangerous to others such as domestic violence. The other difficulty in my mind with these protests is that all of them fail to consider how the very harshness of the American system of criminal justice and social welfare, as well as other elements of our culture, may produce this very violence and crime that is then supposed to have arisen from so much "bad behavior."

28. Nancy Foner, *The Caregiving Dilemma: Work in an American Nursing Home* (Berkeley: University of California, 1995), chapter 2.

29. Nils Christie, *Crime Control as Industry: Towards Gulags, Western Style*, 3rd ed. (London: Routledge, 2001), 13.

Index

About the Author

David Wagner is professor of social work and sociology, as well as the co-ordinator of the bachelor's program in social work, at the University of Southern Maine in Portland. Prior to entering academia he worked as a social worker and labor organizer in Massachusetts and New York. He holds degrees from Columbia University, the University of Massachusetts, and the City University of New York Graduate Center. He is the author of numerous articles in both academic literature and community papers for low income groups, and he has written four previous books including *Checkerboard Square: Culture and Resistance in a Homeless Community* and *What's Love Got to do With it? A Critical Look at American Charity.*